CHANGE AND THE LAW

Change

and the Law

W. Robert Goedecke

Florida State University Press
Tallahassee
1969

A Florida State University Press Book

PRINTED FOR THE PUBLISHER BY
ST. PETERSBURG PRINTING COMPANY, ST. PETERSBURG, FLORIDA

Preface

IT WOULD PERHAPS BE A COURTESY to the reader to indicate the reasons why I wrote this book and what purpose it is supposed to serve. The reason for writing the book was to counteract, in whatever small way possible to an individual private citizen, the growing tendency toward authoritarianism, and the public acceptance of authoritarianism, in America today. The issue between law and personal prerogative is a perennial one, but it appears in different guises in different times and situations. In the United States today, it is an issue as to whether the supreme legitimate authority of the government resides in the Presidency or in the Supreme Court. The Supreme Court represents law, and the Presidency represents personal prerogative. Many sophisticated thinkers have been advocating greater and greater powers for the President, or at least they advocated such strong powers until they discovered a strong President they did not like. This placed them in a quandary, for they had reached a formulation of the issues in which the only alternative to a strong executive was a weak executive, and that did not seem preferable. This book poses the issue in another way: the proper alternative to a strong executive is an executive limited by fundamental law, and the Supreme Court is the guardian of fundamental law. The problems of action and legal direction are found to exist even within the confines of the Court's domain, so that the issues of power and prerogative do not disappear, but rather appear in terms

of arguments for a certain kind of pragmatic jurisprudence of interests. Questions are not begged, but they are placed in the context
of the nature of law, rather than in the nature of personal political
power. If the public accepts the rule of law, then this is the proper
context, and discussions of basic constitutional issues should be more
widespread. That in itself would mean an end to arbitrary and
excessive authoritarianism and would accomplish all that can be
accomplished toward the maintenance of freedom in a free society.

The blunt journalistic editorial about freedom and the abuses of
freedom usually serves no more than to keep indignation aroused
for a day. This work intends to do more and to suggest the foundations of the problem of law and freedom in the basic neglected
beginnings of modern Anglo-American law in Coke's constitutional
struggles and his published works. Coke's works on law were the
first to have the advantage of being duplicated with the modern
printing press for an English audience. That these works severely
limited governmental prerogatives was completely understood at the
time, when they were suppressed by the Stuart kings and then propa-
gated by the revolutionary New Parliament, and such understanding
continued even to the time of Jefferson, who in his private letters
refers to Coke as a Whig and to Blackstone, the new reigning commentator on the laws, as a Tory. But now Coke seems lost in the
past. However, foundations, although underground, still hold up the
building, and modern constitutional freedom cannot be understood
without Coke. Locke presents a practical philosophy of freedom and
toleration and constitutional limitations in politics, something with
which the legalist Coke was not concerned. This also must be understood. Jefferson's political actions, both in starting the opposition
party in America and winning office, and also in stirring responsible
dissent on the Supreme Court, are also part of the action of founding modern freedom.

The second part of the book deals with concrete cases in Supreme
Court history and two different kinds of jurisprudence that were
developed in direct relation to these cases. These are presented in
a slightly different attitude and intention. Justice Field's views represent an admirable concrete development of a jurisprudence of formal
rights. This jurisprudence has to be understood in its concrete opinions on particular issues in order to overcome the prejudices that
several generations of pragmatists have instilled in the reading
public through diatribes on all non-pragmatic jurisprudence. Justice

Field does not represent the "open" formalism that I advocate in this book, but his own argumentation is strong, and his premises and conclusions are relevant to current issues of basic rights. Justice Holmes represents the beginnings of pragmatic jurisprudence. His views are presented as beginning in their historic origins of aristocratic disdain for verbal restrictions and prosaic inhibitions, but developing along with the democratic moralistic views of Justice Brandeis and leading to the meticulous pragmatic syntheses of Justice Frankfurter, in order to show both the range and the actual growth of pragmatic jurisprudence, the "logic of the facts." The study of concrete opinions continues to show the confrontation of pragmatic with formal views of right in law, something which is occurring at the present day. The entire argument of the book concludes with an attempt to indicate that the actual processes of the law embody the proper open acceptance of opposing views, which is stated to be the essence of the rule of law. The law as it exists in the cases and reports is a proper embodiment of the rule of law as developed in history and the liberal heritage of political philosophy and practice. Freedom can be maintained and enlarged by a fuller understanding of the intrinsic interactions of discussion, choice, and proper lawful processes.

In the preparation of this work I owe a particular debt to the great legal scholar William Winslow Crosskey, who first interested me in the problems of politics and basic law. Recent insistent encouragement was given by Donald Clarke Hodges, who helped in every way he could, although his views on the subject are very different from my own. If the style and the language of the book are such that the argument is conveyed to the reader, it is due to the meticulous help of my assistant, Karl Hein. The final aid was the friendly and judicious criticism of the editor, Professor James A. Preu.

September, 1969   W. Robert Goedecke

Contents

Part I

Foundations of Reason in Law

Introduction

MAN'S FREEDOM IN POLITICAL ACTION is the freedom to discuss
and determine alternative courses of action in changing situations. The rule of law guarantees such freedom to talk about alternatives, and decide among them, and the rule of law is the procedure
by which such alternatives are openly discussed. The rule of law is
the procedure by which men are given deliberative freedom among
different proposed courses of action, different values, and different
leaders. The rule of law is not opposed to the rule of men, a claim
often made, but rather is the procedure of open debate among men,
in which both the problems of changing administrations and the
problem of changing situations are open parts of the political and
legal discussion. The rule of law requires talk. The rule of law
requires change in administrations or rulers. The rule of law requires dissent to dominant views as to what the particular commands
of the law are. The rule of law is self-justifying and can be understood only in terms of what it is and what it does. This is the reason
that much modern social science ignores the rule of law in discussion
of sociological or economic approaches to the political order, but
the rule of law cannot be reduced to an aspect of sociology or economics. But whether changes and discussions are in terms of peaceful
talking about alternatives or not makes a great deal of difference in
human affairs. It is the difference between freedom and slavery. It
is the difference between human choice and animal compulsion. It

3

might even be the difference between survival and self-destruction.

The rule of law guarantees freedom, the ability to change policies, the ability to act and determine matters rather than merely react and be trapped in a series of worsening crises. And the rule of law is simply the exercise of the human ability to talk about and deliberate upon changes to be made. The proper moral task of man is to change the world and to determine the world for practical betterment of human affairs. This is both the command given by God to Adam in *Genesis* and the gist of the attack of Karl Marx on Hegelian philosophy, which merely tried to understand the world and not to change it. The question therefore is not whether we are to change and determine our world or not; the question is only how and in which directions? And that problem requires the procedures of the rule of law.

The notions developed in this book will center around the rule of law as deliberative freedom among alternatives. Such freedom can be understood in relation to basic institutions, such as private property and recognized traditions of freedom of speech; or in relation to basic philosophic considerations about practical freedom of opinion and practical judgments; or in relation to the changes and debates of party politics; or in relation to judicial dissents in constitutional law. All of these will be discussed, and roughly in this order: institutions, philosophic bases, political practices, and the special problems of procedure in ultimate formal law.

There are misconceptions and one-sided views of the rule of law, which need to be discussed to make the subject clear. Basic law, the law most connected with fundamental politics and policies, is not a command or a set of commands, nor one value or a set of values. It is a procedure for considering various possible commands and various alternative values. Decisions are made in such a way that the same freedom to make new decisions, in later changed situations, is maintained. The rule of law maintains freedom to choose, and the maintenance of the freedom to choose is the rule of law. If one insists on taking the view of Bentham and Kelsen and other pseudo-scientific analysts of law, that basic law is the command of the sovereign, then those commands have to be seen in terms of radical freedom. In an old Greek story, a visiting centaur was amazed at man who was able to blow hot and cold with the same breath. This is the peculiarity of the basic rule of law, which is intrinsically connected with the ability of man to talk about opposite courses of action: it maintains the ability to blow both hot and cold, and never says "always hot!" or "always cold!"—that is stupidity, not law.

There are two obvious other views which have arisen in the perennial discussions of the province and function of law, which seem at first to be contrary, but need not be.

One view is that the law should be an ideal normative language of directions in which every word means one clear thing in relation to practical direction of affairs, and in which there are clear rules of interpretation of the words in difficult situations, to the end that all things are determined by the words of the law. Normative statements are not the same as scientific and factual statements, and in law they are prior to such fact-statements, which means that the law is established prior to and apart from the facts and situations. If this is done, say the proponents, predictability and stability of conduct and expectation are assured. The law becomes a consistent, orderly, and comprehensive science, making human life well-ordered and peaceful. Such a beautiful logical system, the practical or normative equivalent of *Principia Mathematica,* remains an ideal of many who want things decided once and for all, and clearly, without ambiguity or contrariety.

The second view is that law develops and grows in response to human needs and should change in response to human needs and changing situations. This pragmatic approach is wary of formal definitions and rigid rules. There cannot be rigid rules of interpretation for these legal pragmatists, since all significant or key words are ambiguous in their interpretation of actual circumstances, particularly when one realizes that such application always involves value judgments as well as formal semantic analysis. When Hamilton and Jefferson disagreed as to what powers were given to Congress by the words "necessary and proper" in the Constitution, this was a matter of differences between Hamilton's liking for strong central government and Jefferson's suspicion of the same, and not just a matter of dictionary definitions. Words are grouped in terms of analogies and metaphors and distinctions, varying from case to case and situation to situation. Since words expand or diminish in meaning, or go to the political left or the political right in time, in accordance with how they are used, and since legislators and judges are aware of this flexibility, actual "going values" have to be understood to understand the law. The actual problems and social values of a historical situation are the proper determinants of the law in practice, not the mere instrumental terms. On this basis the pragmatic thinkers view most formal thinking and the rigid use of rules and legal dictionaries as a front for reactionary and insidiously hidden interests and a mask for privilege. When the facts are known such legalisms can be exposed, and since ambiguous and metaphorical usages of terms allow for novel growth and genuine response to needs in law, such use should be accepted. The pragmatists think the future should not be put into any literal straitjacket by the proprieties or interests of the past.

These views seem hopelessly opposed, since one view maintains the priority of the language and norms of the law to situations, and the other view maintains that law should be an intelligent but value-oriented response to prior practical situations. But with an expansion to include oppositions and alternatives, the views can be reconciled.

There should be a formalism in the most general and procedural sense—a formalism of considering arguments and arriving at decisions. Thus there is nothing inherently unrealistic about such procedural forms as *Robert's Rules of Order*: such rules allow for open discussion and for some determinate conclusion to discussion. Such forms do not give a "mechanical jurisprudence," in which all particular determinations are explicit or implicit in the general rules. The latter rules are the end of realistic freedom, while the former rules are the way that freedom can be realized. But unfortunately, the mechanical jurisprudence keeps reappearing as an ideal of those who wish for a science of the law, and instead of the law being a procedure for deliberation and decision, it becomes a rigid substitute for such formally directed practical inquiry into actual cases and situations.

There should also be a pragmatism of relating inquiries and decisions to actual situations and needs. If the pragmatists wish to use the language, the determination of cases in particular instances can be viewed as "responses" to tensions, needs, or problems. However the pragmatists seldom have the openness to admit that men seldom if ever agree on what the problem is and what the response should be. The more open pragmatist admits a pluralism of statements of realistic problems and a pluralism of responses. The law should not embody just one set of values. Pragmatists have found that some values, i.e., their values, are "concrete" and "sensitive," while the values of the others are "abstract" and "formal" or "dated." But in the larger view, which values are "better" than other values is a matter which must *not* determine the procedures of the law. The law should be value-free, not in the naive way desired by positivists, but in the more practical way that the law should allow scope for change in values over time and for differences in values and attitudes at all times.

The question of which values to adopt is itself a matter of deliberation and discussion. The general third theory allows for immediate determinations, which obviously have to be made in terms of some values and not others. It also holds that the rule of law should be open enough to allow for the statement of issues to change and for dominant opinions to go right and left alternatingly over periods of time. Where the pragmatic theory as narrowly conceived took the achievement of "proper, social, concrete" values as a paramount task of the law, as against the wrongheaded values of the "reactionaries," the larger theory deems that what is important is the freedom to move peacefully from one set of dominant values to another. This requires some formal structure, and freedom in such a structure is the rule of law.

This freedom among alternative rules and value applications is intrinsically connected with the basic ability of human beings to talk. Language allows for affirmations and negations, for different formulations of problems in the same situation, and for back-and-forth deliberation about political policies and legal cases. Talking expands freedom, for it increases the awareness of the range of choices and considerations. The procedures of the law allow for discussion and deliberation among free men. Thus, as Locke said, law increases the freedom of man; it does not take freedom away. To be a member of a society of free men, who talk about what can be done and consider various alternatives, is not to be less free than to be alone in the jungle. This false view of freedom, which holds that freedom is basically acting on impulse, has been put forth by such classic thinkers as Hobbes[1] and John Stuart Mill[2] and ends up

1. Thomas Hobbes, *Leviathan*, part I, chapter 14. The second law of nature is "that a man . . . be contented with so much liberty against other men, as he would allow other men against himself."

2. John Stuart Mill, *On Liberty*, chapter 1: "The only freedom which deserves the name, is that of pursuing our own good in our own way, so long as we do not attempt to deprive others of theirs, or impede their efforts to obtain it." The same view, which gives to freedom some sort of pseudo-geographical limits, has been repeated by Bertrand Russell in the twentieth century. See, for instance, his *Freedom versus Organization* (New York, 1934).

in nonsensical dilemmas. They hold that freedom is "doing what you want to do" without further consideration of whether you have thought about or discussed the range of alternatives. Freedom then appears something like the psychological equivalent of a small plot of ground, in which the freedom of others limits my freedom, as their farms limit the extent of my farm. Their freedom becomes a threat to my freedom, and if I could do away with their freedom, I would have more freedom. But this view is wrong. If I lived with a community of intelligent but absolutely subordinate and non-talking apes, then in the view of Hobbes and Mill, I would be more free than if I lived with other free men. But I would lack the freedom to talk and discuss things with other men, to deliberate on public policies, to develop community projects, to read newspapers, to listen to intelligent entertainment, to be aware of alternatives in action and evaluation I personally might never have discovered on my own. If talking is connected with public freedom, then the freedom others have to talk does not limit my freedom, but rather increases it. Thus law gives direction to freedom and increases freedom, as Locke says, and the hopeless task, put forth by Mill when he said that my freedom ends where the freedom of my neighbors begins, can be dismissed as based on fallacious notions. My freedom begins when my neighbors are also free and we live in a society in which practical matters can be openly discussed. When it is realized that freedom means action on the basis of inquiry and deliberation, then it can be seen that the more free my neighbor is, the more free I am. The basic truth ignored by Hobbes and Mill is that we are able to talk about what we want to do and what we should do, and that the more open the talk and discussion about actions and goals and forms, the more free we are. The level of talk and discussion in a free society under the rule of law is higher than that of any alternative society, and higher than that of any viable jungle anarchy. Thus free men aid the freedom of other free men and do not destroy or constrict it.

At the other extreme from Hobbes and Mill are those who hold an "angelic" view of freedom, in which we should always do "the right thing" and believe that maintaining this one right way against all temptation is the only proper exercise of free will. The modern version of this is that man should be consistent in his actions with what he has done before, and this leads us again back to the ideals of mechanical jurisprudence. But man was not meant to be like the stars, never swerving in their courses. Life on earth demands constantly new considerations about changing circumstances and such considerations lead to changes to opposite policies when the situation so warrants. Thus the freedom to talk about practical affairs is the freedom to choose and to change.

In fact, a sign of an oppressive political rule is that the citizens do not talk about pressing practical problems. Criminal trials are conducted in secret, and major policies of government are established without open discussion and are executed in silence and secrecy. Of course, there can be sophisticated perversions of discussion, where people are directed to discuss government policies but with the hidden and secret threat that anything except open adulation will somehow be severely punished. Thus the East Germans "discussed" the new constitution imposed by the Ulbricht government, and the Chinese peasants "discuss" the latest policy changes of the Peking regime, always discovering their entire and total agreement.

Since the nature of language is such that for every proposal there is an immediate counterproposal, to wit, the simple negative of the first, deliberation about practical problems frequently or inevitably involves opposites, which on the linguistic level can be simply affirmations or negations, and on the political level are practical oppositions. This is not to say that all political differences come from our ability to talk, but, given that there are various particular perspectives on practical problems and facts and arguments, it would be most strange if all men arrived at the same opinion with no dissent. Unanimity among citizens is therefore a sign that there has been no real talk and no real discussion. This point was emphasized by Madison as well as Locke and is a reason for the rule of law. The rule of law recognizes differences and guarantees the rights of dissenting and opposing groups. Such dissent is based, as Madison said, in the nature of political man.[3] The dream of a unity of mankind, with all men thinking and saying and doing the same, is in practice an ideal of tyrants and oppressors. The fact is that men divide on affirming and negating proposals and decisions, and law maintains the continued freedom of men to do so.

There are areas of the law where some clear and complete deter-

3. James Madison, *Federalist Paper Number Ten*: "As long as the reason of man continues fallible, and he is at liberty to exercise it, different opinions will be formed. . . . The latent causes of faction are thus sown in the nature of man, and we see them everywhere brought into different degrees of activity, according to the different circumstances of civil society."

mination of the law seems desirable; an obvious area is taxation. It would seem that any tax law should state as clearly as possible what taxes are to be paid for what transactions, property, or income. There should be no contradictions among all the complexities and qualifications, and there should be no loopholes. Also, all the citizens should agree to pay their taxes. But such considerations miss the basic problem of tax law, the formation and creation of such law. Tax laws are of greatest importance to social and economic groups and to political policies, and so in free countries there has always been the greatest demand for talking and debate on the new tax laws. Parliaments and congresses have their historic origin in the rights given to feudal nobility to accept or reject the taxation policies of the king. It is precisely the tax laws, before their final determination and acceptance, which are the source of the most debates and conflicts and discussions. After passage everything should be clear, consistent, and accepted, but before such passage it is tax law which is the prime area for debate and talk, and here the rule of law in basic terms enters, allowing such talk, and insisting that the determinations be made on the basis of talk and discussion, and not arbitrarily and impulsively. The rule of law, for instance with respect to tax law, involves the maintenance of freedom to change the tax law, usually every year or every two years. By having such laws run only for a short period of time, the law itself assures the general public that there will be more discussion and more consideration of alternatives in the future. Taxes are determined but basic freedom is maintained.

The view of other theorists is that such discussion is not needed and that the basic needs and the basic resources of society can be scientifically ascertained. Long-range state planning is taken as preferable, more scientific, and more efficient than continued discussions. But what are the proper goals of such planning? What are the alternatives? Is not the freedom to determine matters of public policy in itself the major value of a free society? These are crucial issues in the world ideological conflicts of today, perhaps even more so than in the past, and it is for this reason that this book wishes to focus attention on the legal foundations of a free society, rather than on the economic foundations and results, although it happens to follow that a legally free society will also be economically more prosperous.

The argument of the book is clear and can be given in a very short space. The legal foundations of a free society are based on the freedom to discuss changes and alternatives. Talking about active changes is the heart of the rule of law. These legal foundations cannot be understood in isolation from actual historic institutional beginnings, philosophic justifications, political activities, technical constitutional formulations of current and actual constitutional law. To give the historical development, we must start with Sir Edward Coke's great founding achievements. At the beginning of the seventeenth century he established the basic rights of the rule of law and public freedom, in his direct fights with Bacon and the Stuart tyrants, and in his writings on property and fundamental constitutional liberties. Coke fought for an independent judiciary and an independent Parliament. He established property rights free from feudal ties of loyalty and royal obligation. He reinterpreted the Magna Carta so that it applied to all Englishmen, not just the medieval barons. He established the basic right to talk about ultimate political and legal policies, and thus laid the historic foundations for the modern rule of law.

The philosophic foundations for the rule of law in modern times have been given most directly by John Locke in his defense of the constitutional revolution of 1688 in England. Locke gave philosophic justification for freedom of speech and opinion in all practical matters, including matters of religion as well as economic policy and political goals. The pieties and subtle oppression of an "establishment" in religion and society were attacked by Locke, and the health of open controversy on all matters defended and guaranteed by the philosophy of constitutional government that he helped usher into the world in 1688. Locke gave the philosophic rationale for the discussion of all practical matters, after Coke had given the institutional and legal grounds. Locke attacked all suppression of opposition views in politics as misguided and vicious paternalism and insisted that the common good could only be defined by and through the processes of open and legitimate discussion.

The political and legal bases of the rule of law in America rest on the legal and philosophic foundations provided by Locke and Coke, but they also depend upon the profound and unique controversies of policy and party at the time of the beginnings of the new government. The agreements and disagreements of policy are explored, the actual peaceful and constitutional changes of government are examined, in order to further the thesis that the rule of

law means law governing basic changes and involves party government and changes of administration, not just acceptance of formal
words. The rule of law in this country rests on the agreeing-disagreements of Hamilton and Madison in *The Federalist,* and on the
acceptance of the "Revolution of 1800," that is, the accession of the
Jeffersonians to office and the peaceful acceptance of the radical
changes of that new government.

Finally, the contribution of Jefferson to the unique system of
constitutional jurisprudence that we have in this country is presented and explained. In America, the rule of law means the ultimate
dominance of the Supreme Court in interpreting the formal Constitution. Jefferson's insistence on open discussion and responsible
dissent by members of the Supreme Court is little known, but has
had enormous effects in guaranteeing the effectiveness of discussion
and dissent at the highest levels of law in America. These considerations are examined in terms of two major dissenting Supreme Court
justices, Justice Field and Justice Holmes. Finally, general considerations about the rule of law anywhere are united with concrete facts
about the rule of law in America, in terms of values and methods of
jurisprudence actually found in Supreme Court opinions, and in
terms of current problems and practices with respect to the principles and processes of law today. A concrete example of the need
for such an "open formalism" is illustrated in the opinions, especially the dissents, of Justice Frankfurter and Justice Black.

Justice Frankfurter and Justice Black represent the paradigmatic
cases in recent American constitutional law of the extremes of
pragmatism and formalism. Justice Frankfurter held to a basic
pragmatic position in jurisprudence, maintaining that the norms
and values of law must come from the community and that legal
terms had meaning only in their factual and evaluated situational
context. For Frankfurter, the norms of interpretation also came
from society and were not a separate legal art of science. The
pragmatic rationalism that Justice Frankfurter recommended within
this view of society, language, and the law involved the serious and
scientific study of what words meant in context, as given by the
norms of society, and not by the values and norms of the judges.
Defining words out of their social context was not proper adjudication, but was "legislation." The application of key value terms,
such as due process, involved an objective and rational judgment
about the going norms of society. Due process cannot be legally de-

fined by other words, since it is always defined situationally, and a verbal and legal definition would be a Procrustean bed forcing the law into an a priori fixity which would have an arbitrary and irrational relation to the various different situations presented to the Court.

In Justice Black's jurisprudence, on the other hand, the problem of the interpretation of the clauses and terms of the Constitution is seen as a matter of discovering the unequivocal meanings of the rules and the legal terms, when the Constitution and the amendments were passed. The rules of legal interpretation should be formal and logical and unchanging, so that new situations can be brought under the law without difficulty. If Frankfurter claims that he maintains self-restraint in not imposing his own values, but rather finding communal values, so can Black maintain he also uses self-restraint, for he does not act on his own private views of right and wrong, but maintains that it is his duty to accept the rules embodied in the language of the Constitution.

Justice Black thinks that there are meanings in the words and clauses of the Constitution independent of situational context, and that such words and sentences can do things; they are not merely passive instruments of social values. Justice Black also argues that his mode of decision is adjudication, while that of his opponents is legislation. His form of argumentation, which can be found in almost any of his constitutional opinions from 1938 to the present time, appeared most remarkably in his dissent in *Adamson* v. *California*.[4] Black dissented to the pragmatic interpretation of words in relation to situational contexts and norms. He argued for an unequivocal meaning of the due process clause of the Fourteenth Amendment in a twenty-four-page argument, and backed up his argument for unequivocal meanings with a thirty-page appendix of historical documentation. Justice Black saw the Frankfurter approach as whimsical and irrational. "I fear to see the consequences of the Court's practice of substituting its own conception of decency and fundamental justice for the language of the Bill of Rights . . . this is to frustrate the great designs of a written Constitution." Justice Frankfurter replied in a dissent in *Irvine* v. *California*:[5] "The effort to imprison due process within tidy categories misconceived its function and is a futile endeavor to save the judicial function from the pain of

4. *Adamson* v. *California*, 332 U.S. 46, 68-123 (1947).
5. *Irvine* v. *California*, 347 U.S. 128 (1953).

judicial judgment. . . . Due process of law, as a historical and generative principle, precludes defining."

This fundamental difference in jurisprudence can be clearly seen in the case of declaring President Truman's seizure of the steel industry unconstitutional, *Youngstown Co.* v. *Sawyer*.[6] Justice Black found that President Truman had, clearly and simply, exercised powers not granted in the Constitution. In that document Congress is to *make* laws, and the President is to *execute* them. The executive order seizing the steel mills was a law, and therefore a matter for Congress, not the President. In other words, for Black, the matter was clearly settled by the *words* of the Constitution and logical application to the present case: "In the framework of our Constitution, the President's power to see that the laws are faithfully executed refutes the idea that he is not to be a lawmaker. The Constitution limits his functions in the lawmaking process to the recommending of laws he thinks wise and the vetoing of laws he thinks bad."

Justice Frankfurter could not abide by such formal and verbal determination. Black had ignored current *historical contexts,* which were the proper grounds of decision:

"To start with a consideration of the relation of the President's powers and those of Congress—a most delicate matter—is to start at the wrong end." Frankfurter started with the First World War, when Congress seized the mills in 1916. Congress had seized them sixteen times since 1916, according to Frankfurter. In 1947 Congress had passed a law providing for future Congressional control over the steel mills. And thus the objective pragmatic judge must see that the words had found their meaning in *historical events,* which should be recognized by a reasonable and non-legislating Court:

"Nothing can be plainer than that Congress made a conscious choice of policy in a field full of perplexity," in its 1947 legislation. The only question was the ambiguous significance of the Defense Production Act of 1950, but that Act had to be read in terms of the established "tissues of historic power," and thus did not change the determination.

Neither Frankfurter nor Black stated that in this case the Court was a dominant power imposing its will as opposed to the President's will. Black was bound by words of the Constitution, and Frankfurter was bound by history. The argument between them did not stop the Court from the exceedingly important action in the *general political*

6. *Youngstown* v. *Sawyer,* 343 U.S. 479 (1952).

scene of insisting that the President withdraw government troops from the steel mills. The argument led in a significant direction, even though it was not a single argument, but argument and counter-argument.

The same was true in *Wolf* v. *Colorado*.[7] Frankfurter and Black agreed on the result, but Frankfurter felt the need to argue with Black on the reasons: "The notion that the due process of law guaranteed by the Fourteenth Amendment is shorthand for the first eight amendments and thereby incorporates them has been rejected by this Court again and again. . . . Due process conveys neither formal nor fixed nor narrow requirements. It is a compendious expression for all those rights which are basic to a free society." Frankfurter found that the security of one's privacy against unreasonable searches was basic to a free society and that such searches were "condemned as inconsistent with the conception of human rights enshrined in the history and the basic constitutional documents of English speaking peoples."

The argument has continued although Justice Frankfurter is no longer the active proponent of his pragmatic views. Thus in *Katz* v. *U.S.*[8] the question arose whether federal agents could legally wiretap a public phone booth. Justice Stewart argued that the extension of the right to privacy (established by Frankfurter in the *Wolf* case) to public phone booths involved the pragmatic problem of whether a phone booth was like an open field or like a private home. Since the man in the booth thought it was private, it was more like a private home, and such basic rights as privacy needed broad interpretation with respect to the needs of civilization. Justice Black objected. The Constitution had no "right of privacy," but only a right against "unreasonable searches and seizures." Wiretapping is not a "search and seizure" at all but rather is a modern kind of eavesdropping, which may be "dirty" but is not illegal: "If I could agree with the Court that eavesdropping, carried on by electronic means, constitutes a 'search' or 'seizure' I would be happy to join the Court's opinion. . . . My basic objection is twofold: (1) I do not believe that the words of the Amendment will bear the meaning given them by today's decision, and (2) I do not believe that it is the proper role of the Court to rewrite the Amendment in order 'to bring it into harmony with the times' and thus reach a result that many people believe to be desirable."

7. *Wolf* v. *Colorado*, 338 U.S. 25 (1949).   8. *Katz* v. *U.S.*, 389 U.S. 347 (1965).

"While I realize that an argument based on the meaning of words lacks the scope, and no doubt the appeal, of broad policy discussions and philosophical discourses on such nebulous subjects as privacy, for me, the language of the Amendment is the crucial place to look in construing a written document such as our Constitution."

Justice Black then turned to an examination of the first and second clauses of the Fourth Amendment, and their historic intent and meaning, and after deciding the meaning was clear, continued:

> In interpreting the Bill of Rights, I willingly go so far as a liberal construction of the language takes me, but I simply cannot in good conscience give a meaning to words which they have never before been thought to have and which they certainly do not have in common with ordinary usage. I will not distort the words of the Amendment in order to 'keep the Constitution up to date' or 'bring it into harmony with the time.' It was never meant that this Court have such power, which in effect would make us a continuously functioning constitutional convention. With this decision the Court has completed, I hope, its rewriting of the Fourth Amendment.

Another strong statement of Justice Black's position occurs in *Berger* v. *New York*[9] where Black indicates, as he has for years, that his mode of interpretation differs from the pragmatic mode: "As I see it, the differences between the Court and me in this case rest on different basic beliefs as to our duty in interpreting the Constitution. This basic charter of our government was written in a few words to define governmental power generally on the one hand and to define governmental limitations on the other. If changes are necessary I think these changes should be accomplished by Amendments, as the Constitution itself provides."

However, the peculiar restraints that reason demands in the jurisprudence of Justice Black have often seemed to outsiders as "judicial activism." Justice Black has been argued against, not only by those in the Frankfurter school of jurisprudence, but by those who argue in terms that took shape in Justice Miller's jurisprudence in the *Slaughterhouse*[10] cases: the Fourteenth Amendment must be seen in the light of the judicial task of "balancing" state and federal relations and powers and must not be construed to change those re-

9. *Berger* v. *New York*, 388 U.S. 41 (1968).
10. *Slaughterhouse Cases (Butchers' Benevolent Ass'n* v. *Crescent City Live-Stock Landing and Slaughter-House Co.)* 16 Wallace 36 (1873).

lations. For these people, Black is not a "legalist" but an "activist" putting the Court into state politics. Thus when Black wrote an opinion that the Mine Worker's Union could legally hire one lawyer on an annual basis to represent workers in compensation cases, as clearly under the freedom of speech, assembly, and petition guaranteed by the First and Fourteenth Amendments against state action,[11] Justice Harlan objected to the usurpation of state police powers; and the lack of "balancing" of powers: "This decision, which again manifests the peculiar insensitivity to the need for seeking an appropriate balance between federal and state authority that in recent years has characterized so many of the Court's decisions under the Fourteenth Amendment, puts this Court more deeply than ever in the business of supervising the practice of law in the various states. From my viewpoint, what is done today is unnecessary, undesirable and constitutionally all wrong. . . . Nothing accords with the traditions and the most elementary demands of our Federal system."[12] Thus the arguments in the law are not just two-way debates, but can involve three or more basic positions on the nature of the law and the role of the Court.

The meaning of "The Rule of Law" does not imply, as particular interpreters suggest, that there is one set of reasons that always work the same way and proceed in the same direction. The rule of law is like a two-bladed axe that cuts both ways with equal force and with equal precision. Those who object to the various directions the law orders and to the various reasons given by the justices may make the basic mistake of the older rationalism—the idea that men should attempt to imitate the stars and always go in the same direction, and that if human reason really ruled, we would all follow the same rules and the same logic and agree on what was right. On the other hand, they may say there are no reasons at all, just rationalizations of emotional attitudes. We are then in the position of obeying the emotions of the five dominant men in a court of nine, who are not under the check or control of the other two hundred million of us. But somewhere in between the false and perfect rationalism of the stars and the animal irrationalism of the emotions there exists the freedom of reason and counter-reason of man. There *is* a mediating position which takes the valuable perspective of both Frankfurter and Black, "pragmatist" and "legalist." This more open,

11. *Mine Workers* v. *Illinois*, 389 U.S. 217 (1968).
12. *Ibid.*

viable and reasonable perspective on the law will be the central concern of this book.

The peculiar ability to reason in the practical sphere and to generalize above particular emotions is directly related to the ability to talk. Philosophically this has been indicated by philosophers as diverse as Aristotle, Hume, Dewey, and William Frankena. The appeal, throughout the latter half of this essay, to the argumentation in the Supreme Court Reports and in the jurisprudence of the more articulate of the justices of that Court, is frankly an attempt to call American society back to its reasonable foundations. The ordinary processes of political democracy are in constant danger of becoming arbitrary or unreasonable because of the constant changes in our society, both of technical advance and simple mobility and growth of population, and also because of the increasing difficulties of reasonable discussion in the context of the mass media, where what counts is "vitality," or quick emotional appeal, or simply scientific Pavlovian repetition of stimuli. The move toward mass totalitarianism, which was acutely analyzed by de Tocqueville more than one hundred years ago, has not quite yet overwhelmed the reasonable restraints and checks inherent in the American system. But the most significant check and the most significant rational direction is given by the basic law of the land and that is both guarded and stated by the Supreme Court. What is difficult to understand is the peculiar way in which the arguments in that Court guarantee the structure of freedom of the American democracy. Compared to science, basic law is difficult and paradoxical. Scientific laws always strive for total structured coherence, while in a free society, basic human laws allow the society to move in various different directions. Scientific laws concern things which are caused by outside forces or events, but the basic law is meant to be above outside forces and events, but limiting at the same time—it is meant to be "self-restraining." Our basic law is self-restraining, but restraining in such a way that alternative conceptions of restraint are permitted and maintained, and alternative conceptions of policy are considered and maintained at the same time. But given that in the processes of hearing various arguments and restating these arguments from the bench, the Supreme Court embodies *structured freedom,* then our basic constitutional law is a law of freedom. The rule of reason exists in our society, not because any one particular view of reason is at the basis of all decision-making, but rather because in law, more than one view of reason is tolerated and accepted: "Reason" is taken to be larger in scope than any one man's view of life and thought. Thus tolerance and reason are the same, just as reason and interargumentation are the same. The law is the embodiment of this larger reason, larger tolerance, and larger argumentation.

The justices of the Court are not "philosophers." The reverse is the case and the only desirable situation. The justices consider themselves "bound" by the approach they take, whether that of adhering to recent precedent, or the meaning of the basic document, or the norms of society, or the balance of powers between state and nation. The accusation that the "other" justices are "making law" is a serious one, as is the accusation that the judges are following their own feelings, their own views of "natural law." A "philosopher" would not take these charges as slanderous or vicious, but within the province of the law they are. This has led to the counter-charge that the justices do not think at all; they simply follow precedent, or when that is impossible, stretch words through devices of analogy or other expansions to cover the new situation, in ways that cannot be formally analyzed except satirically. This is not true either. The justices argue and reason within conceptions of rights and powers which are taken as given, and they argue seriously with the other justices who also feel themselves bound by their conception of the law. The notion of due process is a legal notion; it is not a moral or philosophical notion. Viewed from the perspective of the law, the openness of argumentation among conceptions of law in the Court allows for greater intellectual and philosophic and moral freedom in America than elsewhere, where law and ideology are more closely connected, and where much argumentation is illegal because it is taken to be improper on ideological and moral grounds. In America the law can include argumentations from various philosophies and various "metaphysical" positions. This can be seen in the opinions of Justice Field and Justice Miller, Justice Holmes and Justice Brewer, Justice Frankfurter and Justice Black.

This essay on the development of the law of freedom will illustrate the need for opposition and independence by means of the controversies between Coke and James I; it will show the need to expand conceptions of reason beyond those of any one view through the political and philosophic thought of John Locke; it will present the practical problems of developing historical dissent and ordered change.

The first part of the book, on the foundations of reason in law, moves from institutional and philosophic theories to the political actions of the Jeffersonians, and those actions culminate in the achievement of minority opposing opinions on the Supreme Court. Individual dissenting opinions on the Court have meant the institutionalization of responsible argument on the Supreme bench, the recognition of *reasoned* authority in the law. It is accepted dissent on the Supreme Court which has made our basic law open and reasonable.

The second part of the book is concerned with the various principles of constitutional law, as they have actually developed in cases and opinions in the history of the law. These principles developed in dissent but then were adopted by majorities of the Court later, with various consequences. The dialogue between a formal jurisprudence of rights and a pragmatic jurisprudence of interests, partially presented already in the debates between Justices Black and Frankfurter, will be fully explored in the chapters on Justice Field and Justice Holmes. Field expounded a little known and little appreciated jurisprudence developed from rights basic in the Declaration of Independence and in the Fourteenth Amendment. Holmes developed a well-known but not completely understood jurisprudence of dominant powers and judicial aloofness, which started from notions of a high and aristocratic culture, but developed into later conceptions of ordinary norms of any ongoing community, understood in terms of a nominalism and empiricism rather than in terms of the original Holmesian idealism. This dialogue is important both for the particular cases, which have actually determined the course of American law, and for its exemplification of the general thesis of this book, that reason is exemplified in law in terms of openness to opposing positions. American constitutional law is reasonable because it allows for dissent, and the dissents lead to changes to opposite positions, which in turn lead to new dissents and new oppositions. These oppositions encompass both formalisms and pragmatisms, and it is the ability of the law with its multiple opinions and open argumentation at the highest level to encompass both these opposing jurisprudences which gives law its open formalism and its realism. In its concrete embodiments in history, American law can be best understood as open realism aware of the need for reason in dealing with the constantly changing circumstances of policies and situations.

The rule of technical law in the courts and the rule of law in the sense given here, the open ability to consider alternatives, are finally discovered to be the same. The great problem in American law and politics at the present time is reconsideration of the significance of our heritage of freedom and law. This book is meant to be a recall to the alternatives of reason and debate and away from the compulsions of expediency and impulse. The rule of law, the freedom to dissent and argue, and the rule of reason are the same; without the formally allowed freedom to dissent, there is no reason and no argument, there is no exposition on a responsible level of opposite views of the facts and proper methods of practical life, and the law then ceases to operate. It is to the continued operation of law and the maintenance of freedom that the reasonings of this book are dedicated.

1

Edward Coke, Francis Bacon, and the Foundations of the Law

THE ENGLISH OR ELIZABETHAN RENAISSANCE developed men of outstanding energy in many fields: Shakespeare and Marlowe, Raleigh, Drake, Essex, the Cecils are perhaps the brightest of the men who shone in a period which was democratic and extremely aristocratic at the same time.[1] Two men of formidable scholarship and legal art were educated during this period, men whose political and rhetorical abilities shaped the future of England and the entire Western World. These men were Edward Coke and Francis Bacon. As the great publicist of modern experimental science, Bacon's name is still known and admired, although like Moses, Bacon pointed the way to a promised land of modern technology without seeing it, he himself dying on the desert. Because of Bacon, experimental science became publicly acceptable and not merely a private craft of alchemists and black magicians. The work of Edward Coke in the field of law is fully as important as that of Bacon in science, but Coke is relatively neglected. A man of unending activity in public life and legal scholarship, Coke fought the great constitu-

1. The following works were of great value for the exposition in this chapter: Catherine D. Bowen, *Francis Bacon* (Boston, 1963); Catherine D. Bowen, *The Lion and the Throne* (Boston, 1956); Samuel R. Gardiner, *History of England from the Accession of James I to the Outbreak of the Civil War* (London, 1883); Sir William Holdsworth, *A History of English Law* (3rd ed. London, 1945); Sir William Holdsworth, *Some Makers of English Law* (Cambridge, England, 1938); Herbert Lyon and H. Block, *Edward Coke—Oracle of the Law* (Boston, 1929); F. W. Maitland, *The Constitutional History of England* (Cambridge, England, 1920).

tional battles for freedom against the new Stuart kings, who acceded to the English throne at the death of Elizabeth in 1603, in the person of the weak-legged but strong-willed James VI of Scotland, who became James I of England. One of Coke's greatest accomplishments during the new Stuart oppression was that he survived. Others died or, like Shakespeare, retired to the country, but Coke continued to develop the seminal ideas of modern law and modern liberty despite pressure from James, Bacon, and the times to acquiesce. He fought for the independence of the judiciary and then for the independence of Parliament. He was the basic force in obtaining the king's signature on the Petition of Right. And he wrote the basic volumes of all modern English law, the *Reports* and the *Institutes*.

Coke's *Reports* are his own summations of the issues and the results of hundreds of cases that he either heard personally or discovered in historical searches; they are the basic materials of precedent for modern English Common Law. Coke's *Institutes* are his essays and compilations on the basic laws of property, constitutional rights, criminal law, and court procedures. Since Coke was immediately recognized as the authority in these areas, these writings had enormous influence, not only within the legal profession, but in all politics and all society. The legal foundations for a modern free society were established by Coke and his *Institutes*. Among other things, property was defined in terms of private ownership and rights, and not in terms of feudal allegiance, loyalty to the king, and feudal duties, as had been the case before Coke. *Magna Carta* was interpreted as applying to all Englishmen, not just the barons.[2] Coke has been reviled as a medieval historian, a reactionary in the dawn of the modern age, the dawn seen by Bacon; but in fact his history is interpretation, and in his researches he found what was needed for modern rights and freedoms and ignored what was feudal in the past. There are no guilds in Coke's history, for instance, nor fiefs in the proper sense.[3] Although Coke was a formalist in law and procedure, he was not a nineteenth century romantic pining for the supposed happy times of the Middle Ages, but rather an energetic Elizabethan who lived past his time to assure the function of the rule of law in an age of authoritarianism.

Coke's major adversary in law and politics was Francis Bacon, the

2. Edward Coke, *The Institutes of the Laws of England,* second part, chapter 1 (1640).
3. Coke, first part, chapter 1, sect. 1, on fee simple or *feodum simplex.*

philosopher of inductive logic, experimental science, and the new technology. In these areas Coke had no interest; when Bacon sent him a copy of his *Novum Organon,* Coke wrote on the title page in a large hand, "Ship of Fooles." But Bacon was not only a propagandist for experimental science, he was an advocate of the extreme authoritarian position in law and politics. The law should always bend to the will of the sovereign, and the sovereign should dominate all freedoms of discussion or dissent. Queen Elizabeth found Bacon shallow, and told him so, but James I found him a clever and willing subordinate. James in his political writings maintained that the king stood over his subjects as a "little God" to human beings, and Bacon saw nothing amiss in that view. In practical policies in England, James attempted the role of the tyrant, as did his son Charles. (This led to a revolution in 1640 and to another more successful revolution in 1688, when modern constitutional rights were finally fully recognized.) In law, Bacon favored the jurisdiction of Chancery, in which equity was held to be higher than formal law, and in which the prerogatives of the executive clearly were dominant over the rules and forms of procedure. Such equity jurisprudence had its separate domain in England at the time, maintaining courts separate from the common law courts until the nineteenth century. The struggle between Bacon's Chancery or equity courts and Coke's common law and Parliament is the ancient equivalent of the modern struggle between a formal jurisprudence of rights and a pragmatic call for strong executive and administrative action, as seen in recent constitutional history in the United States: should law predominate or good and "effective" administrators? The latter always seems better in theory but proves oppressive in practice. In any event, Bacon was for the absolute and unlimited prerogatives of the king, and Coke for the limitations of the law. Bacon's prestige as a prophet of the uses of science has led to a glossing over of his practical political views, but he was not only a theoretical authoritarian, he was a willing subordinate to an extremely corrupt, stupid, and deviant king in practice, and when he had total power, as he did for periods from 1618 on, he was unprincipled and corrupt himself. This should be remembered in our day, not only in connection with the maintenance of law and freedom, but in connection with the restatements of the Baconian view that technology, inductive science, and the new logic will solve all human problems. If all reason is subordinate to practice, then there are no restraints on practice.

Bacon and Coke both had gone to Trinity College at Cambridge, and then on to the study of law at the Inns of Court. Coke remembered in later years that he had received an excellent education in college. He took to the study of the law with such avidity that he was recognized as a scholar even before he was admitted to practice, and he won the first case on a fine point of pleading and procedure. Bacon hated his studies at Trinity, and at the Inns of Court he showed more interest in writing literary and philosophic essays than in studying the technical niceties of problems about Blackacre and Whiteacre. He did not practice law at all, until this was pointed out as a defect in his request to be Attorney-General of England. (He then took two cases and prepared brilliant briefs, to show he could do it, and after that never took another private case.) Bacon was a member of Parliament under Elizabeth, but could not get the high public office he so much desired, for he never obtained her favor. Coke was Elizabeth's Attorney-General. Among other things he prosecuted Essex and Raleigh, and with a fierceness that some thought a trifle crude and overbearing. Coke also had a huge private practice and made a great deal of money. In fact, he became one of the wealthiest commoners in England. Bacon and Coke had early begun to feud, their aversions to each other being tempermental as well as philosophical. Bacon wanted the Attorney-Generalship, and Coke got it. Bacon had hoped for the hand and fortune of Lady Hatton, and Coke got her. Bacon was disappointed when he had reached 30 years old and had not achieved any great office or fame. He wrote an angry letter to Coke after the latter had insulted him in public for his lack of legal learning:

Mr. Attorney,
  I thought best, once for all, to let you know in plainness what I find of you, and what you shall find of me. You take to yourself a liberty to disgrace and disable my law, my experience, my discretion. What it pleaseth you, I pray, think of me: I am one that knows both my own wants and other men's; and it may be, perchance, that my fortunes mend, and others stand at a stay. And surely I may not endure in a public place to be wronged, without repelling the same to my best advantage to right myself. You are great, and therefore have the more enemies, which would be glad to have you paid at another's loss. . . . And if you had not been short sighted in your own fortunes (as I think) you might have made more use of me.

But that time is past. I have not written to show my friends what a brave letter I have sent to Mr. Attorney; I have none of these humors. But I haven written for our more particular better understanding of one another. . . .[4]

This was in 1601, before Bacon's rise. The main struggle, on the deepest issues, was in fact yet to begin. Coke would become Chief Justice of the King's Bench, maintain the supremacy of law over arbitrary dictate, and, at Bacon's suggestion, be summarily dismissed. Bacon would become Lord Chancellor, Viscount St. Albans, and, in the vacations King James took from office, the ruling power in England. Then (not without Coke's influence somewhere in the background), he was to be impeached by Parliament and retired in disgrace to the country, to write on the philosophy of science.

The legal and political issues are more significant for our purposes than the biographical and historical particulars. Coke, in his various conflicts with Bacon and James, insisted again and again, and in various and sundry cases, that the due process of the law, which involved proper debates and hearings and public deliberations before decision, was supreme over the arbitrary determinations of executive power. Coke has been called a medievalist and an authoritarian, bringing in the mystifications of forgotten precedents, and peculiar notions of the law as "artificial reason" against modernity and common sense. But this assumes that Coke held the view, which he did not, that everything in law is determined beforehand, even before the processes of argumentation, by the dead hand of the past. Rather, Coke held that the law guaranteed proper processes of talking and argumentation, while Chancery jurisdiction and the King did not.

Chancery jurisdiction always had the power to grant relief from the formalities of the law in unusual cases. It exercised a wholly proper function of particular relief from the general law where the exigencies of the case demanded. But, in case of some direct conflict, which was paramount, the law or equitable relief in Chancery? Coke held that the law was paramount, while Bacon advocated the primacy of the prerogatives of the Chancellor. Practical logic is on the side of Coke: exceptions can be made to general rules and procedures, but if the power to make exceptions is the power to overrule the rules, then the rules become entirely meaningless. Thus the problem of common law versus Chancery is not, as usually stated,

4. James Spedding, *The Letters and the Life of Francis Bacon* (London, 1874), III, 4-5.

merely a power dispute between one policy group and another, but rather it is a dispute between some sort of structure and proper process, and administrative *ad hoc* decisions for every case.

The same problem came up with respect to criminal law. Coke doubted that the King could arbitrarily define any act as a crime simply by his proclamation. This did not mean that criminal law was fixed forever, but that the proper process of enacting criminal legislation was through the consent, i.e., the debate and deliberation, of Parliament. The making of criminal law, for Coke, involved due processes.

Bacon's solution to the problem of Coke's obstinate holding for the due and open processes of general law and legislation was simple: get rid of Coke. Bacon was Solicitor-General to James the First at the time, and his views were accepted in a qualified way: Coke was kicked upstairs, to become Chief Justice of King's Bench. King's Bench had jurisdiction over criminal cases only, and seemed a harmless place for Coke. Bacon thought that the promotion "will thereby turn Coke obsequious."[5]

This did not happen; Coke had a way of discovering basic issues of law and freedom in the very places that seemed to Bacon and James the most insignificant. Thus *Peacham's Case*,[6] instead of becoming a routine administrative persecution of a harmless and powerless intellectual dissenting from the regime, became a major precedent in the legal history of the freedom of thought. Edmund Peacham, a Puritan minister, was charged with the crime of high treason, on the evidence of rumors of lack of patriotism and some completely personal writings discovered in his lodgings at the time of his arrest. Bacon, now the King's Attorney, wanted some more evidence and attempted to persuade Peacham to confess to participation in a large conspiratorial plot against the King. Peacham would not oblige, and Bacon had to report that "Peacham was examined before torture, in torture, between torture, and after torture; nothing could be drawn from him, he still persisting in his obstinate and inexcusable denials."[7]

Bacon then conceived a plan that seemed, in terms of administrative efficiency, simple and brilliant. Why not interview the judges

5. Spedding, IV, 380.
6. James Spedding, *The Life and Times of Francis Bacon* (London, 1878), II, 49-60; Gardiner, *History of England*, II, 273-78; Bowen, *The Lion and the Throne*, pp. 350-54.
7. Gardiner, pp. 275-76.

that were going to hear the case, strongly hinting how the King wanted the case decided, and see whether the judges would convict? Afterwards, of course, the trial could be held, and all the forms observed. But Bacon, of course, ran head on into the very man he had put out of the way in the criminal courts. Chief Justice Coke held that any and all such pre-trial soundings were unconstitutional and against all right and tradition. This conflict involved more than bureaucrats jostling for power, with Coke trying to usurp power for the lawyers. A criminal trial is a process of hearing the arguments and viewing the evidence. As stated before, it is a guarantee of freedom to talk about the issues and the alternatives, leading to some determination of crime, guilt, and punishment. Bacon viewed that process as mere ceremony; Coke viewed that process as essential and necessary for the determination of the issues. Coke did not view due process in a criminal trial as the laying on of the "dead hand of the past," but rather as a present hearing of the issues of the case. The due process of argument, evidence, counter-argument, cross-questioning at the trial should be significant and effective, not ceremonial nonsense, according to Coke. Coke's appeal to tradition is an insistence that the criminal trial should be considered as a serious and reasonable process and not cynically rejected. Bacon did not obtain his pre-trial decision, and, furthermore, Coke wrote the whole case up for posterity in his *Reports*.

Problems of tax law, as well as criminal law, became crucial in the struggle between Coke and Bacon. When Parliament refused the tax policies proposed in 1614, Bacon and James thought of disposing of those taxes which required the consent of Parliament, and thus also getting rid of Parliament and all the talking, dissent, and opposition there. Parliament, in fact, was dissolved. Important Bishops of the Church were allowed to "freely offer" some of their monies and treasures to help the Crown. They did. Soon all important officials who wished to maintain some favor with the King were making "voluntary" offerings. Coke, no angel, did so himself. The extension of this plan again seemed simple and obvious: why not have King James appeal for "voluntary gifts" from landholders and wealthy men in the whole country? The monies of the government would be raised, loyal and unpatriotic citizens separated and properly noted, and no longer would the executive be bothered with the recalcitrance of Parliament. That such ideas have a perennial charm can be noted by discovering how much work has been "volunteered" in modern socialist countries: workers "volunteer" a sixth day of labor free for comrades somewhere, or for a needed harbor; children "volunteer" for simple projects; old people "volunteer" to clean the streets; one sees no force, and everything is freely done simply for the dubious joy of helping the government. Why not? Thus thought or hoped James and Bacon in 1614. (In 1628, King Charles was actually to try a similar scheme, and Parliament was dissolved more or less permanently; money was collected on a voluntary basis, there were no public objections to policies; and a general era of "good feeling" and peace came over the scene for well over ten years—until the Revolution—but that is another story.)

Unfortunately for the plan, in 1614 Coke was consulted. Coke did not, as was his wont, force the issue, but rather shrewdly said that, as a judge, his decision on such an enormous matter would take much time to consider. Realizing what Coke's answer would finally be and perhaps rethinking the plan even in terms of political expediencies, Bacon and James dropped the scheme. Taxation, Parliament, free discussion of the law and politics, talking in the most significant political sense, were allowed to continue for the time.[8]

Finally, in 1616, a direct clash between Coke and King occurred, with the Cokeian notions of the rule of law on one side, and the King's executive power and prerogatives on the other. The case that started the problem involved the legality of church sinecures granted by the King.[9] It was an important case and heard by the twelve leading judges of all England. Two Englishmen, Colt and Glover, had disputed the power of the King to appoint a Bishop *in commendams*, i.e., as a sinecure with the actual duties performed by a lowly agent in residence. The trial had begun and evidence and arguments on the issues were being heard, when King James, acting on reports from his church advisors that his powers were being questioned, stopped the trial.

The twelve judges received a letter from Bacon, the Attorney General, ordering them to report to the King and learn his further wishes. The judges, led by Coke, replied that the letter was illegal and that it was their duty to carry on with the trial and to deliver justice without delay, as stated in Magna Carta.

Could the King stop the whole process of law in its majesty, in a

8. *Ibid.*, pp. 240-41.
9. *Colt and Glover* v. *the Bishop of Coventry* ("Case of Commendams"); Coke's *Reports*; Spedding, *Life and Letters of Bacon*, v. 3.

great constitutional case already begun, leaving proceedings hanging in mid-air, simply at his whim and command? Could the twelve men representing the law stop the executive power determined on one issue?

King James personally called all the judges to council. There he complained of their letter of reply, tore it up before them, and ordered them to mend their ways. Eleven judges fell to their knees and begged forgiveness. Edward Coke remained standing and argued that the delay was a delay of justice and contrary to law.

James asked Bacon, who was present, to give his opinion. Bacon presented his favorite and continually repeated theory that the judges were agents and supporters of the executive power, that the oaths of office required that they always support the King first, and that his orders took priority over all else. Chancellor Ellesmere, head of the equity and ecclesiastical courts, which were much more in the Roman tradition, agreed with Bacon. Encouraged, King James went on to ask another question of the assembled judges: did the King not have the power to stop any legal proceedings whatsoever, at any time the King felt the matter was of royal concern? Could not the King stay any trial, any process, at any time? Eleven judges acknowledged humbly that such indeed was the royal prerogative and that to stay proceedings would be their duty.

The Chief Justice of King's Bench, Edward Coke, stated that when any such case should arise, he would do that which was fit for a judge to do.

James went on to the particular trial at hand: did he not have the power to appoint Bishops *in commendams?* Eleven judges stated that he did and promised to stop any pleader who so much as brought up the matter in any argument henceforth. Coke again refused.

The council was adjourned. The issue was joined.[10]

The administrative problem was what to do with Coke. He was called to a hearing in Star Chamber, and charged with pushing the common law too far and with indecent behavior before His Majesty, at the above meeting. Coke answered that defense of the common law was no sin, but in the tradition "of the fathers." At the council meeting he had been wrong to sneer at the King's Attorney, but his answer that he would act as a judge was not at all disrespectful. The charges were dropped.

10. Bowen, *The Lion and the Throne,* pp. 274-78.

Bacon, shrewdly enough, did not want to make Coke "the great martyr of the Commonwealth."[11] Coke was ordered to leave all other tasks and correct all the errors that could be found in his *Reports,* which, in 1616, ran to eleven volumes. Coke went to his country home for three months, studied his writings, and returned with five sentence changes.

Who knew enough to state that there were more errors? Bacon was helpless before the vast legal learning, and even Ellesmere did not know that much common law. All that Bacon could suggest was that Coke was conceited, that he had "a perpetual turbulent carriage" and that "he made himself popular pulling down government." The King would not act on this.

Bacon then worked up a list of seventeen charges against Coke, with long commentaries on each charge. James ignored this too. Bacon finally realized the best way to handle Coke: simply have no issue at all. Bacon then wrote a model dismissal notice, for the King's signature, with no charges or issues in it whatsoever. King James signed.

Thus Coke was simply dismissed. Bacon's note, signed by the King, was delivered: "For certain causes now moving us, we will that you no longer shall be our Chief Justice."[12] Coke wept. A new and totally subservient man was sworn in as Chief Justice by Chancellor Ellesmere. Perhaps overexcited or senile, Ellesmere died within four months, and Francis Bacon was made Lord Chancellor and Lord Keeper of the Great Seal. Soon after, James went hunting in Scotland with his favorite young man, Buckingham, and Bacon was the acting ruler of England.

For five years, Bacon was in his glory. Parliament was not called. The common law judges no longer gave trouble. Executive power over the law was not questioned. The threat of the rule of law was abated, and all public talking and debate about alternatives to government policies ceased. If one did not like these policies, one could leave the country (and small groups of dissenters did go to Holland and then to Massachusetts). Bacon himself managed to preside over all Chancery jurisdiction, advise the King, help tighten state finances, entertain lavishly, and, in his leftover time, write the *Novum Organon,* which he published in 1617. He remembered to send a copy to Coke.

11. *Ibid.,* p. 382.
12. *Ibid.,* p. 388.

Some particular details of this period must be introduced here, because they became important in the understanding of issues of freedom of speech with respect to open criticism of policy-makers, which arose shortly.

The peculiar politics of this period are overlooked by those who wish to adulate Francis Bacon. King James had begun to show open preferences for young men, and political power revolved around these centers of executive influence and concern. One early favorite, a young Scot named Carr, had been advanced in two short years from gentleman waiter to the Earl of Somerset. When he was implicated in a poison murder case, the trial, in which it is impossible to separate criminal doings and political fabrications, caused him to lose favor. Another young man, George Villiers, was picked (his handsome form elegantly attired), and introduced at Court by a faction which had opposed the group behind the Earl of Somerset. In a short time Villiers became the Earl of Buckingham, and later Duke of Buckingham. Clever and ambitious, Buckingham then made sure that all royal patronage and official appointments be cleared through him, which earned him enormous bribes. James also tended to follow Buckingham's advice on matters of state policy, although Buckingham was only in his twenties.

Francis Bacon, Viscount St. Albans, the great advocate of authoritarian executive power, somehow managed to avoid any critical judgment of all this. In any event, Bacon lived luxuriously enough, through the monies that came to him from royal favor and from bribes. He kept a retinue of one hundred servants, in proper livery of his own design and all "with Spanish leather boots." He had a town house and, in the country, maintained two mansions a mile from each other, with an enormously wide road between them. Money was dispensed or lost as quickly as taken in. He gave one party at Cambridge which cost seven hundred pounds. Servants became rich. When a visitor told Bacon he had seen two servants stealing money openly, Bacon exclaimed, "What can I do?" He perhaps could have instituted the college devoted to the experimental sciences, which had been advocated in the *New Atlantis,* since he now had both the power and the money to do so; but he did nothing to implement in significant practice the plans for inquiry he had conceived in theory.

In practical politics, England became involved in elaborate foreign intrigues with both Catholic and Protestant forces. Lip service was given to helping Protestants, but fear of Spain was always present, and the Spanish Ambassador was a person of great influence at Court. Military expeditions collapsed, policies were reversed without reason, economic conditions at home worsened, and the nation drifted toward a severe economic depression, which finally occurred in the 1620's. Foreign loans went unpaid, although the lavish scale of living of Buckingham was undiminished. Rumors at the time implied that money for the navy or for the Danish loans was spent on his personal toilette.

Coke made a desperate but futile attempt to regain some position by the only route then possible—a connection with Buckingham. He arranged for the marriage of his beautiful young daughter Frances to Buckingham's older brother John. Coke offered thirty thousand pounds dowry, which seemed acceptable to Buckingham and King James. (John was so smitten he said he would marry her in her shift, but took the dowry.) Coke had overlooked asking his wife about the match. Lady Hatton violently resented the whole plan, and took her daughter into hiding. This resulted in an open brawl between Coke and his wife. The marriage did occur but helped Coke's position not one whit. Incidentally Frances Coke Villiers went on to become one of the most notorious and spirited beauties in London society.

But the period of pure executive prerogative was closing. James was greatly in need of money, and the "voluntary offerings" were insufficient. In 1621 he was forced to call another Parliament, and Coke, almost 70 years old, was back in public life, as a member of the House. He immediately became one of the leaders of the opposition.

James needed money, and in return for the monies and taxes granted, Parliament obtained certain concessions and promises. Wars would be waged against Catholic, not Protestant, powers, and the scapegoat for the general discontent with the administration would be the Lord Chancellor.

Bacon was impeached. Testimony as to bribes taken was collected. One of Bacon's defenses was that since he took bribes from both sides, and promised nothing, justice was still accomplished. At King James' suggestion, Bacon pleaded guilty, was heavily fined, dismissed from office, and forbidden to enter London again. He retired in permanent disgrace to the country home he was allowed to keep and wrote and revised his works on the improvement of the human condition.

Coke ended the term in even worse condition. In the *Reports* of this session, Coke's speeches occupy more than one-fifth of the space.[13] He said nothing against Bacon and was not an open leader in the impeachment, but he obviously was a power in the opposition, an advocate of freedom of speech, and a critic of foreign policy, just as spirited and tough as ever. So James had him summarily arrested and thrown in the Tower of London. His houses were closed and searched. He was permitted no visitors, no books, and no paper. At seventy, the great legal scholar, judge, and Parliamentarian was reduced to writing on the walls of his cell with charcoal bits. When asked about Coke, James replied that he had never heard of him.

It was not unknown for men to die in such conditions, but Coke was known as a great leader by important sections of England's people; he had become, himself, an institution of the law. After seven months, Coke was released.

Coke immediately went back to Parliament and was as thorny and demanding as before. He continued as leader of the opposition, powerful both in party counsel and in debate with the Court Party. He kept his ability to quote old statutes and forgotten precedents, as well as an overwhelming skill in debate.

King James finally died, but the Duke of Buckingham continued in power as friend, favorite, and bad advisor to the new King, James' son Charles. Charles rid himself of Coke for a year by appointing him Sheriff of Norfolk. The office required that the man reside in the area for the term. But in 1626 Coke was back in Parliament, fierce as ever. A general economic depression existed, due to causes including a general lack of confidence in the government and some disastrous military campaigns which had been led by Buckingham. King Charles raised the final issue of Coke's political career by decreeing that all discussion or criticism of the Duke of Buckingham was forbidden.

The general issue here was whether the ministers and agents of the policy-making executive power were beyond general criticism. What was involved was not only the policies, but the politicians. Parliament might be limited, as it had been in the past, to discussing whether taxes were acceptable or not. The persons of the King's ministers, the executive agents, might be beyond the pale of discussion. Edward Coke opposed all this.

13. William Cobbett, *Parliamentary History of England* (London, 1806), I, 1399-1403.

Coke alone had the personal power to defy the royal interdict and to overawe the Speaker of the House. Other leaders (such as Thomas Eliot) had been silenced. If Parliament could not discuss Buckingham, perhaps a committee could do so. Parliament moved to become a committee of the whole, the Speaker of the House, a King's man, removed himself, and Coke got up and criticized Buckingham: "Now, shall we hold our tongues? Why may we not name those that are the cause of all our evils? And therefore, not knowing if I shall ever speak in this House again, I shall speak freely. I think the Duke of Buckingham is the cause of all our miseries."[14]

So Buckingham had to stand to Parliamentary criticism. Later, it would become an obvious right to discuss, and even to choose, the ministers of executive action and policy, and such discussion would not be a death-defying challenge. But the first steps had to be taken in that direction, and they were taken firmly by old Coke. (Buckingham survived the criticism but was knifed by an assassin; his successor was thought to be tougher and much worse.)

Coke's second major task was to prepare the Petition of Right, and obtain its full acceptance by King Charles. The Petition declared two main rights against personal rule: (1) all taxes and also any "voluntary" offerings, such as "gifts, loans, and benevolences" to the government, must be discussed and passed by Parliament. Coke wanted to prevent the appearance of obedient and willing cooperation with a tyrannical personal rule, that takes the form of voluntary contributions to government causes; and (2) no man could be imprisoned without cause.[15] The sort of arbitrary imprisonment Coke had suffered himself was to be forever forbidden.

The immediate effectiveness of this petition was nil, for Charles dissolved Parliament and England had thirteen years of "personal rule." But the petition was basic in legitimizing fundamental rights of freedom of speech in later times.

In terms of the general problem of the legal bases of freedom, Coke in the Petition of Right established the right to discuss all methods of government procural of goods and services, and he secured this right by the needed supplementary right of protection of the person against arbitrary government persecution. The methods of governmental terror, used in the twentieth century to stifle any

14. Bowen, *The Lion and the Throne,* pp. 500-501.
15. J. R. Tanner, *English Constitutional Conflicts of the Seventeenth Century* (Cambridge, England, 1928), pp. 62-64.

political opposition and any critical discussion whatsoever, were legally denied by Coke in the Petition of Right. Charles might well have listened to Coke and the Petition. The oppressive rule of Charles without Parliament, with his new ruthless advisor Laud, only led to the radical discontent erupting in a revolution and to the death of Charles himself. Law and freedom of speech are means of settling political problems with the peaceful modes of deliberation and debate; when these modes are not available, violence becomes the alternative procedure.

The Petition of Right was not the end of Coke's legal work, nor was it the culminating achievement of his life. His major work, for later law and constitutional rights, was the preparation of the massive *Institutes* and the *Reports*. Coke, in retirement after the famous Parliament of 1628, worked on both books. He attempted to publish the second and third volumes of his *Institutes* in 1631, but the King refused to allow it. By this time, what had formerly seemed harmless scholarship was understood as establishing powers against royal action. The second volume of the *Institutes* did indeed deal with the *Magna Carta* and other great documents of citizens' rights in English history. The third volume dealt with proper criminal procedures, again against arbitrary imprisonment and the arbitrary torture of earlier regimes. But the books were not burned or destroyed and were immediately published after the overthrow of Charles by the order of Parliament in 1641. Coke's works became established as authoritative presentations of the law, or rather, became the basis of the law after the constitutional revolution of 1688 and endured as authority until well into the nineteenth century. No later interpretations have emphasized basic rights as much as those of Coke. Coke provided the legal basis for modern liberal constitutional government.

If Coke's works on the law had not been written and published, the later developments of constitutional government and a free and open society would have been greatly hindered. This has been forgotten, and the *legal* bases of modern English and American constitutional governments are ignored and forgotten.

What are these legal foundations? They can be roughly limited to four main topics, all of which are still matters of controversy somewhere in the world at the present day: (1) the independence of the law; (2) the notion of independent property; (3) the rights of citizens; and (4) the matter of due process of law.

1. *The Independence of the Law*

The existence of a disciplined and ordered body of learning in the law independent of the direct executive policy-making power gives a basis for the independence of the judiciary from the immediate policies of the current regime. Decisions in the law, no matter how ultimate the issue, depend on professional competence and professional independence, and not direct expediency. The issue is whether the law should be defined as an order independent of present policy or whether it should be "The Command of the Sovereign." The first view was held by Coke, the second by a series of critics, notably Bacon,[16] and after him Hobbes,[17] John Austin,[18] and in the present day such men as Hans Kelsen,[19] the late J. L. Austin,[20] and H.L.A. Hart.[21] On one side is the difficult "artificial reason" of the law, as contained in the tedious volumes of Coke, and on the other side is the view that the executive should not be limited by the law and that the law should be the instrument of government and policy.

But the second view denies the need for what in modern sociological parlance is called the demand for *legitimation* of political power. If the law and the judges are mere tools, they can give none of the required *rightness* to the politicians. Politicians need the independence of the law in order to guarantee the legality of their actions. When Bacon was no longer useful or needed he could be dispensed with easily—other bright subordinates could be found. But although Coke was not useful, he was necessary, and he could not be deposed, for he was the legitimacy the Stuart kings needed.

Thomas Hobbes continues the authoritarian attack on Coke by stressing the ultimate rule and power of the sovereign. Hobbes' direct attack on Coke, in his *Dialogue of a Philosopher With a Student of*

16. Francis Bacon, *The Advancement of Learning*, book eight, chapter 3: "The Doctrine of Universal Justice or the Fountains of Law;" *The Maxims of the Law*, in *Works*, I and VIII, ed. James Spedding *et al.* (London, 1878).

17. Thomas Hobbes, *A Dialogue Between A Philosopher and a Student of the Common Laws of England. English Works*, ed. Sir William Molesworth (London, 1845), III.

18. John Austin, *The Province of Jurisprudence Determined* (London, 1832). See also along almost identical lines, Bentham's *Limits of Jurisprudence Defined* (London, 1798).

19. Hans Kelsen, *General Theory of Law and the State* (Cambridge, Mass., 1945).

20. J. L. Austin, "A Plea for Excuses," remark 7. *Regina* v. *Finney*, in *Philosophical Papers* (Oxford, 1961).

21. H. L. A. Hart, *The Concept of Law* (Oxford, 1961), chapter 4, "Sovereign and Subject."

the Common Laws, concerns only particular rules which are overly complicated and inefficient. Hobbes argues not for revision of these rules within the framework of the common law, but for abandonment of the common law entirely, in favor of a "rational system" of orders proceeding directly from the sovereign. Hobbes entirely forgets, in such revisions, the problems of legitimacy. The same general argument was repeated by Bentham, who supposed that the law could be made a scientific body of rules proceeding directly from the sovereign and in accordance with the "simple and clear" formula of the greatest good for the greatest number. Even in the recent past the late linguistic analyst J. L. Austin has questioned the common law, which he found unreasonable according to "natural reason"; Austin too has ignored general legitimacy as a basic problem.

These opponents ignore the basis of the law as a due process of hearing and weighing of evidence, and listening to arguments from all sides. This process can be either legislative or judicial, but it is properly opposed to arbitrary personal fiat. But the issue as falsely seen by the opponents is that the law, as an outworn set of restrictive conclusions, is opposing progress, which is something obvious, efficient, and natural. What is taken by these opponents to be "natural" differs down through the ages, from Divine Right and Royal Prerogative, to contracted power, to public utility, to the present day's ordinary linguistic usage, or the Marxist's complacent statements of the union of theory and practice in scientific socialist policy. What is taken to be the dogmatism of the law is to be replaced by power or personal belief or a philosophic cult. But the heart of the law, as a history of orderly argument, due process, deliberation over cases, and political policies, is ignored. And the heart of the law has the overlooked factor of legitimacy about it, which the various "scientific" revisions do not have.

Thus Coke, when he moved from King's Bench to Parliament, did not have to change his views on the law, although this is often claimed. When Coke was a judge, he argued for the proper processes of hearing and argument of cases; when he was a member of Parliament, he argued for debate and discussion of new tax laws and of public policies. In both situations there were proper and legitimate ways for deliberating and coming to decisions and determinations. When Coke finished his *Institutes,* he did not distinguish between the law as deliberated upon by judges in law courts and the law as the proper basic rights of Parliament and citizens in general to openly discuss taxation laws and policies in general, because both are necessary components of due process of law.

2. *The Notion of Independent Property*

Coke restated the laws of property in terms which allowed the ownership of property to be considered as a topic independent of current governmental authority. Property in feudal times was one of the feudal ties of allegiance and obligation; there was no free and independent property to be used, leased, or sold at the will of the owner; the fiefholder was bound to the land and to his liege lord. Coke ignored all such feudal relations binding property to political subservience. Thus, most notably, in defining "fief," Coke stated that it meant "inheritance."[22]

In terms of modern economic analysis Coke prepared the legal foundations of capitalism, but he also prepared the legal foundations of political independence. Dissent and criticism of the government could be made without charges of treason, disenfeoffment of lands, and the loss of a means of livelihood, if not life itself. The security of property allowed men to speak and act against arbitrary or ill-considered government policy. Coke himself was an example of a man who had obtained property in the modern free fashion and who used it in a life of political independence. And once title was free and independent, the economy as a whole could move from simple and stagnant agrarianism to modern commercialism and industrialism. Sixty years after Coke, Locke was astonished to find a goldsmith in Lombard Street with a standing credit of 100,000 pounds. Thus Coke's erudite but quite unmedieval *Commentary on Lyttleton*, published as the first part of his *Institutes* in 1628, laid the legal foundations for both capitalism *and* the practical open discussion of public issues. The rights of private property, simply assumed by John Locke in 1690, did not exist in medieval England and would not have appeared so obvious to Locke but for the publications of the lawyer Coke. This conception of private property was, by and large, a creation of Coke. Granted that it was done in the name of an historical commentary on a fifteenth-century text and that it was done in the name of all past precedents and usages, Coke's doctrine, in fact, made authoritative a view never before widely or firmly held, namely the radical independence of property from sovereignty. This view is not, however, universally respected.

22. Coke, *Institutes,* first part, I, sect. 1, "On fee simple."

The attacks by Marx and post-Marxists on private property reduce such property to an instrument of a dominant class, the capitalist class. Private property is a myth used as a weapon in a basic and perennial struggle for total political power. The establishment of property rights by Coke's work and the later political revolution guaranteeing constitutional government are viewed by Marxist historians simply as steps in the rise to power of a new class. Marxists reject private property as a base for *dissent* against the government. But when private property goes, so does dissent and freedom. Both private property and the effective freedom to speak against government policy have been abolished in socialist-communist regimes at the present time. Government plans include the use of all properties within the state as a matter of political right and utility. There are no serious effective objections within the society, because there is no practical way to live while maintaining opposition to the regime. In practical affairs, the threat to abolish the means of life acts as an effective sanction against the higher calls of conscience and the public duty to criticize foolish state policies. Thus without private property, control of speech and even thought is not difficult, and one can discover such renewed government control in any of the totalitarian socialist nations. The practical interrelation of rights of property and livelihood with the higher rights of freedom of speech and thought is frequently ignored by liberals in the United States, who want to have the latter and ignore the former. However, the latter disappears without the former.

3. *The Rights of Citizens*

The third area in which Coke made lasting contributions to the rule of law and basic rights is the area of constitutional rights and the establishment of traditions and precedents against arbitrary government. The second part of the *Institutes* is important because of Coke's *creation* of "traditional" rights of citizens against the executive power. What Coke developed in the *Institutes* was a conception of a society where the citizens were free and equal and had rights which were to be respected by all governing parties. His views have been largely misunderstood and vehemently attacked. He has been called a medievalist who maintained earlier views of limiting restraints on sovereign power, when all modern governments were being "rationalized" toward a conception of some final and unlimited sovereign rule. He has also been called a man who knew nothing about actual medieval conditions and law and misunderstood, among other things, *Magna Carta*[23] (which in the Middle Ages did not give rights to all Englishmen and was not so intended, but protected only the barons, a small group indeed).

As against the former critics, Coke's notion of a government acting within traditional and accepted (and therefore effective) conceptions of right and wrong was maintained in later English history and in the development of the American colonies. Comparison of Locke's view of right with Rousseau's or Kant's reveals that Locke could discuss rights in concrete practical terms, while Rousseau had to call either for an end to all civilization in the name of morality or an acceptance of moral corruption and man "everywhere in chains." Kant discussed rights in a "world of ends" having no direct relation to the practical world around him, where all rights depended on the favor of the King. Kant separated an *ideal* world of law and freedom from the authoritarian and unjust situation in this world. Kant did not hope for a working justice in this world. But Coke's conception of governments *in this world* acting within limits defined by rights has proved viable, although rare. Coke did not say his views were universal. He was dealing with the laws of England, not stating observations about world conditions.

The second charge, that Coke "expanded" the *Magna Carta* and the rights stated there, is correct in a limited way and incorrect in the major way. Without Coke's elaborate commentary and development of the *Magna Carta,* in the popular and authoritative *Institutes,* it would rightfully be regarded as a minor document in the struggle between barons, kings, and popes in the thirteenth century, of little or no practical significance in that era. Because of Coke, the *Magna Carta* is important from the seventeenth century onward and it did apply to all Englishmen. Coke's history is the crucial factor. He could not have written his history without *some* document, but that document acquired its great significance when assigned first place in the traditions of the liberties and rights of Englishmen in the *Institutes.* Coke is himself the major historical basis for the significance of the Great Charter. As with the laws of property, constitutional rights looked very different *after* Coke. *Magna Carta* has had great subsequent effect as a document of rights and consti-

23. See Morris Cohen, *Law and the Social Order* (New York, 1933), "The Conservative Lawyer's Legend of Magna Carta," pp. 19-23; J. R. Tanner, *Constitutional Documents of James I* (Cambridge, England, 1933), p. 176.

tutional rule, and historians who scoff because they do not find this in the thirteenth century should realize they are looking at the wrong time. It was after the printing press, general literacy, and Coke's expanded restatement and commentary in published and widely read books that *Magna Carta* and other documents detailing powers and rights of citizens became important.

4. *Due Process of Law*

The last important aspect of Coke's writings was his dicussions of procedure. The problem of due process of law is never merely one of formal rules but rather of the substantial values of freedom and right. Refusal to take the processes of the law seriously often leads to lynch justice, mob rule, or arbitrary executive action in which any sort of behavior may become criminal. The whole problem of due process, so critical in our own times, will be a recurrent theme of this book. It should be stressed that Coke devoted volumes to the explication of the due process of the law. Due process is not formal and empty procedure but is consideration of basic values of civilization and individual rights. Problems of substantial due process continue to be taken as important or rejected as false in debates on jurisprudence at the present time. Coke did not originate the notions of due process, but he affirmed them for his day, and later reaffirmations (the Fourteenth Amendment) owe much to him.

Coke's groundwork for modern liberalism is vastly underrated. When the peaceful "Glorious Revolution" of 1688 occurred in England, its instigators assumed without articulation much of Coke's work as basic. Locke's famous defense of that revolution is in terms of property and the right of judgment of citizens, but he assumed general standards of *legitimacy* established by Coke. When Locke, the chief defender of the Revolution of 1688, stated in his *Second Treatise on Government* that he would prove that William and Mary were the most *legitimate* monarchs in Europe, whence did he derive his conceptions of a legitimacy distinct from direct political power? From the Stuarts? From Cromwell? No, from Coke. Where did Locke obtain his idea of private property? From Coke. Coke provided the legal bases for a society in which law and right, discussion, fair hearings, and debate have some check on power and in which individual freedom and rights have practical significance. The new government under Parliament and William and Mary guaranteed the rights articulated by Coke.

In the debates on the nature of the law, analytical opponents of Coke's views, such as Bacon, Hobbes, and Bentham, wish to substitute for the flexible, ambiguous laws a systematic body of rules, but these rules would leave the governing power in much more complete control of all practical policies and judicial determinations. On the other hand, Coke's common law is an *open system,* which allows a fair hearing for all arguments, not only with respect to immediate issues, but with respect to revision of general traditions and rules. Due process in common law restricts the rulers and guarantees the rights of the citizens. The problem Coke faced was to restrict the prerogative of the rulers, and he saw the common law as achieving this aim.

Even in the conflict between law and technology represented by Coke and Bacon, Coke's open view does not exclude the programs for the advancement of science. Bacon's views, seen in his *New Atlantis* (and in our time in Thorstein Veblen's work on "technocracy"), assumed that administrators would always benevolently work for the utility and benefit of society. Modern science and technology, said Bacon, could best serve the human estate in an authoritarian political order. The inevitable result was that Bacon saw opposition such as Coke's as reactionary, egotistical, unscientific, and totally lacking in reason, with a popular support that was "artificial." The modern exemplars of Baconian philosophy are those totalitarian countries where all is devoted to national industrial production and useful scientific advances, where independent thought and effective internal opposition to the holders of political power have disappeared, so that all policies are formulated in the name of a general public which submits or accepts in silence, or with an enthusiasm which can be traced to a combination of propaganda and ignorance. Bacon prophesied not only modern science, but modern Big Brother scientific administration which directs all human activities in the name of progress.

In the debate, Coke stood for the maintenance of individual liberties and rights, for individual property rights as against total planning and control, and for limits on all government policymaking. The results of such a constitutional program added up to practical progress. By following Coke's conception of law and constitutional government, England, and later the United States, developed industry, wealth, and most importantly, civilized standards of respect for life far beyond the plans and achievements of the centralized governments of other lands. Coke's rights and freedoms did not mean the end of modernity, but rather the beginning of progress. The rule of law encourages the independent activity of mature citizens who develop science and commerce, agriculture and philosophy, in all sorts of unpredictable ways.

The weakness of the authoritarian alternatives to the liberal notion of private rights has been the weakness or the viciousness of the men who have obtained the position of ultimate authority. Coke's views and principles have provided the means for avoiding or mitigating this catastrophe, and in the perspective of three centuries this has been the source of practical strength against the glamorous seductions and ostensibly rational enticements of unlimited directing power. Again in the Twentieth Century the problem of central planning versus constitutional and legal rights has arisen, and Coke's statement of the issue should not be forgotten.

2

Locke

Locke's work established the philosophic basis for freedom of speech and discussion for all men with respect to all practical affairs. These affairs included for Locke politics, economics, and religion. But most of all, practical life included and involved speech and discussion itself. Locke's first major published work was his *Letters Concerning Toleration* in which he advocated freedom of opinion and of association and argued against the repression of unorthodox beliefs by government censors. Like much of Locke's work, these letters take the form of an argument with an advocate of opposing views: the reader is allowed to realize that arguments exist on both sides of the question and that judgment is required to decide the issues. Emphasis on tolerance, argument, and judgment runs through all of Locke's philosophy, and that philosophy articulates the practical relations holding between talking, the rule of law, and freedom, which may still be a ground for renewed arguments today.

Locke's view of the common good for man depends on the connections between talking, freedom, and law. For there is no way to determine what the common good is except by discussion and argumentation and agreement among citizens who are, in fact, living together. In a society living under the rule of law, common problems will be handled by discussion among all the mature people, with the majority view determining what will happen in each particular instance. Humble submission to the opinions and rules of one man,

45

or a small group of men, in political life is a sign of radical immaturity and is the end of all freedom. Men who take directions from some leader whom they believe beyond all judgment or reproach are children, or even worse, slaves. Law is the proper structure of freedom, since it allows free men to determine their direction for themselves by talking. Or, men can change directions by talking: Locke is a philosopher of peaceful revolution. He articulated the national need for the peaceful revolution which occurred in England in 1688, establishing the rule of law, tolerance of beliefs and statements, and modern constitutional liberalism. In our age, when political options seem divided between the extremes of revolution by violence and unthinking defense of the status quo, Locke's views merit reconsideration. The obvious differences of opinion on vital matters struck Locke as important, and he was concerned with the practical resolution of such differences through thinking and talking, rather than force.

In the "Foreword" to his *Letters Concerning Toleration*, Locke stated his primary thesis: "Absolute liberty, just and true liberty, equal and impartial liberty, is the thing that we stand in need of."[1] Viewed from within, each ideology appears true enough; viewed from outside, all seem to disagree. Such disagreements can lead either to fighting or to thinking, and Locke preferred the workings of the mind: "Dissension unavoidably puts upon us a necessity of deliberating, and consequently allows a liberty of that which upon consideration we prefer." Disagreement is a beginning for deliberation, and deliberation gives us both freedom and final determining choice. Furthermore, if disagreements ended, freedom and choice would be terminated. For Locke, our minds, like water, become stagnant if still too long; activity and controversy are healthy and can be peacefully pursued, as Locke pursued arguments with censors, economists, bishops, and apologists for "Divine Right of Kings."

Volumes of Locke's writings are of this controversial kind, with original essay followed by reply, rejoinder, defense, and answer to the opposing theses of the economist Lowndes, or the churchman Stillingfleet, or Worcester, or whomever. With all this argumentation Locke achieved his purpose: there was nothing sacred left in the realm of practical thought; all things could be discussed, and all freely judged that was relevant to man's life here on earth. (Not that

1. John Locke, *First Letter Concerning Toleration, Works* (London, 1823), VI, 4.

Locke denied the sacred altogether, for God, revelation, and man's final destiny were all matters beyond the limits of practical reason.) But issues of practical life were matters for dissension, freedom, and choice. Locke achieved in the realm of *practical* life what Descartes had achieved in the realm of *theoretical* philosophy in the objections and replies to his philosophy, published at the end of his *Meditations*. Philosophy had been stifled by the pressures of orthodoxy before, but Descartes' arguments with Hobbes, Gassendi, Arnauld, and others had permanently opened this realm to free public reasoning. But while Descartes had carefully avoided talking of practical matters of morals and politics, this is exactly the realm where Locke plunged in to start public arguments and to dethrone taboos. Whether he was always right in his views is not our primary concern, for all opinions of men are only probable, and those who think they have the whole truth are deluded enthusiasts. The primary concern, however, was with freedom of argument and talking and deliberation; the personal prejudices of the leading figures in the Establishment could no longer automatically carry the day, and the rule of law could structure the ensuing freedoms.

There are practical examples of this in economics, religion, and politics. Locke favored hard money and free interest rates as against advocates of devaluation and legal maximum interest rates, an argument which continues to this day. He favored tolerance for Moslems as well as Jews, an opinion astounding at that time, if not today. And he favored a society of free citizens as against authoritarian rule. It is the latter which is the most important aspect of Locke's thought, and in his treatises on government he is least polite to his opponents. Thus in arguing with his opponent on economic policy, Locke is most considerate: "Though Mr. Lowndes and I differ in the way, yet, I assure myself, our end is the same; and that we both propose to ourselves the service of our country. He is a man known so able . . . so learned, so exact . . . that had not he engaged me in the subject himself, I should have troubled the public no more."[2]

But with respect to Sir Robert Filmer and political problems, the tone becomes highly satirical: "Slavery is so vile that it is hardly to be conceived that an Englishman should plead for it. And truly I should have taken Sir Robert Filmer's discourse as an exercise of wit, had not the gravity of the title, and the epistle, and the picture

2. John Locke, *Further Considerations Concerning Raising the Value of Money*, V, 136.

in the front of the book, and the applause that followed, required me to believe that the author and the publisher were in earnest. . . ."[3]

Locke's *Treatises on Government* have their basis in both his views on toleration and in his orientation toward practical judgment, probabilism, and anti-authoritarianism in his large work *Essay Concerning Human Understanding*. Toleration and probabilism are the reflective realizations that no one group, party, or association has a complete monopoly of the truth, although from within a group or party one may believe he has actually grasped the truth. The human understanding operates in terms of empirical data and its own constructions and interpretations of these data, and these human constructions and interpretations are at best useful and probable. The emphasis on probabilism in the *Essay* is not erased by the tone of certitude taken in the political works, for the political certainties start from the premise that men act freely on the basis of their own judgments with respect to the circumstances in which they find themselves and that men differ in these judgments. These principles follow from the conclusions of the work on understanding. People who use their minds discover only one certainty: they are free.

The *Second Treatise on Government* opens with a basic principle and an essential set of distinctions. The principle is that men are born free. The distinctions are between kinds of power and authority. Parental power and authority are for the good of immature children and cease when those children have matured. Business control and authority are for the private good of the individual parties involved on both sides, without any general common good. Slavery is for the good of the master alone. None of these is the same as political power and authority. Political power and authority are delegated power, coming from the citizens, and for the common good.

Locke has been accused of excessive individualism, basing all government on economic relations and at the same time reducing all government to such relations. There is some basis for this in terms of what he says about property, but not adequate basis, and finally it is simply not true. This would reduce the state to the economic relation of employer and employees or a group of individuals making business contracts for their own selfish good. But this is Locke's view of the Hobbesian state, in which there is no freedom and no equality. Locke argues against Filmer who wanted to reduce the state

3. John Locke, *First Treatise of Government,* V, 212.

to economic relations depending upon property, and to authoritarian relations depending upon personal leadership qualities and irrational charismatic factors. Locke argues that, although the arguments typically go together, it is fallacious to combine them, and in fact, either alone is fallacious.

What Locke is *against*, which is why so much time is spent explaining the role of parents, is the reduction of political rule to economic relations or paternalistic controls. Property is explained as arising from individual human operations on the basically common materials of the earth; value in property is seen as deriving from human operations and human convention. The purpose of preserving private property in a developed society is to form a bulwark *against* domination by the executive governmental authority, not to control such authority for the good of one class in society, the propertied class. For Locke, political legislation should be for the common good, and law in its generality should rule both the rich and the poor alike; it should not be for the rich over the poor.

The positive analysis Locke develops is more complex than usually described. The "natural state" of freedom and equality among men is not adequate for the solution of all disagreements, for even though men are social, reasonable, and equal, men tend to see problems from particular and selfish perspectives. Men are not good judges in their own cases because they are partial to themselves. Thus government can first be seen as an arbitration body for disputes. This is little more than a sheriff and a judge, and sometimes such is held to be Locke's final view of the matter. But this is not so. Government, once instituted, develops powers and policies of its own, and in itself government becomes the central problem of society. A first solution given by Locke is to establish a legislative power in the government, responsible to the people through elections, and ruling through general laws and for the common good. But any such legislature needs some executive to enforce the laws, and thus there must be an executive power, hopefully completely and literally subordinate to the legislative power. All this is not only reasonable enough, it is the pattern of constitutional and representative democracy in England and America.

But Locke realizes that clear theoretical distinctions and limitations are not so clear in actual practice. There is a tendency on the part of the executive power to strengthen its prerogatives and expand the area of immediate choices. The executive always sees these uses of power as right, lawful, and constitutional, although the people may not. When has the executive overstepped its bounds, with respect to the exercise of prerogative? This is the final problem in Locke's philosophy, and with it goes the answer, that although there is no clear line that can be drawn with regard to such things, it is *the people as a whole* who shall judge the matter, and *not* the executive power.

Finally, at the very end of the essay, Locke delineates the structure of peaceful changes in the ruling power. If the people have set temporal limits to the duration of the power of the legislative and the executive power, then the power reverts to the people at the end of that time, and the people can then erect new forms or place the old form in new hands. Ideally this is a structure governed by constitutional election not only for freedom, but also for peaceful revolution.

Within this structure of government and the need for some practical limits on executive tyranny, it is presupposed that viewpoints among the electorate will conflict. When arguing against Filmer's authoritarian view, Locke points out that Filmer deduces the rights of absolute power both from God's granting of earthly sovereignty to Adam, and from the mere facts of power itself. But, since no one can say who the direct descendants of Adam are, that is, since no one can say which political view is absolutely correct, then the group in power claims not only power but right. Instead of power coming from right, right actually comes from power. Locke also says that such arbitrary rule can exist in a democracy, as well as in a monarchy; the rulers can take on themselves tyrannical powers, as they did in Athens at various times. The alternative to this assumption of power is law, dissent, and the freedom of views different from those of the policy-makers and power-holders.

The problem of rule by majority vote assumes that there are dissenting groups in the society. At any one time some decisions have to be made. They should be made by the majority, simply because the only alternative is that the minority should make them. But also there is the further consideration that the majority at one time may not be the majority at another time. People may change their minds and a new legislature be elected. The principle of majority rule is of practical value for deciding immediate problems and yet allowing continued freedom for the legal decision of other problems at another time. If one power becomes so overwhelming that there is no impartial appeal against it, then there is no rule of law, and arbitrary exercise of power, which is bound to be abused, is the inevitable result.

Locke's argument is based on premises which identify maturity with ability to judge political issues. He insists that mature citizens will always demand political freedom and that people who accept authoritarian government without question must be immature, and therefore, to some extent, they deserve what they get. Children need to be ruled like children, and adults demand to be respected as adults.

But there is a certain illogicality in mature people that Locke ignores in his polemics and in his defense of the constitutional and peaceful revolution of 1688. People *do* tend to vote for political leaders on irrational grounds. For instance, in the televised debate between John Kennedy and Richard Nixon, during the campaign of 1960, it was thought that Nixon may have lost the election, not because of what he said, but because he looked as if he had not shaved. He did not look as "energetic" as Kennedy, and, in general, he lacked the charismatic qualities of a good popular leader. Selection of leaders on the basis of a public-relations image is a study for sociology. Furthermore, Locke did not view as likely the domination of one class in a free society under law. But the wealthy class can oppress the rest of society using law as an instrument. Such domination of the political realm by an economic class can be studied by economic analysts.

These are possibilities which make sociology and economics significant, but they are also tendencies toward authoritarianism in government. When Locke attacks them, his positive concept of a free and lawful government perhaps involves more than he wants to say; it involves some notion of basic political wisdom on the part of the voting public and the elected representatives in the legislature. It is assumed by Locke that men can distinguish the virtues that make a man a good actor or athlete, from the abilities that make a statesman. It is assumed by Locke that the laws will aim at the common good, and not be for the benefit of any one small group, and that citizens will recognize any deviations from this purpose and have the insight to oppose it. Locke assumes political insight in citizens, which does not have to be vast and all-inclusive, but does have to be discriminating, and he assumes some statesmanship in the persons vocationally active in political life, in and out of office. A free constitutional society requires more than the mere process of growing to voting age.

At the same time, if Locke is correct in his analysis, then the various perversions of a society ruled by laws and legislatures can be identified as corruptions, as deviations, and not taken as the cynical truth about all political order. Locke developed practical standards for legal freedom, and if there is then taxation without representation, or other similar injustices, something is wrong. If citizens elect football coaches or astronauts to the Senate who do not have the necessary political knowledge, the voters have used poor judgment. If one small interested group dominates all government and all other groups, the common good has been ignored. These things all happen, and perhaps, given freedom, such things will always happen sometimes, but even if Locke underrated the possibilities in these directions, he still established goals for structured freedom, rather than turning to an authoritarian elite to set everything right.

The alternatives to a Lockean politics, in the modern world, are derived from Hume on one side and from Hegel and Marx on the other. Hume, writing some one hundred years after Locke, could assume the institutions of a free society as part of an inherited tradition. Hume therefore argued for a free and open society, but one which is dominated by a strong executive relying on tradition and customary authority for his powers.[4] The strong executive power is established to maintain and extend the established open society. Hume and Burke[5] both discovered the luxury of being authoritarian and traditionalist in an open and liberal society only because of a century of acceptance of Locke's philosophy of government through law and government responsible to the electorate. In the twentieth century such philosophy has become a philosophy of defense of the status quo through a strong man, whether he is popular or not, and whether or not he executes policies developed by a deliberative legislative body.[6] This executive rule is operated, even in the United States, in the name of freedom, rather than tyranny, because it claims to be maintaining traditions of freedom developed over past centuries, as against the dogmatic ideologies of modern totalitarian views.

On the other side is the basic Hegelian dialectic of master and servant. Presented first in the *Phenomenology of the Spirit,* Hegel's notion of revolutions proceeds from consideration of a struggle be-

4. David Hume, *History of England* (New York, 1850), III and IV. See also L. L. Bongie, *David Hume, Prophet of the Counter-Revolution* (Oxford, 1965).

5. Edmund Burke, *Reflections on the Revolution in France* (London, 1790).

6. Clinton Rossiter, *The American Presidency* (New York, 1960); Carl Friedrich, *Man and His Government* (New York, 1963), pp. 159-99.

tween opposing parties in the name of "recognition," which leads to the victory and dominance of one party or class.[7] The dominating or ruling party, at first energetic, gradually deteriorates under the luxurious conditions of rule, and the unsuccessful party, which is dominated and must work, gradually becomes more realistic and tough. Finally "the workers" overthrow the "decadent" rulers and establish a new victorious equality for all men, with a ruling group "representing" everyone. In Hegel's developing analysis, the executive power in modern times represents everyone and is the universal and true ruling power. The various groups represented in a legislative body see various partial views, which they never transcend, and the agreements among these partisan groups are trivial compromises, not pure universal and true policies. As developed in Marx and post-Marxian thought, this analysis of revolutions was qualified or added to, but not basically changed:[8] current society has been run by an owning class, but it has become decadent and no longer represents the true interests of society as a whole. The new class, the revolutionary workers' class, must overthrow the owning class by force and establish a strong executive power that will rule in the name of the universal interests of all society. This new ruling class of workers' representatives claims that it can rule justly and eliminate the "trivial and secondary" debates among parties and interest groups that were part of the "hypocrisy" of the period of capitalist domination, debates which in truth had nothing to do with basic universal policy developments anyway, all of which had been determined by the ruling class and for the interests of the propertied class.

It is this Hegelian-Marxist theory of political development and change from which contemporary violent revolutionaries get their ideological gunpowder.[9] It is a new and radically different apology for the absolute authority of a ruling executive representing the developing universal interests of all of society, and a new attack on representative legislatures, as partial, biased, and hypocritical. Where Locke's philosophy of revolution is of essentially *peaceful* revolution, and Locke's philosophy of legislation is of *significant* dissent in the legislature, this new philosophy overturns and denies all this. In

7. G. W. F. Hegel, *Phenomenology of Mind*, trans. S. B. Baillie (London, 1910), pp. 236-40, 500-513.

8. See Schlomo Avineri, *The Social and Political Philosophy of Karl Marx* (Cambridge, England, 1968) and Nathan Rotenstreich, *Karl Marx* (Indianapolis, 1968).

9. Mao Tse-Tung, *Selected Works* (Peking, 1965).

none of Hegel's or Marx' writings is the possibility of a peaceful change of regimes even suggested: any change must be a total change, involving a change in all values, and it must be a violent change, overcoming the violent resistance of the old order.[10]

The general political structure which developed in accordance with Locke's ideas in England and America can, without any great difficulty, include both the philosophies of Hume and of Hegelian universalism within the purview of structure of discussions of immediate policies and peaceful changes.[11] We have had periods of complete traditional acceptance of the established institutions of property and business freedom, such as Hume thought most beneficial in the political order. In the United States, such periods have been marked by an ascendency of the Supreme Court as the guardian of traditions and established practices and interests. Hume was a friend of Blackstone and Judge Mansfield, those guardians of property and business interests. The entire basis of English and American law in precedent has allowed for a habitual conservatism and inertial stability in American and English law. Thus within the traditions and institutions developed by Locke and Coke, the stability that comes from unthinking appreciation and strong reaffirmation of traditional freedoms can operate as a significant strengthening of the structure of a free society. But the traditionalism and conservatism of Hume, Burke, and Blackstone cannot possibly work where there are no strong traditions of freedom and independent law; such conservatism cannot be exported, although the attempt sometimes seems to be made.

The universality of the executive power, over the regionalism and partialities of the views of members of the legislative assemblies, has been recognized to a degree *within* the Lockean institutions, and in a peaceful, not a violent, manner. In the United States, the President and Vice President are the only officials elected by the entire electorate in a general national campaign, and strong presidents have re-

10. Thus the various writings of Charles Frankel and Sidney Hook interpreting Marx from the standpoint of a pacific social moralism and pragmatism miss not only the dialectical turns of thought but also the commitment to and insistence on violence in practical social action.

11. Thus Hegel in England became translated into the moral idealism of F. H. Bradley, Bernard Bosanquet, and Thomas Hill Green, and in America led to a movement toward higher standards in public education. The political structures of the free societies turned what might have been destructive *Aufhebungs* into pacific social and intellectual movements.

garded themselves as representing the interests of the entire people and have been so regarded by the electorate.

What might seem to be the ideal process of Lockean political procedure, which is a powerful but constitutionally limited legislative body enacting laws only after long debates and deliberations of a searching and comprehensive nature, has been the exception rather than the rule in England and the United States. The period of great debates, between Webster and Hayne, Webster and Clay, or Lincoln and Douglas, was but a short epoch in American political history, as was the similar period of Gladstone and Disraeli, or Macaulay and Mill, in England. Congress and Parliament do their work in committees, and more and more power is found in the executive. In the United States, control of the budget has been moved from the legislative branch to the executive, giving basic original discretion in planning and details to the supposed longer range views and more universal and inclusive outlook of the executive. A strong President is able to attack special interests and bring their power into balance with other forces in the country; this is not so easy for a legislative group or particular members of the legislative group. Senators who crusade on matters of general national importance, such as former Senator Douglas, or former Senator Morse, or Senator Fulbright, are thought to be mavericks, to have assumed powers and functions beyond their proper office, and frequently they achieve notoriety rather than effective results. The President can operate both with publicity and with political pressures of other sorts in a vastly more effective manner.

Furthermore, it is difficult to maintain the charge of the cynical Marxists, that the Chief Executive is a representative of one propertied class only. The rich do not always back the incumbent in office, and the citizenry as a whole, at least a large percentage, may back him. And as power has shifted in the country from clergy and lawyers, to manufacturers, and then to the classes of men involved in distribution and communications, there have been shifts in governmental policies, but without the violent revolutions that ideologists have deemed necessary.

Thus, the Lockean political tradition, involving the settlement of disputes and the establishment of policies by law and through free argumentation, has allowed for the inclusion of philosophic conservatism and philosophic radicalism within its structure and processes, insofar as there was some measure of practical truth in these views.

There is a place for acceptance of a tradition of freedom as a base for free discussion and criticism at the present time, and there is need for representative statesmen who rise above party and region and can properly claim to represent the entire country.

There was a period in recent American history, following the brief McCarthy period, in which not only was the extreme left persecuted and deplored for its Marxist views, but the conservative right was ignored and scorned. University professors who openly professed to be followers of Hume, Burke, Adam Smith, and John Stuart Mill were quietly dismissed from leading liberal institutions and, in a process of guilt by association, were associated with the lunatic right and Hitlerism. The *Open Society* of Karl Popper became an ideological dogma of the liberal establishment, in which only one sort of philosophical view and one sort of practical determination of political policy were acceptable. The ideology was accepted because it "looked right" from the inside, and other views were ignored or taken as "enemies." The author saw a paper written by a responsible conservative of the time, in which he lamented the fact that it was impossible to enter into a dialogue with the dominant liberals and with liberal opinions of the day; debate, discussion, and open deliberation were not available as methods of political decision. Granted that there is great difficulty in the Lockean position on tolerance and the preservation of freedom, when it came to deciding how much tolerance should be accorded to those who propose views that would mean the end of all toleration when they obtained political power, still the limits of tolerance can become so narrowed that only those advocating a particular philosophy of life and government are admitted to discussion. This is not the position of Locke; no one philosophy has the monopoly of truth; no one is infallible.

And the claim of the post-Hegelian revolutionary thinkers to have discovered true universality and true unity in the executive power which represents the working classes has been, as some sort of final truth, discredited by the facts. The Chinese universality is not the same as the universality of the Soviet Union, and the most partisan diatribes are directed from one to the other, fully in accordance with Locke's views that men tend to disagree. In the border countries of the Iron Curtain, Rumania follows a radically different foreign policy from that of the others; East Germany is close in policy to Bulgaria, but not to more neighboring countries. The "universal" policy-making of Premier Novotny of Czechoslovakia was discovered to be partial and biased after all, and, in a manner only vaguely like the Lockean suggestions; he was replaced (by the Soviet Union) by an executive who would make policies more acceptable to the judgment of complaining groups of people.[12] Disagreements do not end, as it was supposed they would, with the advent of political rulers making policy for the universal good of all citizens. Rather the harangues and dialectical disputes approach, in the niceties of classification of positions, with rightist deviationists, leftist deviationists, revisionists, revanchists, etc., subtleties of medieval Scholasticism.

And in China, the executive bureaucracy, which supposedly could act only for the good of all the workers and peasants of China, was guilty of what seemed a new sin, but which actually has a long history in the thought and action of man: this bureaucracy was acting to preserve itself, it was acting in its own interest, and to increase its power, rather than acting for the good of the people. But this is exactly what Locke said an executive power would do. The "Red Guard" upheaval of 1966-67 to replace the incumbent bureaucratic power with a new group of incumbents, was required only because of the absence of any election procedures or conception of peaceful change of administrators and administrations. And yet what will prevent the next bureaucracy from establishing itself as a self-perpetuating organized power? Violent revolutions every four years? The means defeats the end. Thus the turning to economic factors and to a "universal" executive, with emphasis on work, production, gross national product, or other clear material goals, does not end political dispute; it only renders political disputes more violent. The alternative to the open political deliberation and acceptance of peaceful determinations under law, as advocated by Locke, is not utopian science, but rather emotional and violent impulse. If men are not allowed to talk and express viewpoints and disagreements, they will either revolt, or they will become mere slaves, inhuman cogs in an inhuman productive process.

Turning back to Locke's thought, his orientation in the *Essay Concerning Human Understanding* is practical: "Our business is not to know all things, but those which concern our conduct."[13] Locke denies that such practical judgments are absolute, or arbitrary, or based on social conformity. Just what is the proper basis of the prac-

12. Unfortunately, the replacement, Mr. Dubček, was himself later replaced by Soviet tanks.

13. John Locke, *Essay Concerning Human Understanding, Works*, I, 5.

tical judgment and reason for Locke? That basis is in the *process* of action, judgment, and reflections; it is the *use* of our understanding and experience in practice which is preferable to deductions from any set of a priori assumptions. Practical reasoning is industriously, cautiously, and judiciously "going down the road," rather than starting from supposed absolute principles or reaching some textbook conclusions. In Locke's view, it is only the fanatics and the shallow relativists who believe in absolute beginnings or in mere arbitrary preferences in practical life. Locke urges the practical use of reasoning. A planned final chapter of Locke's *Essay,* which was omitted because Locke judiciously revised and reflected on it until the end of his life (and then it had grown too large for its place as a concluding chapter), is called "On the Conduct of the Understanding." The correct conduct and use of the understanding as the ultimate sum of practical wisdom is the final recommendation Locke was working toward. The essay is a study of the practical fallacies the human mind can make in reasoning, the so-called "informal fallacies" of modern logic, which can be endless, as Locke's task of clearing up disputes involving practical matters is also endless.

In the first book of the *Essay,* Locke denies absolute principles apart from *their use.* Mathematical principles are discovered, if at all, in use, and so are basic moral principles. "For all reasoning is search, and casting about, and requires pains and application."[14] For Locke, the trouble with "children, idiots, savages, illiterates" and, in general "the greater part of mankind," is the lack of *actual use* of their understandings, not any lack of potential grasp of basic axioms. Men have been unaware of moral rules, or have denied any such rules, or have known them but not used them. But according to Locke, it is only the actual use of moral rules which matters.

The place of human action, human creations and constructions, and human operations in knowledge is fully explored by Locke in the *Essay.* It is not to our purpose to comment on this here, other than to say that Locke never held a "spectator theory" of knowledge, but rather stated that all human knowledge involved human effort, action, and participation. On the other hand, Locke is not a pragmatist pure and simple; he believed in a non-pragmatic *real world* to which our scientific efforts refer, and thus the fact that theories *work* does not prove them to be *true,* but only *probable.*

With respect to the particular problem of free will, Locke's em-

14. *Ibid.,* p. 79.

phasis on the *use* of reason is frequently ignored, but it is essential in his views. Men who do not use their reason are simply impulsive hedonists; other men use their reason to check desires and impulses, but finally the *most* active and reasoning men use their reason to change the character of what they find agreeable and disagreeable. Thinking and deliberation can give us power over our very characters, and over what we find to be pleasant or painful. The use of thinking increases our freedom and does not limit or decrease it, as those believe who equate freedom with following impulses. Through the use of reason, goals can be chosen: "It is a part in the conduct of men toward their happiness, neglected to a degree, that it will possibly be entertained as a paradox, if it be said—that men can *make* things more or less pleasing to themselves."[15]

In the final sections of the *Essay,* Locke reflects on the processes of reasoning. What distinguishes the good reasoner and the prudent man from the unreasonable man and the fanatic is that the first is aware of the difficulties of judging and knowing in this world. He is aware that thinking men tend to differ; he knows the strong irrational force of tradition and previous views on man's judgment; he is aware of the egotism that accompanies any statement of opinion. The enthusiastic fanatic, on the other hand, does not reflect on these difficulties and assumes that his opinions are those of the Divine, that he has total contact with ordinary reality and complete communication with other men. He ignores problems of language barriers, different value perspectives, and the established commitments of history.[16] The careful thinker never forgets linguistic problems, psychological problems, and the problems of error, laziness, and presumption, both in himself and in others.

Thus Locke, in the *Essay Concerning Human Understanding,* found the basis for his political philosophy of law and freedom in his study of the proper *uses* of reasoning powers in practice. Such uses are seen to lead to problematic judgments subject to revision, rather than to dogmatic truths. But the uses of the understanding also may lead to fanaticism and enthusiasm; both uses and abuses are intrinsically connected with the freedom of man to think and act on the basis of thinking or to act without thinking and reflecting. Viewing reasoning pragmatically also offers some justification for

15. *Ibid.*, p. 285.
16. *Ibid.*, chapter 29, "Of Enthusiasm." See also posthumous work *Of the Conduct of the Understanding*, III, 205-89.

preferring the legislative to the executive branch of the government; the legislative, with all its partiality and its arguments, is aware of the perversions and practical fallacies of thought, for they are constant present factors in persuasion and debate. In enthusiastic egotism, the executive tends to act without reflection in the name of fanciful or traditional opinions accepted without question which leads to errors of judgment and to persecution of those who disagree.

For Locke, man's position is such that use of judgment with proper reflection and caution can lead to happiness and a just and peaceful society. Locke is not at all optimistic about all men doing so, for he sees that many men simply adopt the opinions of others, through laziness or through interest in advancement, and others become "true believers," advocating one creed and rejecting all criticisms of it. But there is still a place for proper reasoning in personal and political life, in a government under law and ruled by reflective deliberation and free discussion. This leads to the views in the *Treatises on Government*.

Locke's thesis in his political works is that political judgment should establish the limits of political power. The political power of rulers, not arbitrated by reasoning and judging, is unbounded, absolute, and tyrannical. The basic issue is whether "power" or "judgment" is ultimate and unlimited in political action. Locke takes judgment as ultimate—judgment defines and limits political power, but in itself is not defined by anything else. Political judgment cannot be defined, because it is ultimate. It is roughly the process of deliberating, searching, weighing evidence, evaluating reasons, et cetera, which thus defines the *limits* of power. The recognition of such judgment as the alternative to sheer authoritarianism or sheer exercise of power is the formative principle of Locke's political thought. If power, pure and simple, is taken as the basis of political policy and action, then all distinctions among kinds of power collapse, and political power becomes the same as economic power, the same as the power of the family (the power of "Big Daddy" or "Big Brother"), and finally, the same as that of a master over his slaves. Human judgment distinguishes all these kinds of power. When citizens use human judgment, they will insist on being treated as adults and equals. When citizens do not use their judgment, the powers of rule operate without limit or restraint. When judgment fails to differentiate types of power, a great and disastrous ambiguity arises.

The semantic and practical collapse of relations that Sir Robert Filmer and other proponents of power require is an ambiguous combination of the economic relation and the paternalistic relation. As Locke points out, the authoritarian needs *both* relations for his argument, the *family* relation in order to bring in notions of irrational but moral obedience and the *economic* relation to provide notions of power and direction. The authoritarian, in modern terms, must have the charismatic and irrational sanctions of the family tradition and religion, and the rational proofs and appeals to interest of economic science at the same time. But Locke shows that proper judgment distinguishes these two kinds of direction and authority. If family and charisma are first, then economics is not, and if economic direction is primary, family is not. But vague considerations of power, in the absence of freedom and judgment, lead to the need for both at the same time.

Thus, in modern times, historians following authoritarian views of the primacy of power have traced the Glorious Revolution of 1688 (Locke's revolution) to changes in irrational religious views and the rise of Calvinism and Puritanism, or they have traced it to economic changes and the rise of a new class of merchants and businessmen, or sometimes to both.[17] What is ignored as relatively unsophisticated is Locke's analysis that the changes in 1688 were primarily *political* and that the change was from authoritarianism to popular government under law. William and Mary accepted the limitation of their rule by Parliament. They came to power on the condition that they would recognize the rights of the people; they were constitutional rulers, not arbitrary power-holders. The recognition of constitutional freedoms and governmental responsibilities made the reign of William and Mary "the most legitimate in Europe," not because of tradition and accepted authority, but because of peaceful determination of political judgment.

Locke insisted that there are three kinds of rule: paternal, economic, and political. But this insistence really is the judgment that there *should be* three kinds of rule, since in an authoritarian, arbitrary, and tyrannical government the three kinds actually tend to collapse.

17. See Max Weber, *General Economic History,* trans. Frank H. Knight (New York, 1927); *The Protestant Ethic and the Spirit of Capitalism,* trans. R. H. Tawney (New York, 1958). Also Richard H. Tawney, *Religion and the Rise of Capitalism* (Cambridge, 1934).

In Locke's *First Treatise on Government,* his argument against the authoritarian Robert Filmer takes the form of constantly making this division into aspects of power, when Filmer did not. In the quaint terms of that seventeenth-century discussion, Filmer derives all authority from the authority Adam had over his sons. Locke finds that this authority was of three types: he had economic power over them, for he could leave them his property; he had parental power over them, for they were his children; and he governed them politically. There are three different problems of authority, not one problem. Locke repeats this distinction every time Filmer ignores it.

In modern terms, Filmer maintains simply that those who have power must inevitably dominate those who do not. This theory of domination can be given empirical backing (as in Hitler's regime) as well as an intrinsic appearance of rational consistence and necessity (for, by definition, those with more power can dominate those with less power). Against this, Locke appeals to the distinction between approaches to power in sociology, economics, and political science. Sociological power is not the same as economic power, even if it happens to lodge in the same man, and *the question* of politics is, who shall have power? These differences have to be glossed over in order to picture the inevitability of the operations of behavioristic responses in politics, in which the rulers must satisfy both the deep irrational needs of the public for certain image-types and also determine affairs with the authoritarian efficiency of well-run business corporations, and thus merging right and power into one.

What Locke means by "limited government" follows from the distinction between economic, sociological, and political power. Limited government is derived from political judgment and deliberation rather than sheer power as such, and under limited government, therefore, some separation is made between paternalistic rule, economic power, and political decision. Politics is limited in that it does not become the same as gang-sociology or the economics of an organized corporation. The modern attack on Locke focuses on the view that Locke favored *limited* government, while today we see the need for much greater *extension* of government functions. This is to misconceive Locke's distinctions in a false geographic way, as if Locke came out for a small truck garden, whereas what is needed is a huge farm. What Locke meant by limited government was that the property owners should not automatically dominate the government, and the leaders should not be considered to be on some vastly superior level of humanity from that of the citizens, as fathers to children; these are the limits and distinctions Locke hoped to maintain as the alternative to the unification of economic power and ideological orthodoxy in an elite group.

The program Locke suggests depends upon the assumption or plea that men exercise political judgment. The structure then is simple enough; a legislature which has the duty of passing laws with respect to the welfare of the society and the property and taxation of the citizens is elected by the citizens for regular terms. The executive is to carry out the general laws of the legislative body, and the executive's power is governed by the judgment of the citizens. Property is considered distinct from political power and is identified with the citizens, not with the policy of the government. Paternal prerogative is to be assigned to literal or *real* fathers only, and not to political rulers who are taken to have the same basic abilities and weaknesses as other mature citizens. The rule of law means that men can deliberate about their activities in private lives, which are not entirely subordinated to their public obediences, and that public policy can be a matter of deliberation among alternatives freely discussed. For Locke, no matter how constitutional the structure there will always be problems of the growth and arbitrariness of governmental action and prerogative, and this can only be limited by the continued effective judgment of the citizens.

In discussing the limits of political policy through discussion of alternatives and the avoidance of dogmatic and arbitrary personal rule, Locke assumes that human life can never be raised to some radically new plane of harmony and enjoyment. He is radically against utopian thinking. Such thinking keeps occurring in human political aspiration: it occurred in this country with the views of President Wilson at the end of World War I and before his nervous collapse, and it obviously occurred in early socialist thinking. The politics of utopia always seem to require some magnificent leader, and the fact that such leaders do occasionally exist seems invariably to lead some people to the hope of a utopian politics. The position Locke argued for, therefore, will never be established permanently and securely, safe against all possible refutation or opposition. But Locke would see this argument as a perennial one, and a free society is one in which a great many of the citizens, perhaps a major party, represent an authoritarian and monistic view, based either on tradition or on future hopes or on a complete lack of thinking. But a free society also has a group which believes in political judgment, exercises it, and has an effective say in what happens.

Locke scorned an attitude of clinging to the past, a traditionalism which Robert Filmer embodied. Locke wanted an overthrow of the feudal institutions, dependent on inheritance and loyalty alone. Unfortunately, he underestimated the institutionalized freedoms and rights of the English past. Locke gives no credit to the established legal institutions of England and the traditions of private property and freedom from governmental persecution fought for and established by Coke. This is, purely and simply, a lapse and an inadequacy of his thinking. Like Coke, Locke wants to ignore the feudal and authoritarian past, from which the problems of modern constitutional politics have slowly emerged. Deriving government from a "social contract" avoids deriving problems from the earlier centuries. But in ignoring earlier feudalism and authoritarianism, Locke also ignored the basic institutions of property *as private,* and security of person and freedom of opinion *as legal and traditional.* These basic assumptions of his views would not have been meaningful in feudal legal contexts or Roman law contexts: Coke's thought was basic; Locke extended the freedom and the rights developed by Coke, and these rights became a matter of law and tradition in the Glorious Revolution, but Locke was unaware of the effects of earlier legal foundations on the full development of Parliamentary powers and political freedoms in his day.

In Locke's *Second Treatise on Government,* the "state of nature" is a state of freedom without positive law or overwhelming state power. Locke pointed out that such a condition exists *right now,* among the rulers of the various nation-states. Locke stated that the condition of peace within states is preferable to the peculiar uneasy relations among men where there are no agreements as to law. In Kant's practical philosophy, as embodied in his *Fundamental Principles of the Metaphysics of Morals,* the goal of moral relations among men is a condition where each man is a legislator for all men and obeys the laws which he legislates universally. This seems somewhat like Locke's "state of nature." Locke does not regard that as preferable to the condition of things within a well-ordered free society as it exists now. In ordinary politics and constitutional law, Kant happened to be an extreme authoritarian, a skeptic of the possibility of representative democracy, and a loyal advocate of benevolent monarchy. Kant's attacks on the falseness of British Parliamentary discussions, and the hidden interests which really dominate such purported debates are as vitriolic as the modern attacks of Mao on the same subject. For the sake of a utopian situation, authoritarianism is made preferable to workable freedom in the actual present for Kant, as for Mao. Rousseau's political philosophy is the opposite of Kant's—the utopian age of free men living without politics and constitutional law was the golden age of the past.[18] The noble and sincere savages, living in small self-regulated groups without the hypocrisies of modern civilization, formed the base from which Rousseau could attack the actualities of the present and defend the new democratic tyranny of the *volunte generale,* a public will which rightfully crushed all opposition.

Both Rousseau and Kant wish to subordinate problems of law and free politics to considerations of civilization and accepted moral norms. (In this they foreshadow pragmatism, as will be explicated in Chapter 5.) Rousseau criticizes the norms of current civilization in terms of a simple mythic and noble past; Kant criticizes the norms of civilization in terms of an ideal moral "kingdom of ends"—but both find the ambiguities of civilization and morals more fundamental than the direct formalisms of law and constitutional politics. Locke is on clearer ground in his political position. His politics is workable, while that of Kant and Rousseau is utopian. Locke is not unconcerned with morals, with the informal relations of man to man, and with religion, but these are in no sense matters which have to be determined before political and legal matters. In fact, the establishment of a state of law, peace, and freedom allows such other matters as morals and religion to be discussed in an atmosphere of tolerance and reason, rather than one of witchhunts and holy wars.

Thus the great difference between the ideologies and the political practices of those thinkers and politicians which stem from the Kantian morality of an ultimate and unattainable "Kingdom of Ends" and the practical constitutional politics of England and America is not that one avoids considerations of a society of freedom and equality and concern for others, based on general notions of lawfulness and founded ultimately on both human and divine nature. Locke has such conceptions as much as Kant and, in fact, starts with them,

18. This is true particularly in Rousseau's *First and Second Discourses,* although the theory of the general will is developed only in the later *Social Contract.* It is granted that Rousseau's works are subject to many interpretations; no claim for definitive critical validity is made for the brief generalizations here made.

but does not end with them. Absolute freedom is not viable or practical, and the need is to go beyond the condition that was given us naturally or by God's ordinance. We must go *beyond* anarchism, not work toward that condition. According to Locke, we must *go beyond* the situation where everybody is lawmaker and everyone is executive or executioner. Kant, in the name of culture and strict morality, reintroduced notions of a primitive condition under the name of absolute progress. Kant's men were Rousseau's imaginary savages made rational, but Locke insists that actual savages *were* rational, and that is why they no longer chose to stay in savagery.

It is remarkable how political thinkers concerned with the development of "civilization" after the Kantian utopian tradition *do* postulate a primitive idyllic state, but then discover that *some falsehood* led to the present condition of society. Their strategy is to forecast a new utopia having the primitive virtues of communism and equality, but with modern industry, modern cities, and modern civilization. Thus Marx; thus Veblen. The vastly more practical and concrete thinking of Locke insists that it was no collapse when primitive communism and anarchy were abandoned, but a human achievement of the first magnitude, and that any return to such a state would be a reintroduction to the same problems. Men would differ as to what was moral, with consequent arguments and perhaps wars, and some men would not follow morality in any event. Thus government and authority are practical solutions to a condition of mankind where people have the freedom to operate according to their judgments, but also have the freedom to judge differently from others. Opposed to the Kantian utopia, Locke insisted that there is more freedom with government and law than there would be otherwise, and thus, ideally speaking, men do not give up their freedom when they enter a lawful and constitutional society; they do not take on chains (as Rousseau would have it) but rather they *increase* their freedom: "For Law, in its true notion, is not so much the limitation as the *direction* of a free and intelligent agent to his proper interest, and prescribes no further than is for the general good of those under the law. Could they be happier without it, the law, as a useless thing, would of itself vanish, but that ill deserves the name of confinement which hedges us in only from bogs and precipices. So that, however it may be mistaken, *the end of the law* is not to abolish or to restrain, but *to preserve and enlarge Freedom.*"[19]

19. John Locke, *Second Treatise of Government*, par. 57, *Works*, V, 369-70.

Thus the alternative in politics posed by Kant and Rousseau and that general continental European tradition are quite different from the Lockean alternatives. For Kant and Rousseau, either one accepts the government now in existence, *no matter what,* or one aims at some impossible and practically unworkable utopian anarchic communistic state of absolute morality and freedom. European politics, in this tradition, has tended to become either revolutionary and anarchic or reactionary and autocratic. And in the revolutionary movements, there follow inevitable reactions from a sense of failure or "betrayal" of the revolution. The revolutionary action is supposed to bring about a state of utopian and idyllic freedom; when it does not, movements begin to overthrow the new establishment in the name of the betrayed revolution; the new leaders then institute a purge and kill all the dissidents. This happened in the French Revolution; it happened in the 1930's in the Russian situation, with the Trotskyites being the dissident utopian element announcing the betrayal of the revolution. It apparently is happening in China now, and it has happened several times before in that fantastic fanatical revolutionary situation. All such violent revolutions, all such ensuing reigns of terror, all such inevitable "betrayals" of revolutionary and visionary ideals of a new state of human equality and freedom, come from the backwards idealism and politics of the Kantian morality, wherein an absolute and anarchic freedom is to be obtained by human consent and human achievement, rather than *avoided* and corrected by human political action. Locke maintains in his political theory the practical judgment which he found paramount at the end of his *Essay on Human Understanding.* Practical judgment indicates that it is better for men to have a common and known rule to live by, than to live in an anarchy of individual judgments.

The chief issue in the politics of free societies after Locke is that of a government of men, acting under the direction of their will alone, or a government of laws, in which the executive rulers are under some common bonds with the citizens and cannot exercise prerogative or judgment beyond the considered laws of the land. In Locke, there is no practical question that we are going to have political conditions as we do in fact have them now, and that such conditions and the governments and directions involved are better than any state of absolute equality and absolute freedom and absolute Communism. The practical question is about unreasoning acceptance of authority versus authority developed within reason and consented to by reasonable and adult citizens. This struggle is constantly recurring in a liberally ordered constitutional democracy. But this argument, or rather, this conflict between those peaceful and free men who argue and think about politics and those who do not, is carried on within a peaceful and orderly constitutional structure.

Locke and Kant agree in some rather trivial respects: they do not carry theoretical reasoning past experience. Both wish to direct reason to practical uses, and both, in the practical use of human reason, call for consideration of the rights of others as fundamental in moral and political judgments. But where Locke is careful, cautious, plain, considerate of others, Kant is dogmatically deductive, extreme, complex, and insistent that he has thought of all alternatives. Practically and reasonably, Locke discusses the reality of freedom and a free and orderly society in this world, with men constituted as they are now, and with government constituted as it was in England after the Glorious Revolution. Kant poses the fantastic world of an absolute freedom and equality of citizens, without any government or constitutional order at all: a vision of beautiful anarchical order which has unfortunately gripped later thinkers such as Hegel, Marx, and Lenin and their followers with catastrophic effects on the civilization of the world. Kant's terrible dictum of what he called Enlightenment, "Argue, but Obey," has led to exactly the kind of authoritarian pretentiousness Locke and his fellow revolutionaries despised.

Locke was, to a degree unknown elsewhere in the history of the freedom of thought, a successful practical philosopher. He was not concerned with making glorious but futile gestures, nor was he desirous of establishing postulates for an ideal free society. He was associated with an actual revolutionary movement, and when that movement was successful, he came out of exile and hiding and became the spokesman for practical action and future government under laws and responsible to popular judgment. Thoughts which Locke had developed as early as 1665 were finally published in 1689 and 1690, because then the times were ripe and matters had come to a successful and practical head; without such successes they might never have been published, because they would have had no practical state of affairs to defend. The new sort of constitutional and representative government instituted in 1688 and the philosphy of peaceful and legitimate oppositions among free men who tolerate differences as healthy were part of one and the same practical action and practical deliberation.

3

Jefferson and Madison

S TEEPED IN THE TRADITION of political freedom and law of Coke and Locke, Jefferson applied this tradition to the American situation both in his well-known broad political activities and in the technical and little-known area of Constitutional jurisprudence. In terms of the unique structure of American political institutions, this last contribution is as important for the later history of law and freedom as his earlier activities. In 1776 he advocated the rights of man in the Declaration of Independence. In his organization he continued to advocate the Jeffersonian Republican Party in opposition to the Federalist domination in the 1790's. The interaction of Republicans and Federalists in the founding period is fundamental in the history of the development of modern constitutional and legal structures for freedom. The struggle over the nature of our technical constitutional law was the latest in a series of basic disagreements to develop. All such debates, between authoritarians and those advocating Lockean limits to authority, were settled peacefully and successfully.

The three interesting compromised disagreements between Federalists and Republicans are: the writing of *The Federalist Papers* advocating adoption of the Constitution;[1] the election of Jefferson

1. This writing was done as a compromise between Hamilton and his New York group, and Madison representing the Virginia Jeffersonian group, after the Federal Convention and before the vote on ratification in New York in 1789. As later stated, John Jay's contribution was largely a matter of lending his prestige to the forces favoring the new Constitution.

in 1800 to the Presidency; and the struggle over the nature of final Constitutional authority between Thomas Jefferson and Chief Justice John Marshall.[2] All three are examples of the politics of peaceful or lawful disagreement in action. *The Federalist Papers* advocated the adoption of a Constitution for the country as a basis for further agreements and disagreements. The election of 1800 allowed the full acceptance of party politics on the level of the Presidency, with the cooperation of the losing party with the victorious one and the acceptance of peaceful change of political regimes, policies, and values. The struggle between Jefferson and Marshall led to the assertion of the final authority of the Supreme Court over the administrative and legislative branches of the Federal Government, and then to the development of seriatim opinions on the Court (i.e., separate, personally signed opinions agreeing and disagreeing with the majority opinion). This development of freedom of speech and dissent on the Supreme Court, and with it the overthrow of authoritarianism in American law, occurred in the 1820's, in Jefferson's old age. Long out of office, retired to Monticello, and overburdened with debts, Jefferson continued to advance the policies and structures of freedom, and secured the open confrontation with Marshall needed for open controversy in the law. This development has been crucial in our political evolution; however, most Jeffersonian historians have been concerned with politics in the realms of administration, legislation, and public opinion, rather than in the realm of law. The one historian of American Constitutional Law who has recognized Jefferson's influence, Professor W. W. Crosskey, considered Jefferson's interference and "politicking" in the highest law a matter of unmitigated evil, overthrowing the conservative and authoritarian principles of the earlier Federalists and unfortunately restricting the proper energies of the central administration.[3]

In general, Jefferson managed to combine principles of individual rights and allied conceptions of government structured to recognize individual freedoms with pragmatic conceptions of party politics and practical compromise in an ongoing flexible way that has always enraged his detractors and has often been misunderstood by his friends. Some have termed him a dreaming idealist—they are wrong,

2. This struggle is described in great detail in W. W. Crosskey, *Politics and the Constitution* (Chicago, 1953).

3. *Ibid.*, but see Donald G. Morgan, *Justice William Johnson* (Columbia, S.C., 1954).

for his ideals are always related to practical issues. Others have seen him as a scheming opportunist—they too are wrong; there are always principles of law and freedom operating in the pragmatic dealings of Jefferson. But his combination of idealistic principles and pragmatism can be understood in terms of the basic problems of free and peaceful discussion of principles and the immediate solutions of political problems, crises, and advances. Jefferson did not act alone, as did Coke, but had the help of such brilliant men as Madison, Gallatin, and others. Furthermore, his group was opposed not by shallow tyrants, but by such profound thinkers as Hamilton and John Marshall. The peculiar compromises of the confrontation are a significant part of American traditions. These actions proved the views of Locke that a free people can establish responsible and active rule and continue to disagree on all points. Finally it proved the views of Coke that judges can be independent of all authoritarian pressures.

Jefferson's views of government are complex and are embodied in his actions as a public servant and in his political letters, which number in the thousands. But some summary can be made here. The basic notion is the Lockean man: the social man who recognizes the rights of others but preserves his own freedom and independence of judgment. Thus Jefferson wrote in 1787: "I never submitted the whole system of my opinions to the creed of any party of men whatever in religion, in philosophy, in politics, or in anything else where I was capable of thinking for myself. Such an addiction is the last degradation of a free and moral agent. If I could not go to heaven but with a party, I would not go there at all."[4]

Such a conception is developed with eloquent brevity in the Declaration of Independence: life, liberty, and practical judgment in individuals are basic, and governments are derived from this freedom and should preserve it. The Declaration of Independence is usually misread, with the first paragraph of ringing poetic abstractions taken out of context. But *in context,* these principles were organically related to the detailed list of immediate, pragmatic issues, such as troops being quartered in houses, taxes raised without representation, and judicial trials held far from the scene of the legal issues. Jefferson's work is not abstract, but an indication of the colonists' position on concrete issues. "Life, liberty, and the pursuit of happi-

4. Jefferson to E. Carrington, Dec. 15, 1787, in *Works,* ed. Paul Leicester Ford (New York, 1905), III, 603.

ness" are intrinsically related to immediate rather than utopian issues. Jefferson invoked the basic public right, asserted by Locke, to judge practical issues, and then moved to the practical issues and problems to be judged, by Americans and any other free thoughtful men. Revolution was called for because the only alternative seemed to be continued submission to an oppressive and unreasonable tyrant.

Jefferson did not transfer this doctrine of rights in any mechanical way to all situations of political oppression. It is not well known that when he was American Minister to France, he opposed the revolution there, since he thought the problems involved could be settled with the King, and viable compromises reached without violence. Since Louis XVI was a weak, good-natured, benevolent man, not unreasonable or arbitrary, in Jefferson's judgment political reforms could have been effectuated with his cooperation. The moderate party that Jefferson backed, led by Lafayette, did not succeed, although for a time it appeared that it might. And Jefferson's Republicanism did not prevent him from preferring a continued and reformed monarchy to violent revolution in that situation. This is another proof that Jefferson was not a utopian revolutionary, advocating abstract schemes for their own sake, but a man of practical judgment. He preferred maintaining the monarchy in France to an extremist revolutionary action. Thus Jefferson wrote his analysis of the problems and solutions in France in a public memoir:

> But Louis had a queen of absolute sway over his weak mind and timid virtue, and of a character the reverse of his in all points. This angel, so gaudily painted in the rhapsodies of Burke, had no sound sense, was proud, disdainful of restraint, indignant at all obstacles to her will, eager in the pursuit of pleasures. Her inordinate gambling and dissipations, with those of the Count d'Artois and others of her clique, had been a sensible item in the exhaustion of the treasury, which called into action the reforming hand of the nation; and her opposition to it, her inflexible perverseness, and dauntless spirit, drew the King on with her, and plunged the world into crimes and calamities which will forever stain the pages of modern history. I have ever believed, that had there been no queen, there would have been no revolution. No force would have been provoked or exercised. The King would have gone hand in hand with the wisdom of his sounder counsellors, who, guided by the increased lights of the age, wished only with the same pace to advance the principles of the social constitution. . . . I should have shut up

the Queen in a convent, putting harm out of her power, and placed the King in his station, investing him with limited powers, which, I verily believe, he would have honestly exercised, according to the measure of his understanding.[5]

Jefferson went on to admit that the moderate party of the Marquis de Lafayette had met at his home for discussions, when discussion was still in fashion: "The discussions began at the hour of four, and continued until ten in the evening; during which time I was a silent witness to a coolness and candor of argument unusual in the conflicts of political opinion." Jefferson had hoped for, and had actively aided a party working for, "wholesome and practicable reformation" without violence, regicide, or bloodshed.[6] Jefferson attempted to be more practical than Paine (for the latter had advocated violent revolution in France), but Jefferson's efforts were of infinitesimal effect in Paris just before the Revolution. He returned to the United States to become Secretary of State, Vice President under John Adams, and then, in 1800, President.

From these examples it is clear that Jefferson's politics united basic conceptions of life, liberty, and the pursuit of happiness to pragmatic compromises in actual political life. Such ability to compromise, leading to practical success rather than utopian disillusionment, is shown in the collection of essays written by Jefferson's philosophical and political double, James Madison, and the Tory, Alexander Hamilton. Jefferson and Madison believed in the rights of man and the derivation of government from these rights, which centered mainly on the right of freedom: free speech and free judgment. But such judgment included pragmatic adjustments. While Jefferson and Madison believed in the effectuation of free practical judgment as basic in proper government, this did not involve any dogmatic insistence on the *phraseology* of "The Rights of Man," when such terms would obstruct peaceful solutions to government problems. Thus, in *The Federalist Papers,* Madison does not mention the inherent and God-given rights of man, so basic to the wording and sense of the Declaration of Independence of 1776. The same problems are approached through description of the problems of free discussion in government and protection of property interests.

Thus the unique compromise of *The Federalist* is that the Jeffer-

5. See Sarah N. Randolph, *The Domestic Life of Thomas Jefferson* (Cambridge, Mass., 1939), pp. 131-35.

6. *Ibid.,* p. 134.

sonian thinker, Madison, does not mention anything about the rights of man, and the conservative and authoritarian statesman, Hamilton, does not mention his fears of democracy or his preferences for a strong executive. In these classic papers, there is an agreement on a common practical objective and disagreement over the meaning and goal of that objective, and, further, disagreement is ameliorated to a great extent by practical demands for compromise in the situation wisely recognized by both sides.

The Federalist Papers stand in relation to the Constitution as a campaign document written during the debate about ratification. The essays appeared as newspaper articles written for the occasion in several papers in New York City, from October, 1787, to May, 1788. Although the essays are said to be the work of three men, Jay, Hamilton, and Madison, Jay's contribution was chiefly that of lending prestige to the enterprise; his essays represent a negligible part of the total and can be ignored. Hamilton wrote the great bulk of the essays, sixty-six of the eighty-five. Madison, who had a chief part in the drafting of the Constitution itself, wrote the famous Number Ten, one of the great documents in American political thought, and Numbers Thirty-Seven through Fifty-One. The major disagreement between Hamilton and Madison is the old and perennial disagreement between authoritarian power and judgmental control. This dispute is similar in basic issues to the dispute between Coke and Bacon, and later between Locke and Filmer. Hamilton argued for the needs for "Energy" in the central government, to meet all possible exigencies and dangers, international as well as domestic, and to provide a basis for planned prosperity and commercial success. Madison portrayed the dilemmas of free men freely disagreeing and presented the government as a general forum for discussion of problems and as a *check* on the tendency toward authoritarian control by some dominant faction, which was a feature of all government, but one to be understood and feared.

Hamilton's argument for unlimited power is detailed in the essays from Six to Thirty-Six, but he summed it up briefly in Thirty-One, which starts with a statement of "primary truths" in government. These include: "that every power ought to be commensurate with its object; that there ought to be no limitation of a power destined to effect a purpose which is itself incapable of limitation."[7] Since

7. Alexander Hamilton, *The Federalist No. 31* (New York, Modern Library, 1946), p. 188.

defense in war is incapable of limitation, the power of the central
government is incapable of limitation. To repeat: for Hamilton, the
needs of war mean that the government must have unlimited powers.
Only men who are untractable and have degenerated into "obstinacy,
perverseness, or disingenuity," or men who have "entangled themselves in words, and confounded themselves in subtleties" continue
to disagree with Hamilton's views. The position is restated by
Hamilton:

> A government ought to contain in itself every power requisite
> to the full accomplishment of the objects committed to its care,
> and to the complete execution of the trusts for which it is re-
> sponsible, free from every other control but a regard to the
> public good and to the sense of the people.
>
> As the duties of superintending the national defence and of
> securing the public peace against foreign or domestic violence
> involve a provision for casualties and dangers to which no pos-
> sible limits can be assigned, the power of making that provision
> ought to know no other bounds than the exigencies of the
> nation and the resources of the community.
>
> As revenue is the essential engine by which the means of an-
> swering the national exigencies must be procured . . . the federal
> government must of necessity be invested with an unqualified
> power of taxation.[8]

Here Hamilton is restating the basic argument from the needs of
war for unlimited authority and power, which he had also stated
forcibly in Number Twenty-Three: "The authorities essential to the
common defence are these: to raise armies; to build and equip fleets;
to direct their operations; to provide for their support. These powers
ought to exist without limitation, *because it is impossible to foresee
or define the extent and variety of the means which may be necessary
to satisfy them.* The circumstances that endanger the safety of nations
are infinite, and for this reason no constitutional shackles can wisely
be imposed on the power to which the care of it is committed."[9]
Hamilton remarks that such power must extend to the government
in peace as well as in war, "as the ceremony of a formal denunciation
of war has of late fallen into disuse," (a remark that sounds surprisingly modern) because otherwise "we would be exposing our property and our liberty to the mercy of the foreign invaders,"[10] for we

8. *No. 31,* p. 190.
9. *No. 23,* p. 142.
10. *No. 25,* p. 156.

would be prevented from anticipating distant dangers and would have to wait for the very presence of the enemy forces in our territory before beginning preparations.

Problems of internal dissent are radically minimized by Hamilton, as they must be by all advocates of central power. For Hamilton, there are no real and significant reasons for disagreement inside the society. The goals are clear: defense and prosperity. There have been specious differences between the two great economic interests in the past (between the agrarian interest and the mercantile interest), but their interests are really mutually intertwined and not conflicting. The wisdom of the central government will overcome such emotional differences and factional excesses. "Why has government been instituted at all? Because the passions of men will not conform to the dictates of reason and justice, without constraint." Only jealousy or false abstractions have led men from these "plainest truths of reason":

> The often-agitated question between agriculture and commerce has, from indubitable experience, received a decision which has silenced the rivalship that once subsisted between them, and has proved, to the satisfaction of their friends, that their interests are intimately blended and interwoven. It has been found in various countries that, in proportion as commerce has flourished, land has risen in value. And how could it have happened otherwise? Could commerce, which procures a freer vent for the products of the earth, which furnishes new incitements to the cultivation of land, which is the faithful handmaid of labor and industry in every shape, fail to augment land? It is astonishing that so simple a truth should ever have had an adversary.[11]

With regard to crucial problems of taxation, Hamilton later concedes that there may be division of interest between agriculture and commerce, but the learned professional men in government will act as impartial arbiters to further the general interest.

> The idea of an actual representation of all classes of the people, by persons of each class, is altogether visionary. . . . Mechanics and manufacturers will be inclined to give their votes to merchants. . . . They know that the merchant is their natural patron and friend. . . . We must therefore consider merchants as the natural representatives of all these classes.

11. *No. 12*, pp. 70-71.

With regard to the learned professions; they truly form no distinct interest in society, and according to their situation and talents, will be the objects of choice of each other, and of other parts of the community.

Nothing remains but the landed interest; and this, in a political view, and particularly in relation to taxes, I take to be perfectly united.[12]

Hamilton saw these three groups as comprising the main influences in the government, but the minor differences among landed and commercial interests would be solved by the lawyers: "The representative body, with too few exceptions to have any influence on the spirit of the government, will be composed of landholders, merchants, and men of the learned professions. . . . Will not the man of the learned profession, who will feel a neutrality to the rivalships between the different branches of industry, be likely to prove an impartial arbiter between them, ready to promote either, so far as it shall appear to him conducive to the general interests of society?"[13] Thus Hamilton sees some bases for conflict within society, but these conflicts are "momentary" and "particular" and can be resolved by men who are devoted to the proper "general interest of society."

Hamilton is well aware that problems of taxation are central to government, not only in relation to obtaining means for action, but in the crucial respect of maintaining public consent to the government and avoiding dissension and criticism. Hamilton, without mentioning alternatives, views control over taxation as a matter for the executive power, not the general public: "In order to a judicious exercise of the power of taxation, it is necessary that *the person in whose hands it is* should be acquainted with [the people and the resources]." For Hamilton, taxation is a matter of the judgment of an administrator, a matter of the wisdom of the executive, *not* a matter for continued debate and redeliberation. Taxation is a science:

There is no part of the administration of government that requires extensive information and a thorough knowledge of the principles of political economy, so much as the business of taxation. The man who understands those principles best will be least likely to resort to oppressive expedients, or to sacrifice any particular class of citizens to the procurement of revenue. It might be demonstrated that the most productive system of

12. *No. 35,* p. 213.
13. *No. 35,* pp. 214-15.

finance will always be the least burdensome. There can be no doubt that in order to a judicious exercise of the power of taxation, it is necessary that the person in whose hands it is should be acquainted with the general genius, habits, and modes of thinking of the people at large, and with the resources of the country. And this is all that can be reasonably meant by a knowledge of the interests and the feelings of the people. In any other sense the proposition either has no sense, or an absurd one.[14]

In other words, the taxer will judge the people, not the people the taxes.

Admittedly, Hamilton devotes the later essays in *The Federalist* to a description of the checks on the national power. The system of regular elections and the checks and balances of power within the government will be such checks. But Hamilton also continues to return to the authoritarian view, wherein the government checks the people. In discussing the Senate, for instance, he states:

Such an institution may be sometimes necessary as a defence to the people against their own temporary errors and delusions ... there are particular moments when the people, stimulated by some irregular passion, or some illicit advantage, or misled by the artful misrepresentations of interested men, may call for measures which they themselves will afterwards be the most ready to lament and condemn. In these moments how salutary will be the interference of some temperate and respectable body of citizens, in order to check the misguided career and suspend the blow meditated by the people, until reason, justice, and truth can again gain their authority over the public mind?[15]

For Hamilton, there is no doubt that the respectable people will know what reason, justice, and truth are in public affairs at all times. Similarly, in discussing the Executive, Hamilton discusses the problem of having true judgment prevail over popular error:

It is a just observation, that the people commonly *intend* the PUBLIC GOOD. This often applies to their very errors. But they do not always *reason right* about the means of promoting it. They know from experience that they sometimes err; and the wonder is that they so seldom err as they do, beset, as they continually are, by the wiles of parasites and sycophants, the snares of the ambitious, the avaricious, the desperate ... when occasions pre-

14. *No. 35*, pp. 215-16.
15. *No. 63*, p. 410.

sent themselves, in which the interests of the people are at vari-
ance with their inclinations, it is the duty of the guardians of
those interests, to withstand the temporary delusion. . . .[16]

Hamilton assumes he has grasped *the* truth and *the* right in these
matters; he assumes there is a complete *unity* of interests; he assumes
the man in power is a better judge than the people who are misled by
the multiplicity of interested propagandists.

Finally, Hamilton attacks and derides the notion of a Bill of
Rights, suggested to be added to the Constitution and meant to limit
the power (as the first Ten Amendments) of the government. The
Bill of Rights was added, through the political pressures of Jefferson,
but Hamilton saw no need. First, the provision for the writ of habeas
corpus in the Constitution prevented arbitrary or despotic government and nothing more was needed. Second, Bills of Rights only applied against monarchs, not against popular governments. Hamilton
reviews the work of Coke and Locke and interprets those achievements as having no relevance or significance for modern times: "Bills
of rights are, in their origin, stipulations, between kings and their
subjects, abridgements of prerogative in favor of privilege. Such was
Magna Carta, obtained by the Barons, sword in hand, from King
John. Such was the Petition of Right, assented to by Charles I in the
beginning of his reign. Such, also, was the Declaration of Right presented by the Lords and Commons to the Prince of Orange in 1688,
and afterwards thrown into the form of an act of parliament called
the Bill of Rights."[17] That the Revolution of 1688 was a concession
wrung from the King is an unusual interpretation of the parliamentary act of inviting the Prince of Orange from Holland to England,
but Hamilton ignores all this for the purposes of his immediate argument: "It is evident, therefore, that bills of rights have no application to constitutions professedly founded upon the power of the
people, and executed by their immediate representatives and servants."

The same argument is now used in countries dominated by Marxist thought to explain the absence of rights against the government:
since the government is the agent of the people and acts in their in-

16. *No. 71*, pp. 464-65. Hamilton returns to his Jacobean-Baconian view of an
untrammeled and unhampered administration in this essay: "Energy in the
EXECUTIVE is a leading character in the definition of good government"
(p. 454).
17. *No. 84*, p. 558.

terests, what need is there for any rights against it? Hamilton goes on to sneer that all such notions of rights, and the "volumes of aphorisms" about them, "would sound much better in a treatise of ethics than in a constitution of government."

Hamilton is most upset about demands for rights concerning freedom of the press and freedom of speech: "On the subject of the liberty of the press, I cannot forbear adding a remark or two: I contend, that whatever has been said about it in the constitution of any State, amounts to nothing. What signifies a declaration, that 'the liberty of the press shall be inviolably preserved?' What is the liberty of the press? Who can give it a definition which would not leave the utmost latitude for evasion? I hold it to be impracticable. Its security depends upon the general spirit of the people and of the government."[18]

But what if the spirit of the people is different from the spirit of the government? The answer of the later Federalist Party was the Alien and Sedition Acts, and the imprisonment of recalcitrant and dissident editors. In any event, Hamilton refused to see any problem about freedom of speech; rather than being basic to all discussion of alternative policies and basic to freedom, it was a meaningless issue.

All of this was presented by Hamilton as his part in the defense of the new Constitution in *The Federalist Papers*. He was able to advocate adoption of the new Constitution, although it was "Republican," since it promised the development of energetic administrative power on the national level. But his co-author Madison argued for the new government upon vastly different bases.

For Madison, the goals of government are not given by the exigencies of situation, but rather the very problem of government is to maintain free discussion as to what the goals are. Hamilton separates "reason, truth, justice" from the errors of "passion," but in Madison's critical view, men always get passion and reason mixed together, so that each passionate view seems reasonable to the group involved, and there is no human reason free from emotion. Constitutional limits are important for Madison, for there are many views of justice and right. If the government did control one faction, it would oppress all the others and end the basic freedoms of discussion. "Energetic government" does not necessarily work for the good of all the different groups in society. Reflection leads to the view that restraint is as important as strong action.

18. *No. 84*, p. 560.

Madison did not argue, in his *Federalist* essays, in terms of natural rights. Natural-rights arguments had no practical appeal to New York audiences. Instead, Madison argued from the *unequal powers* of men and from the dangers of faction in a democratic society. He was able to start with the premises of the opposition, Hamilton's views of unequal talents, and reach the conclusions he desired. This is what was done in the famous Number Ten.

That essay starts with an analysis of factions. "Popular governments" are prone to factions, and plans which have no cure for the instability, injustice, and confusion caused by factions in Republican states should not be seriously considered. Madison defined faction as a number of citizens united in policies "adverse to the rights of other citizens, or to the permanent and aggregate interests of the community." Thus, while seeming to disparage popular governments, Madison has established the basic problem which Hamilton never recognizes: there are radical antagonisms and disagreements *within* society, and the peaceful solution of these problems is central to politics. Madison continued and discussed the possibility of the total agreement and harmony that Hamilton assumes: whether we should not give "to every citizen the same opinions, the same passions, and the same interests?" Such basic harmony is impossible, says Madison, *because* men are passionate and *because* they have unequal talents. What seem like the very same premises as those used by Hamilton lead to conclusions of *basic* and *radical* differences in society, which are not to be glossed over, but maintained, and accepted. Hamilton's basic answer of strong wise men in the government is dismissed quickly by Madison: "It is in vain to say that enlightened statesmen will be able to adjust these clashing interests, and render them all subservient to the public good. Enlightened statesmen will not always be at the helm."[19]

Since faction and disagreement are sown in the nature of man, in the nature of property and wealth, and in the nature of government, Madison can dismiss all the assumed unities of goals and ends and all the basic harmonies of economic interests argued for by Hamilton. The following paragraphs from Madison's essay are already well known, but they are quoted not only as a form of political theory, but as a political theory which takes its premises from the arguments of the other side, and rather than mention any inherent rights of man, talks only of property, inequality, and prejudiced judgment,

19. James Madison, *No. 10*, p. 57.

the usual mainstays of the opposition: "As long as the connection subsists between man's reason and his self love, his opinions and his passions will have a reciprocal influence on each other, and the former will be objects to which the latter will attach themselves. The diversity in the faculties of men, from which the rights of property originate, is not less an insuperable obstacle to the uniformity of interests. The protection of these faculties is the first object of government. . . . The latent causes of faction are thus sown in the nature of man."[20]

With this new approach, policy-making in government is not simply forging ahead energetically, but rather pragmatic grappling with dilemmas. For instance, important laws are the determination of the rights of large bodies of citizens, but legislators are all "advocates and parties to the causes which they determine." A law between creditors and debtors ought to be judged by "Justice," but in fact the parties are themselves the judges; "and the most numerous party, or, in other words, the most numerous faction must be expected to prevail." Madison is on ground which cannot fail to interest the propertied reader: debtors are always more numerous than creditors. How can such factions be stopped? Taxation, for Madison, is as important as it is for Hamilton, but as an area of conflict and injustice, rather than as an area for the display of financial genius: "The apportionment of taxes is an act which seems to require the most exact impartiality; yet there is, perhaps, no legislative act in which greater opportunity and temptation are given to a predominant party to trample on the rules of justice. Every shilling with which they overburden the inferior number, is a shilling saved to their own pockets."[21]

The fact that the government is "responsible to the people" is not enough for Madison, for a majority of the people may oppress the rest as much as any tyrant; there is such a thing as a "majority faction" for Madison: "When a majority is included in a faction, the form of popular government enables it to sacrifice both the public good and the rights of other citizens. To secure the public good and private rights against the dangers of such a faction, and at the same time to preserve the spirit and form of popular government, is then the great object to which our inquiries are directed."[22]

20. *Ibid.*
21. *Ibid.*
22. *Ibid.*

The cure is first, representative government, and second, extension of the area of government over a territory large enough to take in so many factions, interests, and regional views, that no one faction can ever predominate. But the cure is in this case not as important as the diagnosis, for it is the insistence on radically opposing views *inside* the society that is Madison's basis for discussing the problems of government. Madison sees oppositions, and he wishes to maintain the rights of the opposing interests to express their views freely and to argue and act in the government. Hamilton saw harmony, but for Madison:

> So strong is this propensity of mankind to fall into mutual animosities, that where no substantial occasion presents itself, the most frivolous distinctions have been sufficient to kindle their unfriendly passions and excite their most violent conflicts. But the most common and durable source of factions has been the various and unequal distribution of property. Those who hold and those who are without property have ever formed distinct interests in society. Those who are creditors, and those who are debtors, fall under a like discrimination. A landed interest, a manufacturing interest, a mercantile interest, a moneyed interest . . . divide nations into different classes. The regulation of these varied and interfering interests forms the principal task of modern legislation.[23]

Madison is able to use the assumptions of inequality among men and the dominance of propertied interests in government to develop the argument for a representative democracy. In other places, but not in *The Federalist,* he begins with the principles of freedom of speech and thought and the equality of men. His general cure for the evils of republican government is more republican government, but he is able to see this as practical support for the authoritarian Federalist position: "We behold a republican remedy for the diseases most incident to republican government. And according to the degree of pleasure and pride we feel in being republicans, ought to be our zeal in cherishing the spirit and supporting the character of Federalists."[24]

Finally, Madison saw a relation between reason and pluralism. Total unity is an effect of a sick society, a society overwhelmed by some unreasonable hostility or total apathy: "When men exercise

23. *Ibid.*
24. *Ibid.,* p. 62.

their reason coolly and freely on a variety of distinct questions, they inevitably fall into different opinions on some of them. When they are governed by a common passion, their opinions, if they so to be called, will be the same."[25] (It was from such basic views as this that Jefferson would later argue that diversity and dissent are more reasonable in constitutional law than uniformity and authoritarian agreement.) Madison concluded his final essay, Number Fifty-One, with a plea for plurality: "It is of great importance in a republic to guard the society against the oppression of its rulers, and to guard one part of society against the injustice of the other part. Different interests necessarily exist in different classes of citizens. . . . In a free government the security for civil rights must be the same as that for religious rights. It consists in the one case in the multiplicity of interests, and in the other in the multiplicity of sects."[26]

Thus was a new modus operandi established between believers in freedom and believers in authority; in *The Federalist Papers,* in the adoption of the new Constitution, and in the subsequent formation of the government, they *cooperated,* although for different public reasons and perhaps for widely different private reasons. With the new government in operation, Hamilton was allowed to show his genius in taxation and finance, and the Federalists could show how energy in government could lead to stability and prosperity through the leadership of the more temperate and respectable elements of society. Cooperating publicly, Jefferson and Madison began privately to build the nucleus of the party of the opposition, disproving Hamilton's thesis that there would be no major opposition. Jefferson and Madison had obtained a Bill of Rights for the Constitution, but the Federalists were in power for the first twelve years and thought they might be in power forever. However, this dream of Hamilton's was not realized.

The ideal unity of a society under a strong executive broke down because the President, John Adams, was not strong. Finances were inadequate. There were diplomatic blunders although there was no war. Chiefly there was great popular dissent and unrest. The Federalists passed the Sedition Act to stop criticism of the weak, corrupt, divided administration of Adams. The Sedition Act made it a crime to write or speak against the president or members of Congress with "the intent to defame" or to "bring them into contempt or disre-

25. *No. 50,* p. 334.
26. *No. 51,* pp. 259-60.

pute."[27] It took from the party publicists of the opposition the right of freedom of speech and destroyed the freedom of the press. The nation was in a crisis. It was hard to tell with whom, England or France, we had the greatest problems. Internally the economy lagged, and the Federalists feared they were losing their political power. The difficulties of Hamilton's smooth reasoning about necessary governmental power to meet the needs of defense against our foreign enemies was now made apparent. The first problem for deliberation was: "Who are our enemies and who are our friends?" In 1798 some people thought France was the enemy; the Alien Act was directed against alien Frenchmen, not against alien Englishmen. But others felt England was the enemy. We fought England later, but it was a matter of some discussion then, and could be so now, as to whether we chose to fight on the right side.

The Sedition Act was meant to stifle all opposition to the Federalist administration and all debate and discussion of alternatives. Jefferson's party used the only weapon available to them, the state governments in Republican control, to announce opposition and to maintain debate and discussion: the result was the Kentucky and Virginia Resolutions, denouncing the Alien and Sedition Acts as unconstitutional.[28] The Sedition Act did not stop dissent but rather greatly increased it, without solving the problem of proper foreign and domestic policies. It proved that the philosophy of energetic government as applied to obvious ends had become bankrupt and defensive and stood shakily without clear goals.

In the last period of Federalist power, Vice President Jefferson was subject to a constant harangue of abuse, insult, and innuendo. The Federalists did not believe the Sedition Act applied against them in their attacks upon Jefferson. Even though he was vice president, he was not considered as a "real" member of the government. But Jefferson insisted on his faith in working compromises despite temporary authoritarian lapses. Even when John Taylor wrote Jefferson, suggesting the secession of southern states since they no longer were represented in the government, Jefferson held fast to his mediating position: "It is true that we are completely under the saddle of Massachusetts and Connecticut, and that they ride us very hard, cruelly insulting our feelings, as well as exhausting our strength and

27. See Irving Brant, *The Bill of Rights* (Indianapolis, 1965), pp. 22-23.
28. See Henry Steele Commager, *Documents of American History*, 6th ed. (New York, 1958); Brant, *The Bill of Rights,* chapter 24.

subsistence. Their natural friends, the three other eastern States, join them from a sort of family pride, and they have the art to divide certain other parts of the Union, so as to make use of them to govern the whole."[29] Jefferson explains this "unnatural situation" as being the result of Hamilton's intrigues and the Federalist use of General Washington for their partisan purposes, but insists that time will bring changes, and "Be this as it may, in every free and deliberating society, there must, from the nature of man, be opposite parties, and violent dissensions and discords; and one of these, for the most part, must prevail over the other for a longer or short time. . . . Who can say what would be the evils of secession? . . . If they show their power just sufficiently to hoop us together it will be the happiest situation in which we can exist."[30] This is Jefferson's "short version" of Madison's argument in *The Federalist Papers,* concerning the eternal factions and changes in a free government in a free society. There is no utopianism here: the doctrine of freedom of discussion, which is really the practical side of the same coin as the doctrine of the rights of man, does not lead to some idyllic state of sweet peace and harmony, but in fact leads to the free-swinging debates of democratic politics, with "opposite parties, and violent dissensions and discords."

Meanwhile Hamilton, out of office, had tried but failed to obtain the appointment to the office of Commander-in-Chief of the Army, first, for himself, and then, for a loyal lackey. As always, he took this as a personal insult from John Adams and began to intrigue against him. He wrote an essay claiming that Adams was unfit to be President and circulated it among his more moderate friends who urged him to destroy it, but then it "fell" into the hands of the Republicans. This was a great help to the Republicans, but Hamilton's last bit of help was yet to come.

The Federalists, of course, hoped to remain in power. Their immediate goal was to carry the elections of 1800. When this seemed to be more and more difficult, various stratagems were devised, but none of the more illegal were carried through. In some sense, the elections of that year were as important to the future freedom of society as were the original foundings of the new government under Washington twelve years before. Washington had come to office simply as the great national leader, the hero of the war and the father of his country. But now leadership was at a much more ordinary

29. Jefferson to John Taylor, June 1, 1798. *Works,* VII, 264-65.
30. *Ibid.*

and partisan level, and the great question arose of whether ordinary party politics could succeed at the highest levels of the government. Some Federalists wished to seize power and dispense with the elections, using as an excuse the need to defend the country against the atheist revolutionary forces of France. But President Adams was too much of a legalist for that. However, Adams was slow in forgiving Jefferson for winning the election, and did not attend the inauguration.

Hamilton caused whatever machinations there were, and then heavily influenced the final choice of Jefferson as president rather than Aaron Burr. Since the Republican nominees for president and vice president were Jefferson and Burr, they received all the votes of the Republican electors in the Electoral College, and this was taken as a tie for the presidency by Hamilton and the Federalists in office. The selection of the president was thus thrown to the House of Representatives, which was dominated by Federalists.

Hamilton controlled crucial deciding votes in the House and could have chosen Burr for president. This would have split the Republican ranks wide open and given the Federalists another chance for the presidency in four years. But Hamilton did not do this. There is some indication that approaches were made to Jefferson, suggesting that concessions be made to certain Federalists in return for the presidency, but Jefferson was not the person to stoop to such bargains with such opponents. Finally Hamilton directed that the votes be swung to Jefferson, and on the thirty-sixth ballot in the House, not taken until February 17, Jefferson became president. The cooperation between opponents, which had started with *The Federalist Papers,* led to the crucial peaceful change of parties in power in 1800. Hamilton paid for this last cooperation with the Jeffersonians with his life, it might be added, since Burr then killed him in the famous duel.

Jefferson's election, the "Revolution of 1800," established the rule of law in the basic democratic procedures of deciding what men and what party would hold office and power for the regular and constitutional terms allotted. Those authoritarians who believe that men always rule, and that the rule of law is a sham, cannot explain such peaceful changes in power, where the men who are ruling step down and out of power and are replaced by other men who then obtain the power. The arguments, the campaigns, the voting, the inauguration of the new regime—all of this is the essence of the rule of law in a free society, and is the contrary of personal rule and personal power, which is not peacefully abandoned at the call of judgment against it. The rule of law in a democratic society *demands* just those wild and emotional conventions and campaigns for the presidency, which are deplored by the "respectable and temperate" classes. Such procedures do not guarantee that "the best man" wins, even if there were such a person, but only that the authoritarian powers of the incumbent administration are not ultimate. These men can be and are replaced through the emotional, because fundamental, process of campaigns, conventions, and voting. The rule of law in a democracy demands and needs party politics to bring about the basic changes in rule peacefully.

It can even be seen that in those states where one party has been overwhelmingly dominant for some time, there are tendencies for an unofficial oligarchical "establishment" to rule as it pleases; this is generally true in Maine or South Dakota, Republican strongholds, as well as in Mississippi or Alabama.[31] The primary nominating conventions may be utter chaos, with fifty or more candidates running for major offices, but the real political powers stay the same, and no real choices are given to the electorate. Amazingly enough, in the most active and economically prosperous states, the two-party system develops fully, and major offices change from one party to the other with fair regularity, as for example in New York and California. This theme could be expanded, but not in this place.

To return to the historic bases of the rule of law with respect to freedom in society and politics: the organization of an opposition party, and the peaceful transition to the politicians and the political values of that party in 1800, is one great basis for the maintenance of freedom in America, and an achievement on the part of Jefferson which equals in practical significance the issuing of the Declaration of Independence. The rule of law in practice means the peaceful transition from one administration to another. Without such changes in regime, words in a document become meaningless. Men always rule, but when different parties take turns ruling, then there exists the rule of law. But there is another achievement, with respect to the more erudite technicalities of the law, which should be credited to Jefferson, and that is the insistence on discussion and freedom on the Supreme Court. To put it paradoxically, Jefferson brought the rule of law to the realm of Constitutional law.

31. Granted this situation has now changed from the 1870-1950 era.

One of the last acts of the Federalist administration of John Adams was to appoint John Marshall of Virginia Chief Justice of the Supreme Court of the United States. Under Marshall's personal power and brilliant intelligence, the Supreme Court became transformed from its earlier weak and ineffectual position to become a bastion of the Federalist outlook. With Jefferson as president, this outlook was now transformed. As before, the national power should be strong, and the interests of commerce and property should be fundamental, but the sound political order basic to this was to be found in the judiciary and the law, rather than in the executive power.

This move was accomplished in the case of *Marbury* v. *Madison*[32] in which the Supreme Court decided that it had no right to enjoin Secretary of State Madison to deliver one of John Adam's "midnight appointment" notices to the appellant Marbury. But after giving this small plum to the Republicans, Marshall, speaking for the Court, stated that the reason was that the relevant section of the Judiciary Act was unconstitutional, and it was unconstitutional because the Supreme Court said so. It is unnecessary to examine here Marshall's syllogisms, which start with man in a state of Nature, and carry through to the purpose of all written constitutions and the proper duties of all courts. Jefferson himself, at a much earlier time, had held the opinion that the judiciary should have a veto power over the other branches of government but at this time it took a strong man to develop the arguments as Marshall did, and since there was such a man, the deed was done.

The Supreme Court under Marshall, in unequivocal terms, also asserted the ultimate power of the national law over the states' sovereign powers, in *McCulloch* v. *Maryland*,[33] the *Dartmouth College Case*,[34] and elsewhere. And the ultimate power of the national law was in the Supreme Court.

Marshall dominated the other members of the Supreme Court and the actions of the Court itself. He instituted the practice of writing all of the major opinions himself, something which had not been done by the three earlier Chief Justices. Marshall was against dissents, which seemed to him to lessen the authority of the Court: the Court should always appear unanimous, and the opinions of the other justices should appear to be the same as those of its chief

32. *Marbury* v. *Madison*, 1 Cranch 137 (1803).
33. *McCulloch* v. *Maryland*, 4 Wheaton 316 (1819).
34. *Dartmouth College* v. *Woodward*, 4 Wheaton 518 (1819).

justice. Perhaps this was the only way that the rule of law could be assured of respect in turbulent and Republican times, but the effect was that the rule of law became to a degree the rule of John Marshall.

John Marshall's insistence, in the name of good fellowship, that all the other justices reside at his boarding house during the term in Washington, also became a means of perpetuating his domination of the Court, for with his strong or "charismatic" personality he tended to dominate the others in their private lives, as well as in the Chambers of the Law. (It was difficult to disagree with Marshall in the formal discussions of the cases, when faced with drinking and eating with him later. The discussions and not the drinking suffered from this, it might be added.) No faction could develop against Marshall, and no dissenting voices could find any permanent foothold. Jefferson's Republican appointments soon became staunch advocates of Marshall's views; the conversion of Justice Story, who was a Jefferson appointee but became Marshall's right-hand man and also one of the great conservative commentators on Constitutional law, is but the most noteworthy example.

However, there was one justice who chafed somewhat more than the rest under this domination, and this was William Johnson. Justice Johnson, a Carolinian, had a strong liberal inheritance from his father and had been given an excellent education in Philadelphia private schools and at Princeton before turning to law and politics in Charleston. He was Jefferson's first appointment to the Supreme Court in 1804. At that time there were high hopes of overcoming Federalist power and John Marshall by outnumbering his forces in the Court. But Marshall converted most of the appointees. Johnson was not so charmed or swayed, but he found his role disappointing and even tried to resign, sending a letter to that effect to President James Madison in 1814.[35] But Madison would not accept the resignation of the only loyal Republican on the Court.

Justice Johnson had been able to sway the Court in one crucial case before the malaise of 1814. Problems of freedom of speech had arisen in Connecticut in connection with local and enthusiastic *Jeffersonian* prosecution of newspaper editors for seditious libel against the government. The case of the two editors, Hudson and Goodwin, went to the Supreme Court despite government efforts to

35. Johnson to Madison, June 16, 1814, quoted in Donald G. Morgan, *Justice William Johnson, supra*, p. 93 (from Madison MSS. in Library of Congress).

ignore it. The prosecution of such a case embarrassed an administration committed to freedom. The case rested on the old common law crime of seditious libel, and by the time it reached the Supreme Court, the Jeffersonians wanted such law declared irrelevant to American national jurisdiction. The Federalists were for a national common law and, incidentally, for punishing Hudson and Goodwin, because such a uniform national law would make commerce easier and more secure. The Jeffersonians were against such a national common law, because the particular crime of "seditious libel" tended to make freedom of speech and the press difficult, if not impossible. Amazingly, no lawyers showed up for either side at the hearing of the case, since the Federalist lawyers defending Hudson and Goodwin wanted the editors punished, and the government prosecution, supposedly attacking them, wanted them released. But the Supreme Court decided the case anyway. This time the Republicans held together over Marshall's objections, and Justice Johnson wrote the opinion: there could be no indictment, since there was no crime of seditious libel against the government, because there was no national common law. He delivered the opinion as that of "the majority of the Court," although there were no dissenting opinions written. His basis for saying that there was no Federal common law is surprisingly pragmatic and, in terms of technical legal thinking, unorthodox: "We consider it to have been long since settled in public opinion that there is no such general common law." Such recourse to public opinion was not part of a Marshallian jurisprudence.[36]

Justice Johnson continued to object to the authoritarianism of Marshall, even in written dissents, but he remembered the general period from 1804 to 1822 as oppressive, as evidenced in his letter to Jefferson on December 10, 1822:

> I was not a little surprised to find our Chief Justice delivering all the opinions in cases in which he sat, even in some instances contrary to his own judgment and vote. But I remonstrated in vain; the answer was he is willing to take the trouble and it is a mark of respect to him. . . . Some case soon occurred in which I differed from my brethren, and I thought it a thing of course to deliver my opinion. But during the rest of the session I heard nothing but the indecency of judges cutting at each other, and the loss of reputation which the Virginia appellate court had sustained by pursuing such a course. At length I found that I

36. *U.S.* v. *Hudson and Goodwin*, 7 Cranch 32 (1812). See extensive commentary in Brant, *The Bill of Rights*, esp. pp. 113-20, 312-16.

must either submit to circumstances or become such a cypher in our consultations as to effect no good at all. I therefore bent to the current. . . .[37]

Justice Johnson bent, but he did not break, and upon Jefferson's urging he regained his morale and continued the struggle to overthrow the authoritarianism of John Marshall. Thomas Jefferson began his correspondence with Justice Johnson toward this goal in 1821. Jefferson began a letter with high praise of Justice Johnson's history of the Revolutionary War in the Carolinas, a book which had diverted Johnson from his frustrations on the Court. Jefferson went on to suggest that Johnson write a full history of the political parties in the United States so that readers could tell the difference between true Republicans and Federalists, since many Federalists had simply switched names, but not principles, in recent times and pretended to be Republicans. But finally Jefferson reached his main point, which was that Justice Johnson should dissent and encourage others to dissent: "A most condemnable practice of the Supreme Court is that of cooking up a decision in caucus and delivering it up by one of their members as the opinion of the court, without the possibility of our knowing how many, who, and for what reasons each member concurred. A regard for character in each being now the only hold we can have of them, we should hold fast to it. They would, were they to endeavor to give their opinions to the world seriatim and publicly, justify themselves to the world by explaining the reasons which led to their opinions."[38]

Jefferson wrote to Justice Johnson *again,* in 1822. Again there is praise of Johnson's book and then a return to the problems of the method of decision of the Supreme Court:

There is a subject respecting the practice of the court of which you are a member, which has long weighed on my mind, on which I have long thought that I would write to you, and which I will take this opportunity of doing. It is in truth a delicate undertaking, and yet such is my opinion of your candour and devotedness to the Constitution, in its true spirit, that I am sure I shall meet your approbation in unbosoming myself to you. The subject of my uneasiness is the habitual mode of making

37. Johnson to Jefferson, Dec. 10, 1822. Jefferson Papers, MSS. Library of Congress. Quoted in Morgan, pp. 181-82.
38. Jefferson to Johnson, Monticello, Dec. 26, 1821, *Works,* Federal Edition, XII, 216.

up and delivering the opinions of the Supreme Court of the US.

You know that from the earliest ages of the English law, from the date of the year-books, at least, to the end of the IInd George, the judges of England in all but self-evident cases, delivered their opinions seriatim, with the reasons and the authorities which governed their decisions. Besides the light which their separate arguments throw on the subject, and the instruction communicated by their several modes of reasoning, it showed whether the judges were unanimous or divided, and gave accordingly more or less weight to the judgment as a precedent. It sometimes happened too that when there were three opinions against one, the reasoning of the one was so much the most cogent as to become afterwards the law of the land.[39]

Thus we have the remarkable prescience of Jefferson, that in American Law the dissent of one day may become the law of another.

Jefferson blamed the change in British practice on Judge Mansfield. Marshall is not mentioned, but his practice was condemned: "Cases are now uniformly prepared in private. Some of these cases have been of such importance and the decisions so grating to a portion of the public as to have merited the fullest explanation from every judge seriatim. It would certainly be right to abandon this practice in order to give to our citizens one and all that confidence in the judges which must be so desirable in the judges themselves and so important to the cement of the union."[40] Johnson's reply has been given in part above. He claimed his situation was no "bed of roses," and that he had no real friends or confidants on the Court. He mentioned the need for dignity on the Court, and suggested rather strongly that most of his colleagues could not give independent opinions because they had none. Johnson thought seriatim opinions would be of no avail on the Supreme Court and advocated instead reducing its membership to four.

Justice Johnson's exposure of Marshall's methods only increased Jefferson's desire to do something about the situation, and rather than acquiescing with Johnson he continued to spur him to change the methods. Furthermore, while Marshall saw unanimity as necessary to ensure respect for the Court, Jefferson saw argument and dissent as the only way to reduce the "growing hostility" to the Court and to restore confidence. He went on, in his next letter:

39. Jefferson to Johnson, Monticello, Oct. 27, 1822, XII, 246.
40. *Ibid.*

I cannot lay down my pen without recurring to one of the subjects of my former letter, for in truth there is no danger I apprehend so much as the consolidation of our government by the noiseless, and therefore unalarming, instrumentality of the Supreme Court. This is the form in which Federalism now arrays itself. . . . I must comfort myself with the hope that the judges will see the importance and the duty of giving their country the only evidence they can give of fidelity to its constitution and integrity in the administration of its laws; that is to say, by every one's giving his opinion seriatim and publicly on the cases he decides. Let him prove by his reasoning that he has read the papers, that he uses his own judgment independently and unbiased by party views and personal favor or disfavor. Throw himself in every case on God and his country; both will excuse him for error and value him for his honesty. The very idea of cooking up opinions in conclave, begets suspicions that something passes which fears the public ear. . . .[41]

By June of 1823 Jefferson had persuaded Justice Johnson to reassert his independence and write his own opinions, whether for the majority view or against it. Justice Johnson also decided, as part of this action, to move out of the common boarding house and live in his own private quarters. After Johnson's move a New York law for the relief of debtors through bankruptcy came to the Court (*Ogden v. Saunders*). It was just this sort of leniency toward debtors that Marshall despised and the Republicans urged. Justice Johnson led the way in maintaining the constitutionality of the New York law, and Marshall was inspired to write his own independent denunciation of the law, his only major dissent. Two other justices wrote opinions also, so that Jefferson's hope of something like seriatim methods of decision was closely approached.

Jefferson then wrote another letter to Justice Johnson and forwarded the whole correspondence to Madison, who was to urge his friends on the Court to write independent opinions. In the letter to Johnson, Jefferson restated the principles of Republican government and attacked the notion of an elite required to rule over unruly mankind. He openly attacked Chief Justice Marshall and restated his view that Marshall's opinion in *Marbury* v. *Madison* on the supremacy of the Court was an *obiter dicta*. But most of all he praised Johnson for his new independence: "I rejoice in the example

41. Jefferson to Johnson, Monticello, March 4, 1823, XII, 277.

you set of seriatim opinions. I have heard it often noticed, and always with high approbation. Some of your brethren will be encouraged to follow it occasionally, and in time it may be felt by all as a duty, and the sound practice of the primitive courts again restored."[42]

The letter to Madison, suggesting he write in similar vein to Todd and Duval, followed the next day: "I communicated to you a former part of the correspondence between Judge Johnson and myself. . . . In a late letter he expresses his concurrence with me on the subject of seriatim opinions. This last being of primary importance I enclose you a copy of my answer to the judge, because if you think of it as I do, I suppose your connection with Judge Todd & your ancient intimacy with Judge Duval might give you an opening to say something to them on the subject. If Johnson could be backed by them in the practice, the others would be obliged to follow suit. . . ."[43] Thus due to the patient urgings of the aging Jefferson and the actions of Justice Johnson, the supreme law in America follows the method of open discussion and open dissent in the published opinions of the Supreme Court, a method which is both modern and democratic, and also a return to the most ancient English practices recorded in the Year Books. Almost half a century after his work on the Declaration of Independence, Jefferson brought about the practice of open dissent in the highest court in the land.

It may be urged that Jefferson did this from *pique* at Chief Justice Marshall and because of purely partisan political motives. But Marshall was never overruled on his ruling in *Marbury* v. *Madison,* and in Jefferson's letters there is no statement that only Jeffersonians should dissent; what Jefferson wanted was responsible argument and discussion, not hidden caucus and authoritarian and unanimous rule. The hidden caucuses remain, but the justices do have the right to present their own opinions in seriatim form, and they do in fact so present them in separate individual opinions, both concurring with the majority and dissenting from the majority opinion, when they so choose (although the justices may also choose to remain silent).

Jefferson was aware of the power of the Court to determine the law of the country through interpretation of that law. In general, he was *for* such power as a check on executive or legislative tyranny. The judiciary was a body, according to Jefferson, which "if rendered

42. Jefferson to Johnson, Monticello, June 12, 1823, XII, 292.
43. Jefferson to Madison, Monticello, June 13, 1823, XII, 295.

independent, merits great confidence for their learning and ability."
At the same time, he thought that such independence did *not* mean
any supposed transcendental superiority to politics, and he keenly
analyzed the political tendency of the great legal sources of his day:

> In the selection of our Law Professor, we must be rigorously
> attentive to his political principles. You will recollect that be-
> fore the Revolution, Coke was the universal elementary book
> or our law students, and a sounder Whig never wrote, nor of
> profounder learning in the orthodox doctrines of the British
> constitution, or in what were called English liberties. You re-
> member also that our lawyers were all then Whigs. But when
> his black-letter text, and uncouth but cunning learning got out
> of fashion, and the honeyed Mansfieldism of Blackstone became
> the students' hornbook, from that moment, that profession (the
> nursery of our Congress) began to slide into Toryism, and nearly
> all the young brood of lawyers are of that line. They suppose
> themselves, indeed, to be Whigs, because they no longer know
> what Whiggism or republicanism means.[44]

It was when the judiciary itself became a faction, and a faction of
the sort opposed by Jefferson, that he worked for the restoration of
independence and integrity to the law, through the development of
freedom of opinion and dissent on the Supreme Court itself.

Jefferson has been much praised and criticized in his role as chief
executive and as a policy-maker on immediate levels of action and
value. His own view of his achievements, which centered on the
Declaration of Independence, the struggle for religious freedom, and
the development of education, is commonly thought to be puzzling
and paradoxical, since he made no reference to his being Governor
of Virginia or President of the United States. But it is conceivable
that Jefferson was true to his basic principles and was more concerned with the establishment of a government of freedom and intelligent discussion of differences and policies than he was with
executive power or the development of any one set of policies at any
given time. Those who search Jefferson's writings, to see whether he
was for "big government" or "small government," whether he was
for the small farmer or the large plantation owner, whether he was
for Negro equality or separatism, ignore the larger scope of Jefferson's view on the nature of a free society: such problems should be

44. Jefferson to Madison, Feb. 17, 1826. In Adrienne Koch and William Peden,
The Life and Selected Writings of Thomas Jefferson (New York, 1944), p. 726.

solved by free and intelligent debate and discussion among free and educated men. The particular policies are to be developed only under the larger structures of a free and reasonable society. Jefferson was able to conceive of men who had to be told what to do and think: his correspondence with the various Indian tribes, while he was president, assumes such dependency, and the Indians are frankly and directly treated as children.[45] Mature and educated men should take the responsibility for deliberation and decision themselves. The law is the guardian of such rights of freedom, but the law itself should exhibit the learning and independence associated with mature freedom. Seriatim opinions are in constitutional law what changes in administration are to the general rule of law. Jefferson helped effectuate both.

Jefferson stands as the American spokesman for the basic rights and freedoms enunciated in the English common law by Coke and in the philosophic literature of the grounds of politics and law by Locke. But more than re-echoing the sentiments of his progenitors, Jefferson merged ideals with a vigorous campaign of pragmatic applications. In *The Federalist Papers*, the Jefferson-Madison position is argued against the Hamiltonian point of view, but the Jeffersonian attitude is tolerant enough to respect Hamilton's position. Jefferson also worked with Hamilton in the same administration and later served as president largely as the result of his arch-rival's influence. Thus in the Amercian political scene, embryonic as it was at the time, compromise, freedom of speech and judgment, respect for individual rights, and the recognition of the significance of dissent, rather than raw power, were taken as ultimate. Law for Jefferson was not a fixed body of eternal verities but a procedure of reasoning and the structure in government and freedom in society to express the reasons, good or bad, for the undertaking of specific programs constitutional revisions, and even the ends of the Republic itself. Jefferson's carrying out of this "open pragmatism" or "higher formalism" will be seen to provide the climate and need in America for the diversity, debate, and far-reaching value of Supreme Court rulings and dissents from Marshall to Field, Holmes, Brandeis and in our own time, the extremes of Justices Frankfurter and Black. Jefferson, it might be said, firmly established *reason* in American law and as a result, the American political and judicial heritage is rooted therein.

45. See Saul K. Padover, *The Complete Jefferson* (New York, 1943), pp. 449-514.

Part II

Principles of Reason in Law

Introduction

THE FOUNDATIONS OF REASON in the law lie outside the technical and specific area of the law proper. As stated, these foundations exist in the development and recognition of institutions which separate the basis of man's economic existence from his loyalty to the current regime, which in England and America meant the development of private property as opposed to feudal grants. They exist also in the development of rights to speak and dissent, which has meant the insistence on an independent judiciary and an independent Parliament and Congress. Such institutional foundations require philosophic interpretation, for where there is neither philosophic nor religious nor economic tolerance on the level of discussion and thought, the institutions of privacy and freedom are ineffectual. Finally these institutional and philosophic foundations culminate in political action and in the peaceful changes in ruling values and ruling men that can come with responsible and reasonable dissent, a recognition of a pluralism of groups in society, and a realization on the part of the rulers that a peaceful change will not be disastrous, and that authority and order can continue. In America these political changes take two forms. The most obvious and most necessary is the change of administrations when a new party elects a new man to the presidency, and such peaceful change is accepted by all. The more specialized and technical constitutional change is that which arises because of the power of justices on the Supreme Court to dissent to majority decisions of the Court. In both respects Jefferson's political and legal acumen played a major role, and the peaceful revolution of 1800, when the Jeffersonian Republicans succeeded to the positions of domination held by the Federalists, is one aspect of the story of the political establishment of the rule of law. The other and crucial but unknown aspect is the revolution of the 1820's, when Justice Johnson, with Jefferson's strong encouragement, withstood the authoritarian pressure of Chief Justice Marshall and insisted on personally signed opinions by justices of the Court and on the right to dissent. This right to seriatim opinions has changed the nature and course of American constitutional law. As Jefferson predicted, it strengthened the Supreme Court in the eyes of a suspicious public, and it allowed for changes in the law, as the dissents of one period were recognized as compelling to a majority in another period. The right of free and thoughtful men to take opposite sides on practical propositions was developed in constitutional law with the recognition of the right to seriatim opinions.

The principles of constitutional law follow from these foundations, but the principles have reference to the intrinsic discussions and issues of the law, and this means technical statements of opinions in particular cases and lines of cases. The next chapters are an exposition of the role of reason in the actual cases of the law. There are two caveats to the reader of these chapters: first, the previous chapters have presented ideas which in their breadth and openness were taken as basic for all reasonable law, while the next chapters present particular views of the law, which are narrower and more dogmatic than the above. Although these views are presented as powerful perspectives, they are not meant to be comprehensive and final, but rather are one-sided and opposite views in the larger scheme of the entire law. Justice Field was a great defender of the rights of man, but necessarily he developed partisan views in relation to his opponent justices when discussing the Constitution, the Fourteenth Amendment, and concrete issues. Justice Holmes was a great defender of a jurisprudence of interests, but he also had a particular aristocratic and idealistic pragmatism, which in the larger debates forms an almost total contrast to the views of Field, and despite its brilliance must also be taken as partisan and somewhat dogmatic. But only in studying such actual concrete legal views can the interplay of principles be realistically understood. Second, the presentation of these concrete views will reach into areas of the law that seem technical and of little interest to the unspecialized reader. Now it is true that some of these problems of jurisdiction, of legal interpretation, of knowledge of precedents, are technical, but at the same time these problems are of fundamental general importance. Discussion of the justice of rates for warehousing in grain elevators is technical but involves far-ranging issues of the basic relations between what is deemed private and public in the legislature and the judiciary. Technical questions of jurisdiction, as between state courts and federal courts, involve the whole question of human rights in our unique but problematic system of independent state governments within the federal republic, and from the *Dred Scott* case to recent cases on criminal rights and voting reapportionment these questions have had great political import.

Although Justice Field and Justice Holmes are presented as holding opposing views, the matter is somewhat different. Justice Field was more directly opposed to men on the Court in his day, such as Justice Miller and Chief Justice Waite, than to the views of the later Holmes. These oppositions are presented, and it may be noted by the discerning reader that the carefully worked out oppositions of that day have been more or less ignored by the more recent pragmatic occupants of the supreme bench. In the cast of Justice Holmes, the presentation becomes even more complex. Justice Holmes tended to be an aristocratic immoralist in his earlier statement of the nature of law and public expediency. Popular law should be whatever the public believes is expedient, even if that dominant opinion has no relation either to truth or to profounder practical wisdom. In *The Path of the Law* he states that the bad man understands the law better than the good man, who unfortunately confuses law with morality. This aristocratic immoralism, however, became associated with the forceful democratic moralistic reformism of Justice Brandeis. "Brandeis and Holmes dissenting" became a common phrase in the Reports for some twenty years. The association with Brandeis changed the philosophic edge of Holmes' thought. The Holmesian heritage is further complicated by the fact that Justice Felix Frankfurter thought himself to be the inheritor of the philosophy of law of both Brandeis and Holmes. But Frankfurter has his own jurisprudence, which can be briefly characterized as an extreme nominalism and an extreme distrust of logical simplicity even in the presentation of views. All of these differences and interactions are developed in the chapter on Holmes and pragmatic jurisprudence. If the reader finds the triadic development complex, it is simply a reflection of the way the facts were. He may be referred to the excellent longer expositions of the scholar Samuel Konevsky on these men, if he wishes more clarity and more facts. Pragmatic jurisprudence is not one clear thing, for in Holmes the norms come from a peculiar idealistic agnosticism, a transcendental Nietzcheanism; in Brandeis the norms are found in the harmony of universal ideals shared by groups and by mankind; and in Frankfurter the norms are found only in surveying the particular and conflicting facts of concrete history. There is obviously a decline in transcendental vision from Justice Holmes to Justice Frankfurter, but at the same time Frankfurter's opinions do represent the perspectives of pragmatism taken at a responsible and literal level of social and legal existence. Finally, there is a dramatic reversal in the course of pragmatic jurisprudence. Chief Justice Warren discovered the pragmatic interest in having a formal jurisprudence and in arguing from the Constitution as supreme law. Thus pragmatism can come full circle and accept logic and fundamental rights and the formalities of legal due process as basic in the needs of a constitutional free society. Chief Justice Warren represents a new view in jurisprudence, in which both formalism and pragmatism are used, depending on occasion and need. Warren represents the pragmatic image of the view maintained in this book, i.e., open formalism. He is an open pragmatist.

Finally, the sixth chapter presents some of the current confrontations of pragmatism, now become conservative, with a vigorous formalism. At the same time, return is made to the basic issue between the recognition of law as primary and ultimate in society and the acceptance of power, the madness of leadership on the basis of personal charisma or manufactured "image" in politics, and the recourse to violence as the final solution of basic practical problems. The fundamental question is whether we seriously are concerned with practical reason and law and freedom and survival, or whether we are to be hypnotized by the ambiguities of power and fear.

4

Justice Field and a Jurisprudence of Rights

J USTICE STEPHEN JOHNSON FIELD was appointed to the Supreme
Court by Abraham Lincoln in 1863. Field had been active in
the Democratic Party in California but was loyal to the Union
cause. Lincoln needed such men on the Court, for Chief Justice
Taney and his colleagues were coming dangerously close to declaring
the war unconstitutional. The court was therefore "packed" with
two more justices, Field and Samuel Freeman Miller of Iowa, to
maintain the northern view against the extreme states' rights view
of the majority of the Court before that time who had decided the
Dred Scott case. (This is of great importance in understanding
Field's views on the Fourteenth Amendment, for he felt, with others
at the time, that the Fourteenth Amendment was meant to overcome
all of the reasoning of the *Dred Scott* opinion.) Justice Field remained on the Supreme Court until 1897, a tenure exceeded only by
that of Chief Justice Marshall, and he developed a habit of dissent
that became the despair of his colleagues. It has been remarked that
the history of the Court during the time was largely that of a duel
between Field and Chief Justice Waite. This is not strictly true.
Field first dueled with his close personal friend Justice Miller in the
Slaughterhouse Cases, over the meaning of the Fourteenth Amendment. When this duel was extended to include the new Chief Justice
Waite, in *Munn* v. *Illinois* and *The Granger Cases*, Waite's more
brilliant and learned colleagues such as Justice Bradley gave him

the arguments to back up his majority opinions; Waite himself was in fact no match for Field in constitutional debate, and it took the entire energies of the rest of the bench to match Field. Whether they matched him or not, they outvoted him, and in important constitutional cases he was usually in dissent.

The question of Field's heritage is important, since his pragmatic detractors wish to accuse Field of responsibility for the extremely conservative opinions about factory legislation and wage and hour regulation which issued from the Supreme Court from the time of the *Lochner* case until the overthrow of such views with the *West Coast Hotel* case of 1936. In these cases, which started with Chief Justice Peckham's majority opinion in the *Lochner* case, a supposed "right to freedom of contract" was developed out of the Fourteenth Amendment, which rendered all factory regulatory legislation and all wage and hour legislation unconstitutional. These reactionary majority opinions are traced back to the dissents of Justice Field. Such heritage is doubtful; the more proper heritage is the method of analysis of cases, which is in terms of the delineation of basic rights within the law. The proper methodological heritage of Field is more correctly seen in the defense of rights by the older Chief Justice White and the present defender of right and formal law on the Court, Justice Black. But this whole question is a matter that can best be understood only after a thorough presentation of Field's position and the pragmatic counter-position has been made.

Justice Field's jurisprudence, as it appears in his opinions, is of great interest because he took the basic rights of life, liberty, and the pursuit of happiness, as stated in Jefferson's Declaration of Independence, to be basic in our constitutional law. The Fourteenth Amendment incorporated these rights into the positive law, if there was any question about their recognition before that time. In the various cases to be presented, Justice Field applied his notion of these basic rights to the developing conditions of modern government, modern industry, corporate finance, conditions of labor, monetary controls, controls over large business complexes, and so on, and at the same time preserved some basic meanings for the terms *rights* and *freedom*. For Justice Field, individual rights had an ultimate value and were taken as the principles of government and constitutional law. The powers of the government were considered as secondary to these basic rights, although obviously such powers at times determined the exact delineation of those rights in practice.

The Supreme Court was the guardian of rights, protecting citizens against government power. If the executive or legislative branches of the government were the final judges of the extent of their powers, there would be no limits on these powers, and thus no individual rights. By "limited government" Field did not mean "small" government, but government (whether large or small) which could be, in some way, *defined.* Thus Field believed that "public interest" was no proper basis for reasoning in law, for the public may be interested in anything, and therefore the public interest is unlimited and indefinable. But "public use" is a proper basis for analysis, since public uses can be *defined.* However, in Field's thought jurisprudence does not establish a set of a priori definitions of words, which are then applied mechanically to cases, irrespective of circumstances; terms are explained and defined in relation to concrete activities and situations, as well as with regard to ultimate principles. Thus "property" for Field meant a butcher's right to pursue his vocation in his own place of business, an attorney's right to practice law, or a teacher's right to teach, since the *principle* of property was that it was a basis for livelihood, and in modern society many livelihoods were related to a specialized occupation, and not to acres of land, as in earlier times. Field similarly discovered property rights in a man's income from services or in returns on capital investments. Field insisted that the worth lying in the older theory of land as value was that such land provided uses and services of definite market value; it is not the land, but the *use* of the land, that is valuable, and similarly it is use that makes capital and vocations of service valuable. In other words, insofar as the law is concerned with values, there are market-values and use-values. There are no values in themselves, for in Field's economics (this does not include basic rights, which are intrinsically valuable) everything which is *useful* may have a market value and thus is property. Consequently, a butcher's income is his property.

Field did not have a legalistic mind that ignored situations; he had a reasoning mind which could incorporate economic thinking into legal definitions, but without abandoning fundamental legal notions of law and right. Jefferson had given *particular* meaning to life, liberty, and the pursuit of happiness in an eighteenth-century context where politics could be based on a society that, he hoped, might remain predominantly agricultural. What Field did was to *redefine* the same terms, life, liberty, and the pursuit of happiness, so that they applied to government and citizen in a society that was increasingly dominated by corporate enterprise of a financial or manufacturing nature. In the view of John R. Commons, the great institutional economist of a generation ago, Justice Field provided the legal bases for capitalism.[1] Granted the aspect of truth in this view, it might be more properly stated that Field *recognized* the growth of capitalism in the United States after the Civil War and *redefined* the basic terms of constitutional law and right, so that they would remain applicable to conditions in the changed urban-industrial society. Freedom and the pursuit of happiness do not require as a material basis a nation of small independent farmers: the same rights can relate to a nation of corporate enterprise, union labor, big government, citizens of different racial backgrounds, and so on.

It was the task of the Supreme Court as a whole to redefine the Constitution with respect to the new conditions of labor, finance, and industry in the period following the Civil War when Field sat on the bench. Majority decisions were not always such as Field thought proper, as we shall see in this examination. Since his argumentation is still applicable, his jurisprudence or rights for an industrial and corporate society merits examination. An apology must be made for Field, with respect to prejudices against him in current judgments by political scientists and American historians. One of the great controversial cases in the history of the modern Supreme Court was *Lochner* v. *New York*: in that case, decided after Field had left the bench, Chief Justice Peckham declared that a New York law limiting the hours of work for employees in the baking industry was unconstitutional. Parts of his reasoning were used later, as in *Adkins* v. *Children's Hospital* in 1924, to establish a concept of a basic "Freedom of Contract" in constitutional law. This notion of "Freedom of Contract" supposedly rendered all state legislation with respect to conditions of industrial work null and void, no matter how detrimental to health and welfare such conditions were in practice. In the uproar among historians and legal scholars about the rigid and unrealistically legal application of this notion of "Freedom of Contract" to attempts at social control of labor conditions, some scapegoat was needed. Peckham's notions of individual rights were thereupon hastily traced back to Justice Field's notions of basic rights, and Field was blamed for the whole thing. Although that

1. John R. Commons, *Legal Foundations of Capitalism* (New York, 1924).

storm is now over, and although most of the leaders in the attack, Charles Beard, Justice Holmes, and Roscoe Pound, drastically reconsidered their attacks on individual rights in their later work and thought, Field's reputation as the mind behind those opinions hindering the social regulation of industry remained without correction. No one has bothered to note that Field's position on corporations allows vastly more social control than even now is deemed legally possible, or that Field's position on freedom of speech is as strong as anything written today by the current defender of that freedom, Justice Hugo Black.

The purpose of examining Justice Field's legal thought, however, is *not* to prove that his policy determinations are the same as fashionable policy determinations today, but rather to indicate Field's interest in the basic legal structure of a free society, wherein governmental policy might develop and change depending on problems and conditions, without endangering fundamental rights. As with Jefferson, it is the larger concerns of deliberation on all policies that are taken as fundamental, not the particular applications, although the ability to go from the larger concerns to the particular determinations is a talent required of the judges of the Supreme Court, and Field developed this ability in his long tenure on the Court. The larger concerns for Field were the protections afforded by the Constitution, tradition, and the Supreme Judiciary to the paramount and fundamental individual rights of life, liberty, and the pursuit of happiness.

The duty of a Justice on the Supreme Court is to maintain the law by interpretation of the Constitution and the various written enactments subordinate to the Constitution, so that these writings find appropriate relation to conditions and conflicts which arise. Field achieved this by means of a general philosophy of rights and of the responsibility of government to achieve and recognize these rights, which has been ignored or misunderstood. This philosophy can be best presented here in terms of the following definite topics: (1) the law on private civil rights; (2) the law concerning private economic rights; (3) public and governmental powers, including the police power, the power over corporations and power over public uses; (4) the law and economics; (5) the law and politics; and (6) the law and proper definitions of terms, such as "rights, powers, and free governments," or "life, liberty, and property," or "due process of law." The range of Field's philosophy goes from eighteenth- and nineteenth-century Constitutional documents to current philosophic problems of definitions in the language of practical affairs.

The Law and Civil Rights

Field's thought on the problems of civil rights includes an uncommon, but not at all unreasonable, view of the relation of the Declaration of Independence to the Constitution. This view is, simply, that the Constitution *supplements* the Declaration, by providing for the institution of proper government, as called for in the earlier document. The Declaration of Independence is fairly clear on the necessity of government to protect basic rights and even calls for such institution: "They are endowed by their Creator with certain inalienable rights, that among these are life, liberty, and the pursuit of happiness. That to secure these rights, governments are instituted among men. . . ."

Thus the Constitution instituted the government called for by the Declaration, since the earlier government, under the Articles of Confederation, proved inadequate. There was no revolution in values between the time of the Declaration of Independence and the adoption of the Constitution, as has been said by certain modern historians, but on this interpretation the Constitution logically followed from the Declaration—because mere declarations, no matter how grand, do not afford any genuine protection or security; for that, government is necessary.

Field's view, that the Declaration of Independence was a basic constitutional document in the country's life, was not so uncommon in his day, and in fact was a view held by Abraham Lincoln. Anyone who traces the famous phrases in the Gettysburg address, about the "founding act" of "our forefathers" four score and seven years before, can discover that this refers to the Declaration of Independence. In Lincoln's view, as in Field's, the Constitution of 1789 supplemented the basic "birth" of 1776.

This is all crucial in understanding how the Constitution is to be interpreted, for this reading allows the Constitution to be interpreted in terms of rules which assume that individual rights are not derived from the government, but rather that government, all government, is derived from individual rights. This interpretation can make a great difference.

The first eight Amendments incorporate into the Constitution certain basic individual rights, insuring *within* the document a legal recognition of rights that might otherwise be ignored. The history of these rights is important in understanding how a basic philosophy of individualism can again and again be used to justify government priorities. The question arose in the case of *Barron* v. *Baltimore*[2] in 1833, as to whether the Constitution protected citizens against *state* governments, with respect to the rights enumerated in the Bill of Rights. The Supreme Court decided that the Constitution offered no such guarantees.

Thus, by 1833 with the Marshall Court, a general jurisprudence of basic individual rights, protected by the Constitution and secured by the governments instituted under the Constitution, was destroyed. The reasons for this decision, beyond the immediate legal reasonings, may have differed from judge to judge. Marshall and Story were not Jeffersonians; they believed in the Hamiltonian and Federalist philosophy of strong central governments achieving order. The protection of rights was not paramount for Hamiltonians. The Southern contingent on the Court wanted to protect the state governments, as forts for the slave power against the threatening powers of the national system. They were no longer interested in individual rights. Therefore, after *Barron* v. *Baltimore*, the Constitution no longer protected citizens against encroachments on their supposed rights by state governments. State governments decided what were rights and what were not.

The general authoritarianism allowed to states as collective powers, so seemingly benign in *Barron* v. *Baltimore*, led to a more drastic interpretation of collective power in Chief Justice Taney's famous opinion for the Court in *Dred Scott* v. *Sandford*.[3] For that decision held that the class of persons to which Dred Scott belonged were never citizens and could *never be* citizens, and the reason for this was that they *were not recognized* by the state governments as citizens. Rights existed only if granted by governments, and the right of citizenship was not granted by governments to Dred Scott and his class: "Every person, and every class and description of persons, who were at the time of the adoption of the Constitution recognized as citizens in the several States, became also citizens of the new political body; but none other; it was formed for them, and for them and their posterity, but for no one else." Taney went on to say that "citizens" and "people" were synonymous terms in the Constitution,

2. 7 Peters 243 (1883). 3. 19 How. 393 (1857).

and that therefore only "citizens" as defined by state governments, were included in the term "people," and Dred Scott and persons of his class had *no rights* whatsoever. Taney went on: since "citizens" were created by state governments, obviously some state governments might recognize persons such as Dred Scott as "citizens" of their state. But they could not legislate for the United States government and could not therefore confer United States citizenship on these persons.

Taney thus developed the notion of citizenship to include two kinds of citizens: state citizens and national citizens. State citizens are persons who have been recognized as "people" by the state, and national citizens are persons who have been recognized as people by all the states at the time of the adoption of the Constitution. From this it follows that there are some persons who might be recognized later as people by some state government, and some persons who might *not* be recognized as people *ever* by other state governments, and in any event could never be recognized as people by the national government.

Now this vicious and arbitrary reasoning, from the authoritarian bases in *Barron* v. *Baltimore*, was still, amazingly enough, the constitutional law on the subject of basic rights at the end of the Civil War. The Fourteenth Amendment was designed to change the law in this particular and to make the peculiar problems of state-recognized citizenship and nationally recognized citizenship *no longer* a bar to the extension of basic rights to Negroes. The language of "persons" and "state citizen" and "national citizen," in the Fourteenth Amendment, was used to directly contradict the language of Chief Justice Taney in the *Dred Scott* case, in which there were persons who were not citizens at all, and some state citizens who were not national citizens. The Fourteenth Amendment gave basic rights to all persons, and gave state and national citizenship to all persons, in order to overrule the *Dred Scott* opinion in every basic thesis: "All persons born or naturalized in the United States, and subject to the jurisdiction thereof, are citizens of the United States and of the State wherein they reside. No State shall make or enforce any law which shall abridge the privileges and immunities of citizens of the United States nor shall any State deprive any persons of life, liberty, or property without due process of law; nor deny to any person within its jurisdiction the equal protection of the laws."[4]

4. 14th Amendment, Sec. 1, adopted July 27, 1868.

Justice Field read this section as overruling *Dred Scott* and *Barron* v. *Baltimore,* and reincorporating *within* the Constitution the inalienable rights stated in the Declaration of Independence. Whatever had been the status of that Declaration before, the general status of rights was now assured, since the same rights were now enunciated *within* the Constitution itself. The rights of individuals were to be guaranteed by *all* governments, and the state governments no longer had the prerogative of declaring who had rights and who did not, nor of saying what these rights were, and what they were not.

The majority of the Court refused to understand the Fourteenth Amendment in this way, so Field's views remain only as dissents. In the peculiarities of the freedom of the American judicial mind, the language of the Fourteenth Amendment was taken to *reinforce* Taney's view that there was a double citizenship in America, with state citizenship determined by the state governments, rather than to *refute* that view. This conflict of interpretation was most fully explored in the *Slaughterhouse* cases and subsequent cases on the same line. But we will save that case and indicate the implications in two cases involving obvious civil rights.

In one such civil rights case, *O'Neil* v. *Vermont,*[5] a New York grocer was convicted by the Vermont courts of selling liquor in Vermont by mail from New York, against the dry laws of Vermont. The Justice of the Peace who obtained jurisdiction of O'Neil found he had done this kind of selling over four hundred times, and simply multiplied the legal penalty by this figure, sentencing O'Neil to a fine of $9,612.40 or seventy-nine years of hard labor. The Vermont Supreme Court reduced this sentence to $6,140 or fifty-four years hard labor. A majority of the U.S. Supreme Court found that the case was entirely a matter of Vermont law. Justice Field thought that basic individual rights were infringed upon: "Had he been found guilty of burglary or highway robbery, he would have received less punishment. It was six times as great as any court could have imposed for manslaughter or perjury. It was one, considering the offenses of which he was convicted, that may justly be termed unusual and cruel." Field held that the forms of the law did not change the nature of the damage, and that in such a case it was the duty of the Supreme Court under the Constitution to uphold individual rights against vicious state action, for there were "great

5. 144 U.S. 323 (1887).

wrongs inflicted, under the form of law, upon the defendant," and these were "wrongs inflicted upon a citizen of the United States."

The first long portion of Field's dissent has to do with Vermont infringing upon the commerce power of the national government, and while clear and cogent, it does not pertain to civil rights. The second part has to do with the rights of O'Neil under the Eighth Amendment, which forbade cruel and unusual punishments. Field thinks such rights are clear, and they hold against the states, particularly since the passage of the Fourteenth Amendment: "The Eighth Amendment was formerly held directed only against the authorities of the United States, and as not applicable to the States, (*Barron* v. *Baltimore*, 32 U.S.). Such was undoubtedly the case previous to the Fourteenth Amendment."

Justice Field then searches into the history of the adoption of the Bill of Rights and of the Thirteenth and Fourteenth Amendments, and concludes:

> While, therefore, as limitations on power, the ten amendments are applicable only to the Federal Government, yet, so far as they declare or recognize the rights of persons, they are rights belonging to them as citizens, and the Fourteenth Amendment, as to all such rights, places a limit on state power. . . . If I am right, then every citizen of the United States is protected against punishments which are cruel and unusual. The State cannot torture him, any more than it can deny to him security against unreasonable searches and seizures, or compel him to be a witness against himself. These rights find their recognition in the Constitution, and against State action in the Fourteenth Amendment.

Justice Harlan agreed, alone among Field's colleagues at the time. Field's view has, in part, become the opinion of the majority of the Court today, largely as the result of the persuasive argumentation of Mr. Justice Hugo Black. Otherwise the fairly clear intention of the Fourteenth Amendment to restore the primacy of rights over state powers was ignored in favor of Taney's views for almost a century. Field's view was to the contrary; basic civil rights belong to persons *as such*, and do not depend on the prerogative power of the state. O'Neil's rights did not depend on Vermont's powers, just as Dred Scott's rights as a person did not depend on recognition by a slave state.

A second case indicates Field's thought on this crucial point with respect to the national government and the rights of aliens. Do aliens have any basic legal rights in the United States? "No," said the majority of the Supreme Court, both then and now. "Yes," dissented Justice Field. They quite clearly are *persons* within the Fourteenth Amendment. In dissenting to the expulsion of a Chinese, one Fong Yue Ting, by the Immigration Department without a trial, an action condoned by the majority of the Court, Field said:

> Aliens from countries at peace with us, domiciled within our country by our consent, are entitled to all the guarantees for the protection of their persons and their property which are secured to native born citizens. . . . The moment any human being comes within the jurisdiction of the United States, he becomes subject to all their laws, is amenable to their punishment and is entitled to their protection. Arbitrary and despotic power can no more be exercised over them with reference to their persons and property than over the persons and property of native born citizens. They differ only from citizens in that they cannot vote or hold public office. As men having our common humanity, they are protected by the guarantees of the Constitution.[6]

To the section of the law requiring the alien to establish residence through the testimony "of at least one credible white witness," Field objected. Why a witness of a particular color? Why not go further and make it some particular archbishop? asked Field. The same problem came up with another Chinese, Wong Wing, who was sentenced to six months at hard labor, before expulsion, by a Federal Commissioner, without indictment or trial by jury.[7] Field held that such treatment was against the Fifth, the Sixth, the Thirteenth, and the Fourteenth Amendments, and said, among other things: "The term 'person' used in the Fifth Amendment is broad enough to include any and every human being within the jurisdiction of the Republic."

Thus it is *not within the prerogative* of the government to decide *who* is a lawful bearer of rights and *who* has no rights at all. All human beings have the same basic rights under the Constitution, as "persons" in the terminology of the Fourteenth Amendment.[8] But Field's view on this is still not the majority view of the Court, no

6. *Fong Yue Ting*, 149 U.S. 698, 754 (1892).
7. *Wong Wing* v. *U.S.*, 163 U.S. 229 (1895).
8. See *Galvan* v. *Press*, 347 U.S. 522 (1954).

matter how clearly it seems to follow from the general language of the constitutional amendment.

As early as 1864 Field maintained the right of freedom of speech against governmental censorship or pressure. When an editor was convicted for publishing attacks on the Reconstruction governments in the South, Field was one of two justices who wished to hear the case, presumably to study the problems of the rights of free speech as against the new governmental powers (*ex parte Milligan*). The Court delayed until Congress could pass legislation taking away jurisdiction of the case from the Court. Field objected to this publicly and was in some danger from the extremists in Congress. A motion to impeach him was made in the House, but failed.

With respect to citizens' rights against state and government loyalty oaths, Field's view was clear: such oaths presume guilt and shift the burden of proof to the citizen who must establish his innocence. Since this is against established rights in criminal procedure, the oaths are unconstitutional. Justice Field *redefined* liberty and property to establish the law that loyalty oaths are unconstitutional, for people who could not take the loyalty oaths could not follow certain professions, and the right to make a living in one's profession was seen by Field as "property." In *Cummings* v. *Missouri*,[9] Field, speaking for a slim majority of the Court, held a Missouri law which required a retrospective loyalty oath (that the citizen had been loyal to the Federal Government during the Civil War) unconstitutional. "Liberty," said Field, included "freedom from outrage on the feelings as well as restraints on the person" and "property" included "these estates one may acquire in the professions." Field insisted that the government did not define rights, but that rights were prior to such government action:

> The theory on which our political institutions rest is that all men have certain inalienable rights—that among these are life, liberty, and the pursuit of happiness; and that in the pursuit of happiness, all avocations, all honors, all positions, are alike open to everyone, and that in the protection of these rights all are equal before the law. The existing clauses of the law presume the guilt of the priests and the clergymen, and adjudge the deprivation of their right to preach or teach unless the presumption be first removed by an expurgatory oath—in other words, they presume the guilt and adjudge the punishment condition-

9. *Cummings* v. *Missouri*, 4 Wall. 277 (1867).

ally . . . the clauses subvert the presumption of innocence and alter the rules of evidence . . . they assume that the parties are guilty . . . they impose penalties without the formality of a judicial trial and conviction.

With respect to a Congressional law requiring the same sort of oath in order to practice law in the Federal system, Field also declared it unconstitutional, along with a slim majority of the Court. A loyalty oath was a punishment without a trial, against the rights of citizens: "It adds a new punishment to that before described and is thus brought within the inhibition against the passage of an *ex post facto* law."[10] Field also found that loyalty oaths were like Bills of Attainder, and as such also unconstitutional.

The dissent held that teaching, practicing law, and preaching in churches were privileges accorded by the government, not basic rights as Field stated. Since they were privileges they could be taken away, and such deprivation was not a punishment. Loyalty oaths were a matter of self-defense, not punishment, and could be understood in terms of the exigencies of the time and the goodness of our leaders: "The history of the time when the statute was passed—the darkest hour of our grave struggle—the necessity for its existence, and the humane character of the President, all show it was a qualification exacted in self-defense, and not a punishment."[11] The dissent shows the pattern of the problem, with the defenders of right arguing for restrictions on what seems arbitrary government power and the apologists for government power pleading the felt needs of the time and the goodness of the people in power. Against this opposing view, Field maintained the right of freedom of speech was not abrogated by circumstances. It was in difficult times that the right needed proper constitutional and juridical guarantees.

Another right, similar to the right of freedom of speech, is the right to maintain silence. Confronted with the demands and powers of a Congressional investigating committee, Field maintained a clear position: Congress could not punish a man who refused to answer the questions of such a committee. Such a man is guilty of no crime under the penal and criminal codes, and if the witness is incarcerated it is without fair trial and thus unconstitutional. Congress has no power to invade private affairs by force. If Congressional com-

10. *Ex Parte Garland,* 71 U.S. 366 (1868).
11. *Ibid.*

mittees believe something is wrong, they may sue in the Courts, as others do:

> Of all the rights of a citizen, few are of greater importance or more essential to his peace and happiness than the right of personal security, and that involves, not merely the protection of his person from assault, but exemption of his private affairs, books, and papers from the inspection and scrutiny of others. . . . Forcible intrusion into and compulsory exposure of one's private affairs is contrary to the principles of a free government. Neither house of congress has the power to make inquiries into the private affairs of the citizen; that is, to compel exposure of such affairs. The courts are open to the United States, as they are to a private citizen, and both can there secure, by regular proceedings, ample protection of all rights and interests which are entitled to protection under a government of a written constitution.[12]

The right against special Congressional investigation into private affairs, in the Fourth Amendment, can be related to the right against peculiar persecution of the Fourteenth Amendment, which guarantees equal protection of the laws. Although the Supreme Court has developed Fourth Amendment rights recently (*Linkletter, Mapp*), they still have not granted citizens' rights against Congressional investigating bodies.

Justice Field held unconstitutional legislation which, on its face or with an obvious implicit intent, was aimed at racial minority groups. The minority groups involved in these cases were not Negroes but Chinese. For instance, a San Francisco ordinance that all prisoners in a city jail must have their heads closely clipped, in the interests of health and sanitation, Field found unconstitutional. Aimed at the practice of the Chinese to wear queues, it was specifically directed against their peculiar customs. This required going beyond the face of the law, but Field found the intent obvious. A law requiring laundrymen to have the written consent of people on their block in order to continue operations, Field also found unconstitutional and prejudicial to the rights of Chinese, who would have vastly greater difficulty obtaining such consent than white laundrymen. Field found that in practice the law had been enforced only against the Chinese. But a law that laundries could not operate from

12. *In re Pacific Railway Commission*, 32 Fed 241 (1887); see also *Kilbourn v. Thompson*, 103 U.S. 168 (1880).

ten at night to six in the morning, Field found constitutional, as a proper city ordinance for quiet at night. Although it hurt Chinese laundrymen most, that did not prevent it from being lawful. There are two considerations here that are important.

The first is that Field held there was *no* constitutional guarantee against special legislation or class legislation as such. Again and again he noted that *most* laws had a special or class character and hurt some people more than others. Laws to enlarge highways or to put in city utilities hurt the people in the way more than the rest. Laws respecting safety on railroads hurt people in railroading more than others. In no sense did this make such laws unconstitutional, if the laws were passed for an acceptable public purpose. Field was not against legislation with respect to a special industry or special problem. Such is the character of most legislation, but this seems to have been forgotten by some later judges. Field never came out against state laws simply because they affected some one class more than another, or hurt one class more than another. But such laws could not be *aimed primarily* at injuring or hurting one class or race more than another. The purpose had to be properly within the power of the state; it could not be aimed at establishing unequal protection before the laws.

On the other hand, unfortunately, it must be said that Field remained silent on issues on Negro civil rights. He objected to federal supervision of state voting procedures when such supervision would have been the only way to ensure Southern Negroes the right to vote. He objected to requirements that Negroes serve on juries as well as whites. He rationalized this by saying that the duty of the Supreme Court was to *prevent* inequitable legislation by the states, but not to intervene to establish equitable conditions: the Fourteenth Amendment provided only *negative* powers for the Federal courts as against state legislation. All that can be said here is that Field was directly aware, at first hand, of conditions of racial discrimination in California, with respect to Chinese, and there he took a firm stand, but he had never been in areas of radical mistreatment of Negroes.

Apart from this important lapse within the area of civil rights, Justice Field stands as a spokesman for major and basic rights of individuals against government action which seems tyrannical or arbitrary. Field held that the Bill of Rights protected citizens against state governments long before the entire court could ever comprehend that view; he held that aliens were, as human beings, persons under the law, when the present law still does not maintain that position. He upheld rights to freedom of speech and freedom of the press and upheld rights against laws exacting loyalty oaths with respect to past deeds and actions, when the general sentiment of the country was for employing such oaths. He insisted on constitutional limits to the prerogatives of Congressional investigations, when these have seldom been maintained by other judges of the Court before or since. And in some areas he established precedents for denying constitutionality to legislation because of its antagonistic relation to the doctrine of equal protection before the laws. All these positions on basic rights follow quite logically from Field's general notion that basic rights are the foundation of any free government. The legal foundations in our government are the Declaration of Independence, the Constitution, the Bill of Rights, and the Fourteenth Amendment.

The Law and Economic Rights

In the area of economics, problems of government monopoly, private monopoly, and government regulation of business led to basic Supreme Court decisions and to Field's dissents. These dissents are misunderstood, since the false statement that his views led to Justice Peckham's majority opinion in the *Lochner* case has been accepted without much investigation.

With respect to the role of government in securing private economic rights, the issues involved in the *Slaughterhouse Cases*[13] and *Munn* v. *Illinois*[14] are paramount. In the former case, Justice Field was strongly in favor of the rights of butchers to work where they pleased and not in premises given by the state legislature to one monopoly slaughterhouse. The majority of the Court, exercising what today would be called "judicial restraint," decided that the acts of the legislature did not violate any of the *national* rights of the butchers and that the legislature was the judge of state rights.

In more detail: in 1869 the Louisiana legislature passed a law giving a monopoly of the slaughterhouse business in New Orleans to one company (which was newly formed just for the purpose), the Crescent City Live-Stock Landing and Slaughterhouse Company. The company did not have a monopoly of the slaughtering itself; any butcher could use the premises for his own slaughtering, upon

13. 83 U.S. 394 (1873).
14. 94 U.S. 113 (1877).

the payment of a fee which included money and certain parts of the animal slaughtered, but the Crescent City Company was to have the only legal slaughterhouse in the city, and butchers could no longer slaughter in their own yards or in any other stockyard.

The case was heard by the Supreme Court in 1873. The Butchers' Association charged that the law was an unconstitutional deprivation of rights under the Fourteenth Amendment, while the Crescent City Company said that the law was a health and sanitation measure, within the police powers of the state.

Justice Miller, speaking for the Court, said that the grant of exclusive privileges to the one designated company was within the police powers of the Louisiana government. Miller started with basic notions of "the full sovereignty of a state." Every state in the United States retained the "full sovereignty" of the British Parliament, except for strictly limited powers granted to the national government. Following Taney, Miller said that the phrase "all persons . . . are citizens of the United States and of the State wherein they reside" distinguished *two separate* citizenships, a national citizenship, of strictly limited range, and a state citizenship, which was determined by the sovereign power of the state. The Fourteenth Amendment changed this only in one respect: it gave civil rights to Negroes, but that was the entire extent of its application.

Justice Miller's pragmatic reasoning allows for various theses besides the strange continuation of Chief Justice Taney's theory of state citizenship and national citizenship. Miller discovers the *real* meaning of the Fourteenth Amendment by going "behind" the words to the sociological intent, and since the intent was to give rights to Negroes, no other persons are covered by the Amendment, even though the surface reading says "persons" and not "Negroes." Miller not only does not define what he means by "police power" but even states that there can be no definition; the term is "incapable of any very exact limitation." Furthermore, Miller argued, in terms that sound like Justice Holmes or Justice Frankfurter, that to read the Fourteenth Amendment in any other way would make the Supreme Court a judge of state powers: "Such a construction would constitute this court a perpetual censor upon all legislation of the states, on the civil rights of their own citizens, with authority to nullify such as it did not approve." This, Miller found, would be too great a departure "from the structure and spirit of our institutions."

The proper function of the Court, according to Miller, is to balance the different sovereign powers, the state governments and the national government: "This Court has always held with a steady and even hand the balance between State and Federal power, and we trust that such may continue to be the history of its relation to the subject." To declare the law about butchers unconstitutional would be to upset the balance.

Finally, the rights of the butchers have not been infringed anyway; the law simply controls the place where the butchering must be done. The fee is not any deprivation of basic rights.

Thus, by interpreting the Fourteenth Amendment so that no change was made from the decisions in *Barron* v. *Baltimore* and *Dred Scott* v. *Sandford*, Justice Miller saved the "traditional structure of our institutions." What some might have interpreted as the rule of law protecting basic rights, Miller interpreted as "perpetual censorship on state legislation on local matters." Justice Miller did not have to define any of the crucial terms he used, except to define "persons" as meaning "Negroes only"; and he does not *really* abandon the dominant role of the Court, since the Court still *balances* state power and national power, but these powers are not seen as oriented toward individual rights. "Sovereign powers" just are what they are and can't be defined at all.

Justice Field differed from all this, particularly concerning the nature of citizenship, the power of state government, and the extension of the word "persons" in the Fourteenth Amendment. For Field no "balancing" or "self-restraint" was needed, for the Louisiana law was an open infringement on the constitutional right of the butchers to follow an ordinary calling of life unimpeded by any state-created monopolies. Monopolies had been illegal in common law since the days of Coke, and the Fourteenth Amendment was specifically designed to give to the Federal court system the power to protect such rights, which had been given to the states alone because of *Barron* v. *Baltimore* and Taney's *Dred Scott* opinion. If no change were contemplated, asked Field, why was the amendment passed, for it then "unnecessarily excited Congress and the People of the United States" on its passage? Field thought it was passed so that the rights of all citizens would be protected. The right to pursue the ordinary occupations of life was such a right, and this right was infringed by the slaughterhouse monopoly granted by the Louisiana legislature.

For Field, the Fourteenth Amendment "protects citizens of the United States against deprivations of their common rights by State legislation." For Field, the Fourteenth Amendment was made to abolish the heinous distinction made by Taney between state citizenship and national citizenship: "A citizen of a state is now only a citizen of the United States residing in that state." This clear and logical, as well as realistic, view of citizenship in this country has yet to be accepted fully and completely, but it is the reading of the Fourteenth Amendment alternative to Miller's interpretation. Field read the Fourteenth Amendment as a change from the earlier doctrine and a new development in the area of guarantee of rights: "If it does not do this, it was a vain and idle enactment."

Among the rights of citizens "must be placed the right to pursue lawful employment in a lawful manner, without other restraint than such as affects equally all persons." This means protection against "hostile and discriminating legislation." This is a crucial point in the perennial argument centering on this view. Justice Field does start with individual rights, and if state legislation is injurious to these rights, it is unconstitutional. Now critics have charged that this view makes *all* state legislation impossible, and, most particularly, the regulation of working conditions in industry, because of a supposed "right," which was later discovered by the Court, to contract to work under any conditions whatsoever. One could add the right to buy adulterated food, and then pure food and drug regulations would be unconstitutional, and so on. This argument *ad horrendum* does not apply to Justice Field, for he clearly delineates the proper legislative powers of the state. These legislative powers or "police powers" could be broadly defined, and were by Justice Field: they were all laws and regulations affecting the health, good order, morals, peace, and safety of society. The state is the judge of what is right and proper within the range of these powers, and the Court cannot be a "perpetual censor" over every act of the state. But if these powers come in conflict with a basic constitutional provision, then they can be assailed in a judicial tribunal. In this case, "the Act of Louisiana went far beyond the province of a police regulation, and created an oppressive and odious monopoly, thus directly impairing the common rights of the citizens of the state . . . it was believed that the Fourteenth Amendment had taken away the power of the State to parcel out to favored citizens the ordinary trades and callings of life."[15] Furthermore, the amendment clearly applied to *all* citizens, and not just to Negroes. To narrow the application of

15. 83 U.S., *op. cit.*

the amendment to Negroes only would be to interpret the amendment as class legislation, and basically inequitable.

The crucial inequity of the Louisiana law was the creation of a *legal* monopoly. This is not the same as the simple dominance of one company in a field or what might be called an economic monopoly, but it is much more; one company was granted by the state the sole right to operate in one field. Field objected to this in 1873, just as Coke had in 1608, as favoritism of the most arbitrary sort: "All monopolies in any known trade or manufacture are an invasion of the privileges of the citizen, for they encroach upon his liberty to acquire property and to pursue happiness."[16] Field quoted Coke's *Reports*: "A monopoly is an institution or allowance from the sovereign power of the state, by grant or otherwise, to any person or corporation, for the sole buying, selling, making, working or otherwise using of anything whereby any person or persons are sought to be restrained of any liberty they had before, or hindered in their lawful trade."[17] The slaughterhouse company was such a monopoly, and therefore the slaughterhouse monopoly was void.

Thus Justice Field does not extend the area of rights past all tradition, as charged; the opposite is the case. The Louisiana law would have been void and illegal in England under common law, for over two hundred years. It was Taney and Miller who violated "the spirit of the Common Law," not Field.

For Field, the basic rights extend from the case of monopolies, to the Declaration of Independence, to the Fourteenth Amendment. The right to be a butcher was one of the traditional liberties of the English law. The right to make a living among lawful occupations without arbitrary interference was established in principle in the Declaration of Independence, and now the Fourteenth Amendment made that Declaration part of the basic law of the country: "The Fourteenth Amendment was intended to give practical effect to the Declaration of 1776 of inalienable rights, rights which the law does not confer, but only recognizes." This does not mean that these rights automatically exist in every land, but rather only where they are secured by a free government. The equal protection of rights is basic in a free society, and particularly in the United States: "This equality of right in the lawful pursuits of life is the distinguishing privilege of citizens of the United States. To them, everywhere, all pursuits, all professions, all callings are open. The state may pre-

16. *Ibid.*   17. *Ibid.*

scribe such regulations for every pursuit as will promote the public health, secure the good order and advance the prosperity of society, but within such regulations, the pursuit or calling must be free to be followed by every citizen. This is the fundamental idea on which our institutions rest, and unless adhered to in the legislation of our country, our government will be a republic only in name."[18]

This fundamental right of equal protection under the laws has nothing to do with the right of labor to organize nor with the right of the state to impose time or wage limits on labor. In fact, Field is defending a butchers' union in this case. It means simply that the Constitution protects citizens against a government-sponsored monopoly. This is not a matter of calling "natural rights" out of the empyrean blue, for such rights were guaranteed by the positive law of the Fourteenth Amendment.

Justice Field had been relatively quiet during the first ten years of his tenure on the Supreme Bench, from 1863 to 1873. But the *Slaughterhouse* case started him on an unending argument over basic constitutional principles. He insisted that government could be defined in terms of its purposes and that the fundamental purpose was the guarantee of the rights of the citizen. When a prohibition law of the State of Iowa came before the Supreme Court, Justice Miller stated for the Court that the law was within the police powers of the state. Field agreed, but in a concurring opinion. After agreeing with the Court, he distinguished this case from the *Slaughterhouse* case, which he continued to hold as contrary to basic law. First, the police powers could be defined and were not vague and indefinable. Second, it was against basic rights to have the state parcel out ordinary callings of life to favored citizens. The Fourteenth Amendment extended the protection of the law over all rights of all citizens, and against the arbitrary action of state as well as national governmental power.

Some ten years later, Justice Field still dissented. The Republican legislature had been voted out with the termination of the Reconstruction Period in 1876, and the new legislature had repealed the charter of the Crescent City Slaughterhouse Company, although that charter extended for twenty-five years. Was this revocation of the charter legal? The Supreme Court held that it was. Justice Field concurred with this decision; the state cannot contract away its police powers. But, furthermore, since there never was a valid charter for

18. *Ibid.*

the monopoly, the charter had *always* been void. He went on, again: police powers are held with reference to the health, safety, peace, and good order of the community. These powers and their uses are not subject to scrutiny or review by the Federal courts in any ordinary legislation, but these powers cannot conflict with any constitutional provision. Legislation cannot encroach upon rights in the Thirteenth, Fourteenth, and Fifteenth Amendments. The granting of a monopoly was such an encroachment; it was always void.

Field expanded his argument from the amendments, to the Declaration of Independence, and to even more general statements of the basic nature of rights: *"certain inherent rights lie at the foundation of all action, and upon recognition of them alone can free institutions be maintained."*[19]

It is difficult to see why Field's dissents in these cases should be seen as the first step in the defense of buccaneer corporation capitalism. Field objected to legislation which infringed on the rights of a group of skilled laborers. The legislation did not do this by the proper method of state inspection of slaughterhouses, but by the improper method of creating a private corporation as a private monopoly of all slaughterhouse business. For Field this was an infringement on rights. For Justice Miller and the majority of the Court, no individual rights were involved, only powers—state powers versus the powers of the court and the nation. For Miller rights are what the state legislature says are rights. Somehow Justice Miller's opinion has been classified as "liberal" and Field's reactionary, although Miller followed exactly the reasoning of Taney in the *Dred Scott* case, while Field considered the effects of the Fourteenth Amendment.

The Extent of the Police Power

The second case is more extreme. In *Munn* v. *Illinois,* the state passed a law regulating the storage rates of grain in grain elevators.[20] This was done in accordance with a section of the Illinois Constitution of 1870, which specifically and literally empowered such legislation. It was generally felt that the various owners of some fourteen warehouses in Chicago had a monopoly of grain storage and were exploiting the farmers by charging unreasonably high rates. The legislature fixed "reasonable" and lower rates.

19. *Ibid.*
20. 94 U.S., *op. cit.*

There is evidence that the majority of the Supreme Court knew that Field would object. Chief Justice Waite gave the majority opinion, which deals at great length with the fundamental purposes of government and the traditions of the common law, but there is gossip that the opinion was written by the intellectually stronger Justice Bradley and then presented by Waite in order to have the authority of the Chief Justice behind it.[21] Justice Field never seemed to have had the ability to persuade men, but his arguments did give rise to the need for strong counter-arguments. For some pragmatic thinkers, this case is simply a problem of whether or not to have government control of business, but for Field it was vastly more complicated. As will be seen, Field was *for* government regulation of corporations; but he was against defining private property, by means of the vague term, the unlimited and indefinable term, "public interest." Public powers extend to public *uses,* not to public interests, since the public is interested in everything. Regulating rates of private business would be taking private property and would involve payment of compensation, as in the exercise of prerogatives of eminent domain.

In the majority opinion, it was held that the property was part of a "virtual monopoly," that it was "clothed with a public interest," and therefore subject to state regulation.

Unlike Justice Miller's reasoning, Waite's argument is not a matter of pragmatic balancings of various powers and interests. Waite stated there was one question and one answer. The question was: "Does the Illinois law deprive Munn of property without due process of law?" The answer was simply "No." Munn retained all his property rights in the warehouse, although the rates were regulated. The rates were regulated because the virtual monopoly of the grain storage business by the elevator owners was a matter of public interest.

Waite stated that the ultimate ends of government can be defined so as to allow regulation: "The very essence of government" is "the establishment of laws requiring that each citizen so conduct himself and so use his property as not unnecessarily to injure another." If sovereign power or police power needs to be defined, it is "the power to govern men and things for the public good."[22] Society is produced by a compact which commits each member to obey all the laws. This

21. See Peter Magrath, *Morrison R. Waite* (New York, 1963), chapter 10.
22. 94 U.S., *op. cit.*

is quoted from the Massachusetts Charter. When a person enters society, he necessarily sacrifices some rights and privileges. Under its general power, the government not only regulates the conduct of citizens toward one another, it also regulates the *manner* in which each shall use his property, if such regulation is necessary for the public good. The control of warehouse rates is such a control of the *manner* of use of property to prevent injury to others. The traditions of the common law in both England and America were that regulations of prices and charges were perfectly legal: "It is apparent that down to the adoption of the Fourteenth Amendment, it was not supposed that statutes regulating the use, or even the price of the use, of private property necessarily deprived the owner of his property without due process of law." It had been customary in England and America to regulate rates for ferries, wharfs, and common carriers. The basis for such regulation was the public interest. Waite did not deny that there was a difference between public and private, but only insisted that the determination of what was public was a matter for the public interest. He discovered precedent in an ancient British tract *de Portibus Maris* by Sir Matthew Hale: "When private property is affected with a public interest, it ceases to be *juris privati* only." Public interest, therefore, founds public right and power: "Property does become clothed with a public interest when used in a manner to make it of public consequence, and affect the community at large. When, therefore, one devotes his property to a use in which the public has an interest, he, in effect, grants to the public an interest in that use, and must submit to be controlled by the public for the common good."

From this, Waite proceeded to a long statement of the particular facts; the grain production of seven or eight states had to pass through these warehouses on the way to the Eastern seaboard, and these warehouses had a virtual monopoly of this public trade. The owners were not entitled to compensation, for the controlling fact was the public power to regulate. Public power may be abused, but for "protection against abuses the people must resort to the polls, not to the courts."

Mr. Justice Field dissented.[23] He could not accept Chief Justice Waite's definition of government, his definition of the police power, or his definition of private property. But he particularly dissented to Waite's introduction of the principle of "public interest" as permit-

23. *Ibid.*, pp. 135-55.

ting public regulation. For anything can be a matter of public interest, nothing can be said to be assuredly private, and all constitutional limitations are ended: "The principle upon which the opinion of the majority rests, is, in my judgment, subversive of the rights of private property, heretofore believed protected by constitutional guarantees against legislative interference."[24]

For Field, the warehouses in Chicago were not any more public than most other businesses; in fact, they were not public at all.[25] Therefore the question is whether the state has the right to regulate the price for the use of private property in a private business. If businesses are private, then they are private. Laws, and even constitutions, cannot make them public. The distinction is not a matter of public will: "The declaration of the Constitution of 1870, that private buildings used for private purposes shall be deemed public institutions, does not make them so. The receipt and storage of grain in a building erected by private means for that purpose does not constitute a public business. . . . There is no magic in the language, though used by a constitutional convention, which can change a private business into a public one. . . ."[26] Justice Field continues to emphasize the point, which in truth is the critical point in his whole position: "A tailor's shop would still be private, even though the assembled wisdom of the state should declare that such a place was a public workshop. One might as well attempt to change the nature of colors. . . ."

If Waite is correct, and it is given to the public to define what is private and what is public, then private rights are at the mercy of public opinion. But the essence of a free and constitutional government, for Field, is just that private rights are protected, and they must be protected just as much against invasion by the public as against invasion by other private parties. Unlike Waite, Field does not see that individual rights are sacrificed upon entering into society. Society and government rather are necessary for the protection of private rights. While Waite emphasizes a fictional social contract developed by efficient causes in explaining the powers of government, Field emphasizes the formal and final causes of government, which he sees as the protection of rights necessary to free

24. *Ibid.*, p. 142.
25. *Ibid.*, p. 154: "The business of a warehouseman was, at common law, a private business, and is so in its nature."
26. *Ibid.*, p. 138.

individual action. For Waite, there is an implied relinquishment of private rights by citizens in the face of the public interest; for Field, the *function* of the public is distinguished from the immediate *interests* of the public, and the function rather than the interests is what should be regarded by the court.

For, as Field points out, practically every business is one in which the public has an interest. The legislature might even fix the rent of apartments used for residences, without reference to their cost of erection, and "If the owner does not like the rates prescribed, he may cease renting his houses."[27] The public is interested in textiles, publishing, the manufacture of appliances and utensils of every variety; "Indeed, there is hardly an enterprise or business engaging the attention of labor of any considerable portion of the community in which the public has not an interest in the sense in which that term is used by the court."

To summarize this point: Field states that the difference between public and private is defined by their different *natures*, and it is not a matter of opinion. If it were a matter of opinion, obviously public opinion would be controlling, and the result would be the regulation of many businesses which nobody now believes to be subject to regulation.

Justice Field next considers the question of "regulation" in relation to "deprivation" of property. He holds that regulation is deprivation, stating a position he held with tenacity throughout his long term on the bench. Property is the *use* of something. From this it follows that the value of property is the value of its use. Rent is the value of use for a period, and control of rents or rates for use is control of the value of the property: "The doctrine of the court, that title and possession alone are property, appears to me to destroy for all useful purposes the efficacy of the constitutional guarantee. All that is beneficial in property arises from its use and the fruits of that use; and whatever deprives a person of them deprives him of all that is desirable or valuable in the title and possession."

Field now turns to the Constitution and the meaning of its limitations: "The Fourteenth Amendment, it is to be observed, places property under the same protection as life and liberty. Except by

27. *Ibid.*, p. 143. Rent control is the ultimate *ad horrendum* suggested by Justice Field in this case. In *Budd* v. *New York*, regulation of the price of milk in small village groceries is suggested as a possible incredible result if Waite's principle is allowed to stand. 134 U.S. 517, 534: see *Nebbia* v. *New York*, 291 U.S. 502 (1937).

due process of law no state can deprive any person of either. The provision has been supposed to secure to every individual the essential conditions for the pursuit of happiness, and for that reason should never be construed in any narrow or restricted sense."

What follows is Field's explication of the Fourteenth Amendment. I believe it is an excellent summary of his basic position, and also it indicates Field's clear separation of "liberty" and "property," a distinction which does not exist in Brewer's or Peckham's jurisprudence, or in Beard's, McCloskey's, Commons', or Pound's reading of Field's opinions:

"No State shall deprive any person of life, liberty, or property without due process of law" says the 14th Amendment to the Constitution. By the term "life," as here used, something more is meant than mere animal existence. The inhibition extends to all those faculties by which life is enjoyed. The deprivation, not only of life, but of whatever God has given to every one with life, for its growth and enjoyment, is prohibited by the provision in question.

By the term "liberty" as used in the provision, something more is meant than mere freedom from physical restraint or the bounds of prison. It means freedom to go where one may choose, and to act in such manner, not inconsistent with the equal rights of others, as his judgment may dictate for the promotion of his happiness—that is, to pursue such callings and avocations as may be most suitable to develop his capacities and give to them their highest enjoyment.

The same liberal construction which is required for the protection of life and liberty, in all particulars in which life and liberty are of any value, should be applied to the protection of private property. If the legislature of a State, under pretense of providing for the public good, or for any other reason, can determine, against the consent of the owner, the uses to which private property shall be devoted, or the prices which the owner shall receive for its uses, it can deprive him of the property as completely as by a special act for its confiscation or destruction. If, for instance, the owner is prohibited from using his building for the purposes for which it was designed, it is of little consequence that he is permitted to retain the title and possession. Or if he is compelled to take as compensation for its use less than the expenses to which he is subjected by its ownership, he is for all practical purposes deprived of his property, as effectually as if the legislature had ordered his forcible dispossession.

If it be admitted that the legislature has any control over the compensation, the extent of that compensation becomes a mere matter of legislative discretion. The amount fixed will operate as a partial destruction of the value of the property, if it falls below the amount which the owner would obtain by contract, and as a complete destruction, if it be less than the cost of retaining its possession. There is no protection of any value under the constitutional provision which does not extend to the use and income of the property as well as to its title and possession.

Thus "freedom" is action as judgment may dictate for the promotion of happiness. "Property" is the use of something, and the value of property is the value of the use. Legislative regulation of the value of use, such as controlling rates for the use of grain warehouses, is legislative regulation of the value of the property and is deprivation or even destruction of property in practical terms. Therefore the court must protect the use and income of private property or the court is not protecting property at all.

Field does not, in his opinion, consider whether there is a monopoly in the economic or commercial sense. He would probably have disregarded factual studies proving that the fourteen warehouses in Chicago were in a state of economic competition, rather than monopoly, for this is not the issue. The issue is the right of the public. Field reiterates here what he has said elsewhere: the public and the government can make all sorts of regulations for the peace, good order, morals, and health of the community. These regulations will affect the uses and value of private property, and no compensation need be paid to the owners. In cases where the government appropriates or regulates private property for particular public purposes, it must compensate the owners of the property. But *warehousing* is *not* a public purpose or activity, and the government made no effort to *compensate* the warehousemen for the loss in their property. Warehousing is private, both by common law and by the nature of the business—and the government should not take over the warehouse business.[28] The fact that the warehousemen can charge prices higher

28. *Ibid.*, pp. 113-38. This means that the positive law is limited not only by the Constitution and common law but by the essential difference between the area of actions and things covered by public law and the area of action and things covered by private decision. The fact that the control of the warehouses was vested in the state legislature by the Constitution of Illinois did not matter to Justice Field. The Constitution was simply wrong: "The statement by the Illinois Constitution of 1870 that these businesses are public institutions does not make them so." 94 U.S. 113-38.

than their costs for the use of the warehouses means that they have extremely valuable property.

It might be pointed out by an economist that any large difference between capitalized returns and construction costs in the warehouse business (if there is free entry into the business) would lead to the new construction of warehouses until these two factors balanced; that high rates thus encourage needed construction of new facilities; and that the regulation of rates discourages the needed construction indicated by the market price and thus tends to create a permanent shortage of warehouse space for grain in Chicago. But the economist is taking the public *interest* as primary, indicating that it is to the public interest to avoid regulation. Field does not take the public interest as primary; in fact, it is his point that *if* the public interest is taken as primary, the public can deliberate and act with regard to *every* business and *all* private property. The public is limited to regulations for public uses, and private uses are free from public regulation. Thus there is an explicit rejection by Field of the principle of the public interest determining law and legal control of economic enterprise. Legal control can only be based on right, which is based on *actions* and *uses,* and not interest. Thus while Waite sees public use, public interest, the common good, and public right as all covering the same ground, Field distinguishes between public use and public interest. Public right extends only to *"public use,"* a much narrower and *more definable* area than *"public interest."*

There is also an implicit rejection by Field of the philosophy that private interests or class interests determine law and the legal control of economic enterprise. This is a direct implication of the principle he fully enunciates elsewhere, and repeats in this opinion, that public property and public power cannot be used for private purposes.[29] But it would be against Field's jurisprudence to have suggested that the warehouse regulation was a law for the benefit of the private interests of the farmers as against the private interests of the owners of the warehouses. If the law is for ends recognized as public, using means within the public power, no judicial notice can be taken of what private interests are served by the law: these things are the concern, not of the judiciary, but of the legislature.[30]

29. 16 Wall 689 (1871); 20 Wall 655 (1875).

30. *Ex parte Newman,* 9 Cal. 502 (1859). Public problems are solved by the democratic process. But not all problems are public problems, and the Court limits the democratic process to consideration of its proper problems only, accord-

To summarize: Field's rejection of Waite's argument about the existence of a "virtual monopoly" of grain handling by Munn does not stem from confusion about economic processes or from reactionary protection of propertied private interests as opposed to agrarian private interests. A consideration of interests simply is not fundamental in Field's thought.[31] A consideration of private rights, including rights to the uses of property, is fundamental. From this it follows that control of private business by the government is unconstitutional.

Justice Field's thought is stated clearly in the Munn case, because of the point for point opposition of the philosophy of Chief Justice Waite. Waite held that persons sacrifice rights in order to live in society. Field held that persons enter society to protect rights not otherwise protected. Waite stated that monopoly is defined in economic terms; Field stated that monopoly does not exist where there is no law preventing other businesses from entering the same area and therefore is defined in legal terms. Waite held that property is defined in terms of title and possession and that control of rental rates is not touching the essence of property, but merely a control of its manner of use. Justice Field stated that all the value in property for the owner comes from the benefits of its use and that to lower the money return on the property is to lower the value of the property itself. If the property is not beneficial, it is of no value, and if the returns from rentals are lowered, it is of less value than before. Therefore regulating the rates of using the warehouse is a lowering of the value of the property itself, not simply an incidental regulation. And finally, Chief Justice Waite indicates that *public interest* is the basis for public *control,* while Justice Field states that public interest in all its applications is so widespread that it cannot be the basis for public control and that only *public use* is a proper basis.

Justice Field indicated in the *Munn* dissent an *analysis* of rate

---

ing to Field, and he objects to Waite's allowing the public itself to determine the scope of its own powers.

31. Economists from the time of Adam Smith have been concerned with a maximization of production and distribution of goods according to resources of material and labor and actual demands of purchasers. This is not Field's concern, although he apparently read Smith's *Wealth of Nations* and Mill's *Principles of Political Economy,* and was conversant with the thought of the American economist David Ames Wells. Economists tend to consider the economy as a whole, and as a single system; Field is concerned with the rights of workers, or the rights of property owners, in particular situations—and even in particular situations, interests are subordinate to the rights involved.

regulation which would have clarified the matter from that day to this if his thought had been followed. Regulation of the rate of use is identical with regulation of the value of the property in actual practice, as Field indicates. The attempt to relate rate structures to property values, as if they were two independent entities, is therefore impossible: the prices for *use* determine the practical value of property under consideration. However, continuing attempts have been made to relate rates to costs of construction, or supposed costs of replacement, or a complicated valuation of property based on five variables, or on the amount of money "prudently" invested in the property, as opposed to money supposedly imprudently thrown in—all these criteria assuming that there is some value to the property apart from the use and that there is some value to owners of business property apart from the net income they derive from the property. What Justice Field wished for was legal recognition of the facts of life about the value of property. A farm is only as valuable as the value of the products grown on it, and the same principle applies to a warehouse, or railroad, or power company: the value is determined by the income. Justice Waite's thesis that rate control is incidental to the value of property is therefore false to actual facts; rate control is control of the value of the property.

The later history of such legislative rate control is filled with various attempts to achieve an "objective" standard for such rates, apart from the finding of the rate commission or the Federal court, i.e., the attempt is to avoid the truth that the setting of the rate determines the value of the property. In *Smyth* v. *Ames*,[32] Justice Harlan found that rate regulation had to be based on the "fair value" of the property, and he tried to isolate factors for such valuation, apart from the rate setting itself. Said Harlan:

> In order to ascertain that value, (1) the original cost of construction; (2) the amount expended in permanent improvements; (3) the amount and market value of its bonds and stocks; (4) the present, as compared with the original, cost of construction; (5) the probable earning capacity under the prescribed rates; and (6) the sum required to meet operating expenses, are *all* matters for consideration, and are to be given such weight as may be just and right in each case . . . what the company is entitled to is a *fair return*. What the public is entitled to demand is that the services are *reasonably worth* the price.

32. *Smyth* v. *Ames*, 169 U.S. 466 (1898).

This peculiar mixture of measurable and evaluative factors was thought to be a modification of the *Munn* v. *Illinois* ruling, for in the *Munn* case no consideration was given to the problem of fairness to the company involved at all.

The problem of "fair" return was approached by Chief Justice Hughes in the *Minnesota Rate Cases*.[33] Hughes attempted to examine every major accounting figure relating to assets and earnings. Some different appraisal figures on the same properties by different accountants varied as much as 50 per cent, or $5 million. Finally Hughes took the findings of the Master in Chancery as to "reproduction costs," rejected gross earnings for net earnings, and estimated the latter at 4.1 per cent to 3.5 per cent of "reproduction cost" estimated net value. These earning percentages were then adjudged to be "unreasonably" low, and it was adjudged the company did not get a "fair return." But despite all the array of figures, the results are obviously both arbitrary and a matter of subjective evaluations.

In a dissent in *Southwest Bell* v. *Public Service Comm.*,[34] Justice Brandeis suggested that the accounting base be the amount of money "*prudently* invested" in the company. Brandeis criticized estimates of reproduction cost as involving "opinions" and "predictions." But so obviously does a notion of what is a "prudent" investment. Brandeis did indicate that the companies involved in rate hearings knew that it was the determined rate that mattered and that officers and their attendant lawyers spent more time worrying about the next rate hearing than they did about providing public services. In a dissent in the *St. Joseph Stock Yards*[35] case Brandeis indicated that problems of evidence as to "fair value" had become unreasonable, with 1,648 pages of evidence and 1,358 pages of additional tabulations, besides verbal evidence taken in court. Brandeis suggested turning the whole problem over to "highly trained and especially qualified" administrators, i.e., the rate-making commissioners. To review decisions was to question the virility of the rate-makers: "Responsibility is the great developer of men. May it not tend to emasculate or demoralize the rate-making body if ultimate responsibility is transferred to others?" However, Chief Justice Hughes insisted, in that case, that the question as to whether the rate decision "had passed beyond the limit of reasonableness into the forbidden

33. *Minnesota Rate Cases (Simpson* v. *Shepard)*, 230 U.S. 352 (1913).
34. *Southwest Bell* v. *Public Service Commission*, 262 U.S. 276 (1923).
35. *St. Joseph Stock Yards Co.* v. *United States*, 298 U.S. 38 (1936).

area of confiscation" required "judicial scrutiny of the entire rate-making process, including reasoning and findings of fact." To give all over to the rate commission was to place rights of liberty and property "at the mercy of administrative officials."

To indicate the difficulties of judicial determination in the absence of defined rights, such as Justice Field wishes, the reader can examine some of the questions which arose. In *Driscoll* v. *Edison Light and Power*,[36] for instance, Justice Reed had to decide such questions as the following: is 6 per cent or 7.8 per cent a "fair return" on capital in the capital market of today? Can net assets include an amount for "going concern value"? Can the legal expenses of appealing the rate commission schedule be admitted as proper "costs"? Could salary raises given by the company be properly disallowed as expenses by the rate commission?

Justice Frankfurter's reaction to this, in his dissent, was to exclaim: "The determination of utility rates does not present questions of an essentially legal nature." Justice Frankfurter wanted to go back to the Waite opinion in the *Munn* case. That at least avoided the problem of a fair return *apart* from open market price and return, which had been attempted by Harlan, Hughes, and Brandeis. But all the later judges wanted to avoid facing the fact that establishing the rate for use, for all practical purposes, established the value of the property.

Could one go from the real value of the property to the return on it? In fact the causation and determination went the other way. Justice Field attempted to state this in his dissent in the *Munn* case. Justice Field thought there were other ways of legally controlling *incorporated* public utilities and railroads, but that is a matter for later discussion. As far as individually owned business property was concerned, lowering the price for its use was lowering the real value of the property, a kind of confiscation without compensation. This could be done in established cases of *public usage,* but not in the vastly more ambiguous and far-reaching cases of *public interest,* for the rights of the individual were more basic.

Now, much later, in an 1890 case, *Budd* v. *New York*,[37] Justice Brewer stated that *he preferred* a government which allowed laissez-faire competition to a "paternalistic government"; the latter, he went on to say, "is repugnant to me." Brewer made it a matter of *his*

36. *Driscoll* v. *Edison Light and Power Co.,* 307 U.S. 104 (1939).
37. *Budd* v. *New York,* 143 U.S. 517 (1892).

preferences and *his* political opinions, and thus laid himself quite open to Holmes' attack, that he was simply substituting his prejudices and biases for those of the legislature and that if the matters concerned political preferences, they should be left to the legislature. But Justice Field did not reason in this way; he reasoned about the bases of government in individual rights and about the nature of the value of private property in relation to the rental price for its use. In fact Field was not against government regulation, if it was equitable. But somehow Brewer's egotistic prejudices have been attributed to Field by later historians. Field, however, was reasoning from the Fourteenth Amendment.

Law and Economics: Corporations

There is an area where the public does properly determine the sphere of private rights. This is the area of corporation activities. For Justice Field, corporate powers were clearly a matter to be defined by public legislative action.

In cases decided at the same time as the *Munn* case, a group called the *Granger Cases*,[38] Chief Justice Waite held that the legislatures had a right to regulate the fares, since the railroads were "clothed with a public interest." Justice Field dissented, but *not* because of the rate regulation. The railroads were corporations, and in the corporate charter were provisions that the rates must be reasonable, as defined *at law*. Furthermore, the railroads were common carriers and as such, in common law, in a business always defined as public; therefore the state could regulate them as common carriers. Field dissented because Waite had justified the regulation on the basis of public interest, rather than public use. This left the delineation of "reasonable rate" entirely arbitrary and would have a damaging effect on future investments. Some definition would have been preferable to no definition, but, according to Field, Chief Justice Waite gave no definition of "reasonable rate."

But the vastly more important line of cases with respect to public control of business enterprises began with *Paul* v. *Virginia*.[39] It is usually thought that Justice Field concurred with Chief Justice Waite, in the view of the latter, that corporations were "citizens," or "persons," and as such entitled to the rights and privileges of the Fourteenth Amendment. It is one of the ironies of interpretation of

38. *Granger Cases*, 94 U.S. 150 (1877).
39. *Paul* v. *Virginia*, 95 U.S. 357 (1878).

that document that the Supreme Court gave legal privileges to incorporated business enterprises, while nothing was done for "second-class" human beings for almost one hundred years. But Justice Field did not include corporations under the classification of "persons," and if his views were now followed, there would be little or no dispute as to the problems of governmental control of these enterprises. State corporations could operate only in the state of their chartering and under whatever supervision the legislature desired. National corporations would be chartered by Congress and also would be whatever controls Congress desired. The rather simple and basic legal logic, by which the parent legislature could place any restrictions it desired in the charter of the created corporation, has been rendered useless by the opposing doctrine of Chief Justice Waite and Roscoe Conkling.

The first case in which Justice Field expressed an opinion on corporations was *Paul* v. *Virginia*. This was in 1869, but no mention of the Fourteenth Amendment was made. His views are quite clear: "Corporations are not citizens. The term 'citizen' applies only to natural persons, not to artificial persons created by the legislature, and possessing the attributes which the legislature has prescribed." Field expands this indicating that corporations chartered in one state have no intrinsic right to operate in any other state:

> A grant of corporate existence is a grant of special privileges to the corporators, enabling them to act for certain designated purposes as a single individual, and exempting them from individual liability. The corporation, being the mere creature of local law, can have no legal existence beyond the limits of the sovereignty where created . . . having no absolute right of recognition in other states, but depending for such recognition and the enforcement of its contracts upon their assent, it follows, as a matter of course, that such assent may be granted upon such terms and conditions as these states may think proper to impose. They may exclude foreign corporations entirely . . . or they may exact such security for the performance of its contracts with their citizens as in their judgment will best promote the public interest. The whole matter rests in their discretion.

In this early case, Field correctly predicted the results of the alternative doctrine: the corporations of any one state (in fact the states with the most lenient corporation laws) operate at will in all the other states:

> [Otherwise] an extraterritorial operation would be given to
> local legislation utterly destructive of the independence and
> harmony of the states. At the present day corporations are multi-
> plied to an almost infinite extent. . . . It is not too much to
> say that the wealth and business of the country are to a great
> extent controlled by them. And if their corporate powers could
> be exercised in other states without restriction, it is easy to see
> that with the advantages thus possessed, the most important
> business would soon pass into their hands. The principal busi-
> ness of every state would, in fact, be controlled by corporations
> created in other states.

Justice Field indicates perfectly legal methods of government control, including supervision of all transactions, strict notions of
accountability of the officers, not only to shareholders, but to the
state, and publicity for all affairs, among others: "It might be of the
highest public interest that the number of corporations in the state
be limited; that they should be required to give publicity to their
transactions; to submit their affairs to proper examinations; to be
subject to forfeiture of their corporate rights in case of mismanage-
ment, and that their officers should be held to a strict accountability
for the manner in which the business of the corporation is managed,
and be liable to summary removal."

Thus, Justice Field's doctrine of corporation law allows for full
and complete control of corporations, at the will of the legislature,
through the power of placing such controls either in the original
charter or a revised one. The dominant position now existing in
American law is that corporations are "persons" under the protection of the Fourteenth Amendment and therefore entitled to operate
outside the domain of their original incorporation, as "citizens of
the United States." Other states cannot control them, and the original state, as a matter of fact, cannot either, although, as stated, there
is competition for the taxes that are concurrent with incorporation
so that some states create extremely easy incorporation laws. The
United States government cannot exercise the kinds of internal supervisory controls over state corporations that Field advised. The
government can threaten corporations with dismemberment through
anti-trust action, only if and when a corporation dominates a sales
market. Thus no one controls U.S. corporations on ordinary day-to-
day transactions. The situation is similar to what would occur if
policemen could only shoot to kill, without any lesser powers of

control: much would be unnoticed. The anti-trust action can break up the corporation, but lesser, detailed regulations of prices, officers' responsibilities to stockholders, etc., are now impossible. But this is not Justice Field's fault. The responsibility lies with Chief Justice Waite.

In a peculiar *dictum* preceding the opinion of the Court in *Santa Clara County* v. *Southern Pacific Railroad*,[40] Waite states: "The court does not wish to hear argument on the question whether the provision of the Fourteenth Amendment to the Constitution, which forbids to a state the power to deny to any person within its jurisdiction the equal protection of the laws, applies to corporations. We are all of the opinion that it does." Waite's use of the word "all" was unjustified, since Field was not of that opinion. In a case on the Circuit Bench, just before this case, *San Mateo County* v. *S.P.R.R.*,[41] Justice Field had adjudged that a county assessor could not assess the property of railroad corporations using different standards of evaluation than in the assessment of other property in the county. This was an arbitrary exercise of the power of assessment, and Field held that as such it went against equal protection of the laws. He argued there that the *stockholders* of corporations were persons, but he never said that the *corporation* itself was a person. But, in any event, Field simply ignored Waite's dictum, although it had tremendous effect in corporation law as a precedent for other cases to this day.

Thus, in *Ruggles* v. *Illinois*[42] Field declared that the State of Illinois had the right to place in the charter of a corporation the provision that the corporation abide by the state price-regulating laws: "No proof was made that the rate prescribed by the legislature was unreasonable. Under previous decisions of the Court, the legislative rate is to be taken as presumptively reasonable. I do not give any weight to *Munn* v. *Illinois* . . . but that case does not relate to corporations or to common carriers."

In *Georgia* v. *Smith*[43] Justice Field also allowed control over railroad corporations and still was angry about the *Munn* case:

> The incorporation of the company, by which numerous parties are permitted to act as a single body for purposes of its

40. 118 U.S. 394 (1886).
41. 17 Fed 722 (1874).
42. 108 U.S. 526 (1883).
43. 128 U.S. 174 (1888).

creation, the grant to it of special privileges, and the obligation to transport all persons and all merchandise, affect the property and employment with a public use, and where the business is thus affected it is subject to legislative control. . . . There have been differences of opinion among the judges of this court in some cases, as in *Munn* v. *Illinois,* but none as to the doctrine that when such public use exists the business becomes subject to legislative control in all respects necessary to protect the public against injustice, and oppression.

In *R.R. Co.* v. *Gibbs*[44] Field restates the identical doctrine: "Being the recipients of special privileges from the state . . . their business is deemed affected with a public interest, and subject to legislative control." It is restated in even stronger form in *Maine* v. *Grand Trunk Railway:*[45] "The privilege of exercising the franchise of a corporation within a state is generally one of value, and often of great value. It is natural, therefore, that the corporation should be made to bear some proportion of the burdens of government. As the granting of the privileges rests entirely within the discretion of the state, whether the corporation be of domestic or foreign origin, it may be conferred on such conditions as the state in its judgment may deem most conducive to its interests or policy."

In the above case, the corporation had demurred to the taxation plan of the state, whereby Maine placed a tax on all assets of the corporation, even though most of these were entirely outside the boundaries of the state. Field ruled that it made no difference.

In *Minn. and St. Louis R.R.* v. *Herrick,*[46] Field also explained the role of special legislation and stated that railroads, and any other business, were included legally under specific laws. Special legislation has to do with establishing regulations for one class or industry in a society. Field believed such legislation was necessary, proper, and constitutional. He would not have agreed with Justice Peckham, who thought otherwise in the notorious *Lochner* case. In this case a state law was in issue which declared that the railroad should pay workmen for damages caused by the negligence of other workmen, when such injury cases arose, and that "assumption of risk" no longer applied to stop such suits: "The objection seems to rest on the theory that legislation which is special in character is within

44. 142 U.S. 386 (1891).
45. 142 U.S. 217 (1891).
46. 127 U.S. 210 (1889).

the constitutional inhibition, but nothing can be further from the fact. The greater part of all legislation is special, either in the objects sought or in its application. [Field gives instances of the building of bridges, utility mains, and street widenings.] And when such legislation applies to particular associations, it is not open to objection if all the persons brought under its influence are treated alike."

Justice Field's doctrine of the strong and unlimited control of corporations by the chartering legislature applied to all businesses, not only to railroads. He said the same with respect to the mining business in *Horn Silver Mining Company* v. *New York*:[47] "A corporation, being a mere creature of the legislature, its rights, privileges and powers are dependent solely on the terms of its charter. . . . The granting of rights, and privileges, which constitute the franchise of a corporation, being a matter resting entirely within the control of the legislature, to be exercised in its good pleasure, it may be accompanied with such conditions as the legislature may deem most suitable to the public interest and policy." The same doctrine applies to insurance businesses as corporations, as Field stated it in *Home Insurance Company* v. *New York*.[48]

Justice Field's doctrine does not deny the reality of corporations, but corporations are not viewed as persons and are not able to obtain the protection of the Fourteenth Amendment. A corporation is neither a person nor a contract but the result of a charter. It has no personal rights or contractual rights but only charter rights, which can be changed by the legislature of the jurisdiction at any time. States do not have to recognize "foreign corporations," i.e., corporations chartered by other states, except on the terms they choose to establish. Thus, no corporation can claim the privileges granted in one state as binding on the legislatures and courts of all states. Under Waite's doctrine, the rights established by one state can be held as binding on all states, as the privileges and immunities of a citizen of the United States.[49]

A practical conflict of the two doctrines concerning corporations occurred in the case *Pensacola Telegraph Company* v. *Western*

47. 143 U.S. 305 (1891).
48. 134 U.S. 594 (1889).
49. *Kentucky Finance Corp.* v. *Paramount Auto Exchange Corp.*, 262 U.S. 544; *Santa Clara County* v. *SPRR*, 118 U.S. 394; *C. and L. Turnpike Co.* v. *Sandford*, 164 U.S. 578; *Atchison, Topeka, and Santa Fe* v. *Vosburg*, 238 U.S. 56; *Dartmouth College* v. *Woodward*, 4 Wheaton 518.

Union Telegraph Company.[50] Following an act of Congress allowing telegraph services along postal roads, Western Union began to
run wires along the line of the Alabama and Florida Railroad Company. The Pensacola Company already had its wires strung along
that railroad right of way. It had been granted an exclusive privilege
of telegraphic service in Florida by the state legislature. The Court
ruled that Western Union, a New York corporation, had the right,
by virtue of the act of Congress, held constitutional under the Commerce Clause, to compete with the other service and could build its
lines along the road. Field dissented:

> There can be no serious question that the State of Florida
> possessed the absolute right to confer upon a corporation cre-
> ated by it the exclusive privilege for a limited period to con-
> struct and operate a telegraph within its borders. . . . The
> exclusiveness of a privilege often constitutes the only induce-
> ment for undertakings holding out little prospect of immediate
> returns. . . . It has, therefore, been a common practice in all
> the States to encourage enterprises having for their object the
> promotion of the public good, such as the construction of
> bridges, railroads, turnpikes, and canals, by granting for limited
> periods exclusive privileges in connection with them. Such
> grants are held to constitute contracts, and to be within the
> protecting clause of the Constitution prohibiting any impair-
> ment of their obligation.

Since corporations arise from state charters, which are like a special contract with the incorporators, they do not extend privileges
beyond the scope of the contracting parties: therefore New York
cannot give the Western Union Company rights in Florida:

> A corporation can have no legal existence beyond the limits
> of the sovereignty which created it . . . the recognition of its
> existence even by other states, and the enforcement of its con-
> tracts made therein, depend purely on the comity of those States,
> a comity which is never extended where the existence of the
> corporation or the exercise of its powers is prejudicial to their
> interests or repugnant to their policy. [Assent to recognition]
> may be granted on such terms and conditions as those States
> think proper to impose. They may exclude the foreign corpora-
> tion entirely; they may restrict its business to certain localities
> [etc., etc.]. The whole matter rests in their discretion.

50. 96 U.S. 1 (1879). (See Crosskey, *Politics and the Constitution*, pp. 42ff.)

Field correctly notes the consequences of the opposing position:

> The position advanced, that if a corporation be in any way engaged in commerce it can enter and do business in another state without the latter's consent, is novel and startling.—Let this doctrine be once established, and the greater part of the trade and commerce of every state will soon be carried on by corporations created without it. The business of the country is to a large extent controlled by corporations, and it may be of the highest public interest that the number of corporations in the state should be limited, that they should be required to give publicity to their transactions, to submit their affairs to proper examination, to be subject to forfeiture of their corporate rights in case of mismanagement, and that their officers should be held to strict accountability for the manner in which the business of the corporations is managed, and be liable to summary removal. All these guards against corporate abuses the state would be incapable of taking. . . .

By this time, it should be clear that the usual charges against Field as a protector of corporations and the unscrupulous captains of industry of the time against governmental control are false. Field was concerned about such abuses, and his doctrine of corporations would have allowed the states to prevent such abuses.

Justice Field's views have been upheld by the legal historian W. W. Crosskey, who in *Politics and the Constitution* stated that the power of states to charter national businesses was absurd. He noted that Field's doctrine in his dissent in the *Pensacola* case would have corrected the matter and would have led to national incorporations by Congressional charter of all businesses operating on a national or interstate scale. Field deplored the fact that directors and other corporate officers are held to no standards, such as the directors and officers of national banks are held to now under the national banking acts. All the various "exposés" of corporation executive behavior in modern times, from Brandeis' *Other People's Money* through Berle and Means' *The Modern Corporation and Private Property* to Burnham's *The Managerial Revolution,* assume that there is no proper legal way in which officials and directors can be held to strict accountability both to stockholders and to the public at large. They all ignore the proper definition of the rights of a corporation, as stated by Field, and the consequent wide legislative or public powers held by the chartering legislature over all corporation matters.

Justice Field was more drastic in his views of public control over corporations than the modern liberal critics, such as A. A. Berle, ever are, in their wildest and most "socialistic" proposals; and yet Field is directly in line with the earlier traditions of the common law. As Crosskey notes, the New Deal reforms might have done something about the matter, but the "modern" lawyers employed assumed that corporations operated as persons, mostly chartered in Delaware, under the Fourteenth Amendment and that nothing could be done directly. There are some amusing stories about these administrators calling corporation officials to Washington and *hoping* they would come, since they were not sure if they had any jurisdiction. In fact, until Joseph Kennedy, Sr., entered the Maritime Administration, they were not coming. Several industries never turned in legally demanded schedules to the N.R.A.; Washington did not know what to do about it. The obvious control through national charters for all national corporations would have solved the situation.

There is one exception to the general trend to take away state powers over its own corporations, a North Dakota case that came to the Supreme Court in 1954, *Asbury* v. *Cass County.*[51] North Dakota had passed a law preventing any corporations from owning farm property in the state. Chief Justice Stone stated that such exclusion was within the province of the legislative powers and quoted Field's opinions, *Paul* v. *Virginia, Pembina* v. *Pennsylvania,* and *Horn Silver Mining* v. *New York,* ignoring all other contrary opinions announced by the Supreme Court and also ignoring the general consequences of taking Field's views seriously today. But this case is a minor and unnoticed one. In general, the law is that state legislatures have the power to legislate for the entire country with respect to chartering national corporations. In what was termed a "novel and striking" dissent, Justice Hugo Black objected to this general Waite doctrine in *Connecticut General Life* v. *Johnson*[52] since he could not see how corporations were either "born" or "naturalized" in the United States, and the Amendment talks only of such persons.

There is no pressure or demand at the present time for more political or governmental control over our corporations, and thus it would seem that little will be done about changing existing corporation law. But there is little complaint where the strict state regulation is enforced, as with insurance companies and banking

51. 326 U.S. 207 (1946).
52. 303 U.S. 77 (1938).

institutions. The Federal Government has the power to institute anti-trust suits against corporations which monopolize sales in an industry, but whether there is such a monopoly in fact is a question which involves the presentation of thousands of pages of data by the lawyers on both sides, hearings which frequently extend over a year or so, and doubtful definitions of "monopoly:" Does monopoly depend upon the slope of the supply curve projected for the industry? If so, at what point does the lack of slope become monopolistic? There are rumored to be situations in particular industries where the dominant company, with excellent management and high standards of efficiency, keeps its prices high, in order to allow the badly managed and inefficient companies in the field to remain solvent; otherwise an anti-trust suit would threaten. Most recently there have been stories of price-fixing in the drug industry, in which the costs of the expected Federal suit were supposedly planned for and a fund set aside for that purpose out of the higher earnings. All this could be avoided by returning to Justice Field's concept of corporation supervision and placing nationally operating corporations under the supervision and chartered control of the appropriate legislative body —Congress. The Constitution gives Congress control over "Commerce among the several States"; the Waite doctrine has relinquished this control to the states, with respect to corporations; or, rather, there has been no obvious and direct governmental supervision of such nationally operating corporations. They have, in fact, returned to a peculiar state of nature, neither under local supervision nor under direct national supervision. This has perhaps accounted for the fantastic success and the powers and the flexibility of the larger corporations. This absence of legal control over corporations lends credence to the widely held view in this country that economic power rather than political power is paramount. These corporations seem to be economic powers only, although in fact they have a sort of quasi-political status, since it is not obvious that the state legislatures which chartered them have any power over them.

To return to the older view of corporations, and at the same time insist on Congressional chartering of national corporations, would not be a step on "the road to socialism." Does anybody hold that banking is now "socialistic," although the appropriate government supervisors can look at the books at any time, and officers and directors are required to make public any transactions involving their activities with banking monies? Furthermore, the ancient and proper purpose of incorporating charters was not simply to benefit the persons who received the franchise; it was to promote some venture for the benefit of society, for the common good. This public function of commercial corporations has been forgotten in the modern analysis of corporations as power-and-control relations among executives, stockholders, minority stockholders, and employee unions. The public is not thought to have any control or policy-making powers. But this takes away the fundamental purpose of the legislative grant, the chartering act.

The supposedly modern and liberal solution to the problem of unsupervised corporations was to create large labor unions, which would "balance" the power of the large business enterprises and thus achieve a form of justice through "counter-vailing powers." Thus the Norris-La Guardia Act of 1932 explicitly created such "balancing" powers: "Whereas under prevailing economic condition . . . the individual unorganized worker is commonly helpless to exercise liberty of contract and to protect his freedom of labor, and thereby to obtain acceptable terms and conditions of employment . . . it is necessary that we have full freedom of association to negotiate the terms and conditions of his employment." Perhaps to some degree such a solution was proved viable; but perhaps there is substance to the charge that in some industries corporations and unions work together to the detriment of the larger public interest; and finally, perhaps large-scale and legally uncontrolled organizations develop in *another* realm, that of labor. Without denying labor the right to strike or the right to organize, it would still be possible to subject labor unions to the *same* legislative supervision as other commercial organizations and business corporations.

And finally, with respect to the practices in Marxist countries: although these nations supposedly operate on philosophies of *economic* determinism and orientation toward workers, in fact what occurs is *total political* determination of everything in the sphere of manufacturing, finance, and distribution. In order to avoid that alternative, in which there is no possibility of constitutional limitations on government power and no possibility of individual rights and freedoms, the perfectly legal and perfectly traditional and constitutional alternative of establishing supervisory control over corporations through limitations and qualifications placed in the charter, by states for state corporations, and by Congress for national corporations, seems both feasible and logical. The maintenance of a free political life and a free economic and commercial order may depend upon establishment of the ultimacy of the rule of law over both the separate spheres.

Law and Economics: *Labor*

Let us turn from the problem of corporations to the problem of labor per se and public control over the conditions of labor and work. Here Justice Field was explicit: the government could control such things as the hours and conditions of labor. In fact, it had to control these, since otherwise the power of capital is unrestrained with respect to labor, and the moral and physical debility of the workingman is the result. Such views were held by Justice Field from an early dissent in California in 1857, to opinions given in 1890.

In the early case, *Ex parte Newman*,[53] the California legislature had passed a law forbidding business on Sundays. The California Supreme Court held it unconstitutional as a violation of religious liberty, particularly for the Hebrews. Field, in a strong dissent, stated that the law had nothing to do with religion; it had to do with the hours of labor. The government had the duty to protect labor, and that included protecting those who labored from a seven-day working week. Such laws were within the power of the legislature, since they were aimed at the health and well-being of the community. The facts of the workingman's situation with respect to his employers should be taken into account:

> It is no answer to the requirements of the statute to say that mankind will seek cessation from labor by the natural influences of self-preservation. The position assumes that all men are independent, and at liberty to work whenever they choose. Whether this be true or not in theory, it is false in fact; it is contradicted by every day's experience. The relation of superior and subordinate, master and servant, principal and clerk, always have [*sic*] and always will exist. Labor is in a great degree dependent upon capital, and unless the exercise of the power which capital affords is restrained, those who are obliged to labor will not possess the freedom for rest which they would otherwise exercise. . . . The law steps in to restrain the power of capital. Its object is not to protect those who can rest at their pleasure, but to afford rest to those who need it, and who, from the conditions of society, could not otherwise obtain it. Its aim is to prevent the physical and moral debility which springs from uninterrupted

53. 9 Cal 502 (1859).

labor; and in this aspect it is a beneficent and merciful law. It gives one day to the poor and dependent; from the enjoyment of which no capital or power is permitted to deprive them. It is theirs for repose, for social intercourse, for moral culture, and, if they choose, for divine worship. Authority for the enactment I find in the great object of all government, which is protection. Labor is a necessity imposed by the condition of our race, and to protect labor is the highest office of our laws.

Justice Field strongly rejected the doctrine, then generally prevalent, of "assumption of risk." By that doctrine, the worker, in contracting to work for a company, assumed the risks of working under the conditions and with the other workers in the situation, and therefore the company was not liable for any injuries he incurred when at work. Thus the employer avoided any responsibility for conditions of work and was not obligated to remove dangerous equipment, or to protect against dangerous working conditions. Field disagreed with this doctrine, in *Chicago, Milwaukee, and St. Paul R.R.* v. *Ross*[54] and in *B. and O. R.R.* v. *Baugh.*[55] In both cases Justice Field noted that in practice the laborer is in a position of dependence on the orders of a superior, and thus accidents are the responsibility of the company. In the first case Field gave the opinion of the Court; in the second case the first was, for practical purposes, overruled and elicited a characteristically vigorous dissent from Field. Field's dissent covered the entire problem of the conditions of labor, the common law, and the protection of individual rights by the government and the courts. The dissent is also remarkable for a statement that Field makes to the effect that there was now (that is, after 1890) more danger to individual rights from the national government than from state governments, and therefore that the rights and powers of states should be broadly interpreted as a means of protecting the individual against the oppression of the national government. Field indicated that this view was somewhat different from the view he once held upon the matter of states' rights. This may be viewed as an inconsistency, but it is not inconsistent with Field's fundamental principle that government exists for the protection of individual rights. The problem for the courts is not to "balance" state and national government, but rather to understand our dual State and Federal system of government as a device for the protection of individual rights.

54. 112 U.S. 377 (1881).   55. 149 U.S. 368 (1896).

Law and Economics: Money

Justice Field strongly opposed any power the national government had simply to print money. The government could float loans on its credit, giving negotiable bonds in return, but these were not legal tender. The government had the right to control interest rates, for by common law the government had always had such a right. But printing unbacked paper money, as the government had done during the Civil War, was a form of "theft," and the resulting inflationary results were an unwarranted and free gift to all debtors who could pay their debts using the reduced currency. When the Legal Tender Acts were declared constitutional and an earlier decision reversed in *Knox v. Lee*,[56] Field presented a forty-seven-page dissent, quoting largely from traditional conservative authorities, Marshall, Story, Hamilton, and Daniel Webster. The law operated as an impairment of the obligations of contracts and was therefore unconstitutional. Field continued to dissent to the majority opinion that such "Greenback" legislation was constitutional in at least five more cases that arose before the Court, but his dissents were without effect.[57]

To sum up: where individuals were involved in businesses which could be defined as involving *"public use,"* or where individuals had received the special privilege of a corporation franchise, they were subject to governmental regulation. Although strongly opposed to the majority view in the *Munn* case, that the public had the right to control anything whatever that was an object of *public interest*, on the ground that such a doctrine destroyed all constitutional limitations and all individual rights, Field was for such legitimate public control of business, finance, and labor as seemed required by both modern conditions and the protection of private rights and the public good. He was, in fact, for much more control over corporations than is now dreamt of, and obviously would not have been against the New York law regulating the hours of labor in the baking industry, which was the basis for the *Lochner* case and Peckham's statement about the liberty of contract holding priority to any legislation for the health and safety of factory workers. Field's statements about the rights of individuals did not mean that there was no public

56. 78 U.S. 457 (1868).
57. *Legal Tender Cases*, 79 U.S. 457; *Dooley v. Smith*, 80 U.S. 604; *Vaughn v. Telegraph*, 81 U.S. 258; *R.R. Co. v. Johnson*, 82 U.S. 195; *Maryland v. P.R. Co.*, 89 U.S. 105; *Julliard v. Greenman*, 110 U.S. 421.

good, nor did it mean that there were no general legislative powers, the "police powers" to regulate industrial and financial conditions for the public good. But there were limits to such powers, and the law could not be defined simply in terms of the public *interest*, expressed by laws passed by majorities in a legislative body.

Law and Politics

Justice Field's conceptions of the interrelations of law and politics were by no means naïve, mechanical, or formalistic. The sovereign power in the United States resided in the people, not in the government itself. The government might have the power to override the proper rights of the people, but the limits on such usurpation were elections and the restraints of the courts. However, the ultimate source of power for the courts was the people and the legislative and executive branches of the government. Field experienced the strong hand of political power in the Court-packing of President Grant who placed two new justices on the Supreme Court to reverse the decision declaring Greenbacks unconstitutonal. When the case was reheard, the decision was reversed. Field was on the commission to investigate problems of fraud and chicanery with respect to the crucial election of 1876, when two sets of returns, Democratic and Republican, came from some vital Southern states. The Electoral Commission voted along straight party lines, and Hayes was elected; Field noted that most of the members did not even bother to examine any of the evidence.

Field's early experience in California was both political and legal. He was disbarred from practice by an emotional state judge, when Field had dared to question his authority on a point of law. When the case was appealed and reversed, the judge simply disbarred him again upon his return to court. Field ran for the state legislature, was elected and, in the revision of the judiciary laws that he accomplished, sent the judge off to the wilds of the northeastern part of the state. Field also, in the legislature, drafted the civil procedure and criminal law of the state. Field was a friend of one of the early Democratic "bosses" of the state, David Broderick, who was later killed by Judge Terry of the State Supreme Court. (Field's bodyguard later killed Terry, who had been threatening Field.)

When Field first came to Washington, a California property case came to the Supreme Court, and the majority was against Field. He went to his friends in Congress and instigated the passage of a law covering the situation which took jurisdiction away from the Supreme Court and decided the matter the way Field thought it should have been decided. Thus Field did not view the law and the Court as a sacred cow. When the majority of the Court seemed to oppose Field's positions in cases he considered basic, such as the *Slaughterhouse* cases and the *Munn* case, Justice Field considered running for the Presidency. Many justices then were running for the Presidency, particularly Salmon Chase and David Davis, but Field's purpose was somewhat different from the usual motivations in the matter: he wanted to pack the Court back the other way, toward his views. He ran for President, attempting to obtain the nomination of the Democratic Party in 1880. In a letter to his friend John Norton Pomeroy, the legal scholar, Field stated that his hopes, if he attained the Presidency, would be to reform the judiciary. He would place "solid men" on the Supreme Bench. He would help clean up the overloaded docket by establishing a special court for patent infringement cases, which he thought could be handled by a special and subsidiary court (as they are now) and another special court for corporation law cases, which he also thought could be handled by a separate and subordinate court. Field had always thought that the law on corporations was clear, with corporations subordinated to government chartering and regulating powers, and he did not think that aspect of the law of ultimate constitutional importance. The Supreme Court, Field thought, should limit itself to basic issues and problems of constitutional rights and governmental powers.

However noble his intentions, Field failed miserably in the balloting at the Democratic convention, and the Democratic candidate, Hancock, lost anyway. But Field remained aware of the importance of the Presidential powers with respect to the membership of the Court; one of the reasons he remained on the bench in his last years was that he intensely disliked the Cleveland group within the Democratic Party ranks and would not resign and give President Cleveland the power to appoint one of his men during the last four years, 1892-96, of that split administration.

However, the basic logic of Justice Field's thought required that, in a free society, law be paramount to political policy-making. This is perhaps difficult to understand in terms of the various theories of jurisprudence which have almost overwhelming popularity today. The modern theories assume that *all* political action, whether in law, in the administration, or in Congress, is a matter of *compromise* among pressure groups or interests. The mode of *all* politics is persuasion, using vague and emotive terms as proper and essential on the verbal level. There are levels other than the verbal, which are taken as more important: the basic social biases or social attitudes of the men who have the power to make the decisions and the basic power relations among the various groups competing for fulfillment of needs or wants through political action.

Justice Field was perfectly willing to see such compromising adjustment among interests as the area of legislation and administration, but the area of the law was a matter of proper ultimate *definitions* and logical argument rather than emotive vagueness. Thus, life, liberty, and the pursuit of happiness had to be *defined*. Public *use* was preferable to public *interest* because the former could be defined. And these, in law, were not just *verbal* definitions, since the definitions of the law also defined the *situations* involved. The "police powers" of the state legislatures could be defined; the laws then enacted were not to be made matters for review on the basis of the emotional preferences and attitudes of a majority of the justices on the bench, but rather a matter of guaranteeing defined rights with respect to defined public powers. With respect to problems of property, a *realistic definition* of property was called for, because such would establish the clear limits of public power and the clear grounds of private and constitutional rights. Property was to be defined in terms of *use* and the income from use, for two reasons: first, this was the traditional notion of property from the time of Coke's statements on, and, second, because realistically use and income from use are in fact what make business property important; the mere title to property without the power to derive any income from it makes such property wholly without value. To employ vague and emotionally "positive" terms such as "the public interest" to decide cases at law did not define anything, rather it made for endless litigation. It made for the sort of appeal of every single rate-making case to the Supreme Court that Justice Field wanted to avoid. Field's jurisprudence demanded a logic in a sense understandable to the best of the pragmatists: moving a situation from the realm of the indefinite and problematic to the realm of the defined. As he stated in the *Granger Cases* dissent: "the opportunity was presented to the Court to define the interests involved, and this has not been done."[58] Such definition, in terms of the realities of the situation, not simply

58. *Granger Cases,* 94 U.S. 150 (1877).

in terms of legal formalities alone, was what Field sought and achieved, but mostly in the posture of dissent.

In the twentieth-century discussions of jurisprudence, there has been a reduction and devaluation of legal reasoning to rhetorical use of emotive terms, and there has been a behaviorist reduction of even this to persuasive language, so that even the persuasive rhetoric supposedly simply veils the realities of power and pressure. There have been notable exceptions to this main current, notably in the jurisprudence of Mr. Justice Hugo Black and in the legal scholarship of William W. Crosskey. There is always a latent belief in rational argument and defined terms implicit in the "sociological jurisprudence," "realistic jurisprudence," and the "behavioristic jurisprudence" of various authors. These proponents assume that *their own arguments* and reasonings and definitions of judicial action are to be taken seriously, and make sense, and must be accepted or refuted on reasonable grounds, even though they deny such significance to the argumentations from judges on the bench. It can be granted that styles in basic appeal, even by justices on the Supreme Court, have changed since the nineteenth century. Justice Field's insistence on the recognition of individual rights and the securing of such rights by the institution of government has been compared to Justice Bushrod Washington's famous dictum that American law followed from "the rights of citizens in all free governments." Even though this concerned rights, Washington's views have been called "natural law" doctrines, with that term taken in its most pejorative and empty sense. But Chief Justice Marshall appealed to the bases of governments in the rights of a free people, not only in the famous argument in *Marbury* v. *Madison,* by which he established the power of the Court to define constitutional limitations altogether, but also in his lengthy and reasoned dissent in *Ogden* v. *Saunders*[59]—the only dissent in a major constitutional case Marshall ever wrote.

Fundamental arguments have shifted to the problems of the epistemology of making determinate practical judgments when reasonable men differ, to problems of the interpretation of language, and to issues of "activism" versus "self-restraint." Dissenting arguments are in terms of *future* consequences and "impartial sensitivities to traditions" rather than to the basic argued foundations for government, such as were developed by *both* Waite and Field in their opinions in the *Munn* case. Both Waite and Field argued about the

59. 12 Wheat 122 (1824).

foundation of government, the nature of the maxim "Thus use your own so as not to injure others," the relation of public power and private rights, and the nature of property. The *Munn* case indicates several theses in exemplary form: it illustrates Jefferson's plea for responsible thinking on crucial ultimate issues by members of the Court on a seriatim basis; it illustrates the general thesis of this work, that intelligent men can *and do* disagree about fundamental issues of policy and the reasonings for policy; and finally, because of the nature of the arguments as reasoning from fundamentals, the case places the nature of judicial exposition above the usual persuasive and *ad hoc* rhetoric of political debate and compromise. If the Supreme Court is to have a dignity and esteem above that of the other branches of government, it should properly depend upon the rational range of its arguments and the acuteness of the analyses of the reasoning presented. Such argumentation was present in the *Munn* v. *Illinois* opinions.

But apart from the general problems of styles in jurisprudence and the significance of legal argument, Field in particular thought that there should be a clear delineation of the area of private rights and public power. This distinction between public and private should not be solely in the hands of the public, but should remain within the bounds stated in the Constitution, particularly the Fourteenth Amendment, and those bounds should be guaranteed by the Courts. Thus politics, in the normal course of events, would operate within the law.

Justice Field did not deny the Constitutional guarantees of citizens' rights through the assurance of regular election of lawmakers and executive officials, but rather assumed them as a matter of course. The basic problem was to maintain the proper distinctions between various areas of action. The private sphere was to remain private. The public sphere was to remain within its proper bounds, limited by the basic aim of securing individual rights to life, liberty, and the pursuit of happiness. Within the government, the legislature was to make the laws, which were to be enforced with the traditional prerogatives of policy interpretation and decision by the executive, and the judiciary, as an independent body, was to guard the bounds.

In a routine case, marked by Field's characteristically strong dissent, President Cleveland had fired the incumbent territorial judge for Alaska, McAllister, and replaced him with another man, in what seemed like a simple matter of party politics and acceptable spoils of office. McAllister's suit for his salary for the remainder of the year was denied by the Court since no constitutional issue was involved. Not so, said Justice Field—the issue was the independence of the judiciary from executive prerogative. If judges could be fired at the will of the executive, because of differences of opinion or outlook, then all the principles of the Revolution of 1688 were forgotten and lost. The Statute of 13 William III, passed by the Parliament of 1689 and signed by the new King, William, was passed to express the discontent of the new constitutional Parliament with the previous administration of justice, which had been subservient to the will of the executive. The same principles applied in America: "Whoever here is clothed with judicial office, cannot be restrained from the fearless exercise of its duties by any apprehension of removal, in case he should come athwart the will or pleasure of the appointing power."[60] Field went on to quote the Declaration of Independence, which had complained of the lack of justice in the colonial courts, the Constitution, the Federalist Papers, and various early American and English cases. The principles did not abate because of the complacency or the cynicism of the times.

To sum up: Field, in Supreme Court opinions and dissents over thirty years, developed a jurisprudence in which broad and realistic definitions of powers and rights were fundamental in law, and it was the task of the Court to so define the law that such rights and powers could be exercised with proper precedence among them in the modern world. Obviously the realm of politics would be the realm of conflicts of interests and powers, but such a realm could be delimited by law, and the struggles would have constitutional bounds and structures. Field maintained that the rule of law could prevent class struggles from becoming matters of open violence, while otherwise there was no device for the assurance of peace. For those who think that "compromise" and "arbitration" are the better and more civilized forms of amelioration of social conflicts, Field's jurisprudence is fatuous. Nevertheless, this was Field's opinion, and in 1890, with growing labor unrest in the country, and with obvious and increasing differences between the wealthy and the poor, the owners and the workers, Field stated in a short address:

As population and wealth increase—as the inequalities in the conditions of men become more and more marked and disturb-

60. *McAllister* v. *United States,* 141 U.S. 174 (1892).

ing—as the enormous aggregation of wealth possessed by some corporations excites uneasiness lest their power should become the dominating one in the legislation of the country, and thus encroach upon the rights or crush out of business the individuals of small means—as population in some quarters presses upon the means of subsistence, and angry menaces against order find vent in loud denunciations;—it becomes more and more the imperative duty of the Court to enforce with a firm hand every guarantee of the Constitution of the private rights of the citizen.[61]

With the maintenance of defined areas as the proper task of the Court, rights would be protected and freedom would be maintained and secured by the public through the government. For Field, the Court had an importance of "immeasurably significance," the "negative power" of "declaring the law," which was the "only safety of a free and popular government."[62]

With respect to the disciplines of economics and sociology in relation to the law, Field has been called a master economist of laissez-faire finance capitalism by the late institutional economist John R. Commons. But Field's view that the value of property was the value of the produce or return on that property can be traced back to feudal English law; Field simply applied the same views to modern warehouses, railroads, and the like. Field was not for wild and unrestrained "free enterprise" among *corporations* and wished to treat them as a special class of entities created by legislative fiat, with the officers and directors having the legal duties of the strictest trust and fiduciary agency law. The actual development of corporation law was not in accordance with his views. Field always took a *legal* view of monopolies, never an economic view: a monopoly was a grant of exclusive privilege by the government. The fact that some few owners dominated an industry, as in the *Munn* case, did not concern Field, for he thought that anyone could break such a monopoly, since there were no *legal* restrictions on entering the business. Field went so far as to maintain that the San Francisco water company was not a monopoly in the strict sense of the term, since other water companies were not *prohibited* from building their water mains and selling water in San Francisco. Wherever businesses were involved in activities that had a "public use," such as common carriers (i.e., railroads), they were, in Field's view, subject to reasonable regu-

61. Centennial Address of 1890 (1890 U.S. *Reports,* Appendix).
62. 168 U.S. 713 (1896).

lations and required to offer reasonable prices for their services. But this was simply the common law doctrine on the subject. Justice Field grew to be a close friend of the economist David Ames Welles, but their correspondence concerned the legal aspects of economic activity, not the workings of the economic system *per se*; for Field, that was not the province of the law.

Field recognized the rights of minority groups and individuals under the law, but also thought that American law represented values of Western civilization, not Oriental civilization. Any human being, within the jurisdiction of the United States, was entitled to all the constitutional guarantees of rights of the person. But this did not mean that the Chinese were not different in their religious views and their views of civilized behavior. Field did not hold to the ancient Stoic notion of the same cosmopolitan law for all religions and all civilizations, or at least he did not feel that American law was adopted to such widespread application. In private letters to John Pomeroy and even in opinions from the bench, Field stated that the Chinese would not adopt Western ways of life, and that if they were allowed to migrate to the United States in unlimited numbers, there would be major problems of civilizations which did not harmonize confronting one another. Thus he was for the treaties which ended immigration, while at the same time he defended the personal rights of particular Chinese in the country, not on a sentimental basis, but for the reasons embodied in the literal wording of the Fourteenth Amendment. Although in later life both of Justice Field's distinguished brothers, David Dudley and Cyrus Field, worked for the adoption of international codes of law and international peace tribunals, there is no evidence that Justice Field took any interest in such idealistic and cosmopolitan gestures; the rights with which he was concerned were embodied in the positive law of the Constitution and the amendments.

Finally, Justice Field's heritage is improperly traced to Justice Peckham, Justice Brewer, and to the decisions concerning "liberty of contract" of the otherwise great Justice Harlan. When these latter gentlemen were at their worst, it was almost true that no state legislature could pass any regulatory law whatsoever, since such law would have been an infringement on the previously held "rights and freedoms" of the citizens before the law. Thus regulating the baking industry stopped the freedom of bakers, and allowing unions to organize stopped the freedom of employers to fire anyone they chose, and so on. But Justice Field allowed full scope to state regulations, for the sake of health, the protection of the physical security, the prosperity, the peace, etc., of the community. He had brushed aside objections to railroad legislation as class legislation with the argument that practically *all* legislation affected one class more than another and thus was special in aim or application. Later the Supreme Court did a great deal of soul-searching as to whether state laws could protect women or whether the state could pass laws with respect to the baking industry and the health of the workers in that industry. But this was not an inheritance from Justice Field. It was Brewer, not Field, who stated from the bench, that "the paternalistic theory of government is to me odious."

This sort of non-argument set the stage for Holmes' brilliant rebuttals, that the Court was not sitting to impose its own prejudices over the views of the legislatures of the various states. It was Holmes, in fact, who rescued the role of reason in constitutional law from those men who would have reviewed all state legislation on the basis of *undefined* rights and proper "police powers" which somehow had to operate without disturbing any previous relationships. But the *true* heirs of Justice Field's mode of jurisprudence are Mr. Justice Hugo Black, Mr. Justice Abraham Fortas, and Professor Crosskey, all of whom argue logically, in terms of rights clearly and literally defined, and in the context of the proper constitutional clauses, and in terms of proper definitions of governmental powers, also as literally interpreted from clauses in the Constitution. The tradition of logic, law, and rights, which Field saw as including Edward Coke, the Revolution of 1688, and Jefferson's Declaration of Independence, is not entirely dead in the world today, even if scorned by the rhetoricians of compromise and the scientists of power.

5

Holmes and the Complexities of Pragmatic Jurisprudence

T HE FUNCTION of seriatim opinions in jurisprudence is illustrated in its largest scope by the dissents of Justice Holmes and their subsequent embodiment in majority opinions. Justice Holmes attacked not only particular interpretations of rights, such as a purported right of workers to work long hours in totally unregulated industries, but also the whole jurisprudence of rights. He replaced such a jurisprudence with a jurisprudence of interests, real or purported, as developed in public opinions and legislative activities. The function of the law was to recognize interests, not to guarantee rights.

Holmes' background stemmed from the literary aristocracy of Boston. His father belonged to the same literary club in Boston as Emerson, Longfellow, Whittier, Dana, Sumner, the elder James, and the elder Adams. That aristocracy had been praised by Holmes' father, the once famous Autocrat of the Breakfast Table, in humorous fashion:

> We are forming an aristocracy, as you may observe, in this
> country . . . a de facto upper stratum of being, which floats over
> the turbid waves of common life like the iridescent film you may
> have seen spreading over the water about our wharves,—very
> splendid, though its origin may have been tar, tallow, train-oil,
> or other such commodities. Of course, money is its corner stone.
> Money kept for two or three generations transforms a race,—I

don't mean merely in manners and hereditary culture, but in blood and bone. Money buys air and sunshine, in which children grow up more kindly, of course, than in close, back streets; it buys country places to give them happy and healthy summers, good nursing, good doctoring, and the best cuts of beef and mutton. When the spring chickens come to market—I beg your pardon—as the young females of each successive season come on, the finest specimens among them, other things being equal, are apt to attract those who can afford the expensive luxury of beauty. The physical character of the next generation rises in consequence. It is plain that certain families have in this way acquired an elevated type of face and figure, and that in a small circle of city-connections one may sometimes find models of both sexes which one of the rural counties would find hard to match from all its townships put together.

The weak point in our aristocracy is its lack of valour. It is very curious to observe of how small account military folks are held among our Northern people. Our young men must gild their spurs, but they need not win them. The equal division of property keeps the younger sons of rich men above the necessity of military service. Thus the army loses an element of refinement and the moneyed upper class forgets that it is to count heroism among its virtues. Still, I don't believe in any aristocracy without pluck as its backbone.[1]

This self-conscious defense of aristocracy, not entirely uncommon in a society that is slowly losing its power to others, as Boston was to New York, was part of the heritage of young Holmes. He became the embodiment of his father's literary and semi-humorous aspirations, particularly after he was wounded twice as a young and daring officer in the Civil War. He was discharged as a lieutenant colonel in 1864, in all the maturity of his twenty-three years. Holmes had attended Harvard College, and now he entered Harvard Law School, where he took his degree in two years. He became a lecturer at the Law School in 1870. In 1880 he delivered his famous lectures on *The Common Law*. The substance of these lectures was that the early foundations of the law had been in the irrationalities of vengeance, and that the modern bases should be founded on impersonal considerations as to coverage of losses. (His second thesis in that work, that the modern theory of conveyance is based on an identity

1. Oliver Wendell Holmes, Sr., *The Autocrat of the Breakfast Table* (New York, 1915), pp. 250-51.

of persona between buyer and seller, has been properly ignored.) He became a professor at the Harvard Law School and then Chief Justice of the Supreme Court of Massachusetts. On that bench he made some notable decisions on behalf of the interests of labor.[2] A Boston Brahmin with labor learnings was just what Theodore Roosevelt thought the U.S. Supreme Court needed, and he appointed Holmes a justice of that Court in 1902. At sixty-one, Holmes' major career, which was to be thirty-one years of dissenting, began.

As soon as he reached the highest court, the dissents of Justice Holmes came thundering out, affecting the character of American jurisprudence for generations. The first great dissent was in the *Lochner* case. In that case, a New York law restricting the hours that laborers could work in the baking industry was declared unconstitutional by a majority of the Supreme Court. Justice Peckham stated that the rights of the workingman outweighed the police powers of the state in this case. The Court developed a constitutional "right" to work long and dangerous hours in a totally unregulated industry —the so-called right of "freedom of contract." Justice Holmes attacked the supposed "right," and he attacked the whole jurisprudence of rights that went with it. For Holmes, the whole legal structure of rules and rights was properly to be based on public policy, not on logical deductions from the Constitution. The only limitation on public opinion is the traditions of the civilization. This famous dissent in *Lochner* v. *New York* reads:

> I regret sincerely that I am unable to agree with the judgment in this case and that I think it my duty to express my dissent.
>
> This case is decided upon an economic theory which a large part of the country does not entertain. If it were a question whether I agreed with that theory, I should desire to study it further and long before making up my mind. But I do not conceive that to be my duty, because I strongly believe that my agreement of disagreement has nothing to do with the right of the majority to embody their opinions in law.
>
> It is settled by various decisions of this Court that State constitutions and State laws may regulate life in many ways which we as legislators might think injudicious or, if you like, as tyrannical as this, and which equally with this interfere with the liberty to contract. Sunday laws and usury laws are ancient examples. A more modern one is the prohibition of lotteries.

2. *E.g., Vegelahn* v. *Gunter,* 167 Mass 92 (1897). See Max Lerner, *The Mind and Faith of Justice Holmes* (New York, 1947), pp. 3-27.

The liberty of the citizen to do as he likes so long as he does not interfere with the liberty of others to do the same, which has been a shibboleth for some well-known writers, is interfered with by school laws, by the Post Office, by every State or municipal institution which takes his money for purposes thought desirable, whether he likes it or not. The Fourteenth Amendment does not enact Mr. Herbert Spencer's *Social Statics.*

The other day we sustained a Massachusetts vaccination law . . . United States and State statutes and decisions cutting down the liberty to contract by way of combination are familiar to this Court. . . . Two years ago we upheld the prohibition of sale of stock on margins for future delivery in the constitution of California. . . . The decision sustaining an eight-hour law for miners is still recent. . . . Some of these laws embody convictions of prejudices which judges are likely to share. Some may not. But a constitution is not intended to embody a particular economic theory, whether of paternalism and the organic relation of the citizen to the State or of *laissez faire.* It is made for people of fundamentally differing views, and the accident of our finding certain opinions natural and familiar or novel and even shocking ought not to conclude our judgment upon the question whether statutes embodying them conflict with the Constitution of the United States.

General propositions do not decide concrete cases. The decision will depend on a judgment or intuition more subtle than any articulate major premise. But I think the proposition just stated, if it is accepted, will carry us forward to the end. Every opinion tends to become a law.

I think that the word liberty in the Fourteenth Amendment is perverted when it is held to prevent the natural outcome of a dominant opinion, unless it can be said that a rational and fair man necessarily would admit that the statute proposed would infringe fundamental principles as they have been understood by the traditions of our people and our law. It does not need research to show that no such sweeping condemnation can be passed upon the statute before us. A reasonable man might think it a proper measure on the score of health. Men whom I would certainly not pronounce unreasonable would uphold it as a first installment of a general regulation of hours of work. Whether in the latter aspect it would be open to the charge of inequality I think it unnecessary to discuss.[3]

With this dissent the lines were drawn between Holmes and those

3. *Lochner* v. *New York,* 198 U.S. 45, 74 (1904).

who held in some more or less traditional fashion to the formal law of precedent and legal rights of liberty and property. And this dissent is only one small part of a larger jurisprudence of interests which Holmes with consummate brilliance presented in his legal opinions and in a constant outpouring of essays, speeches, and letters. Justice Holmes is but the first of a trio of pragmatic justices, and although they do not share the same positive views, they share the same negative view of the older formal jurisprudence of rights, stated clearly in the opinions of Justice Field. In the trio of Holmes, Brandeis, and Frankfurter, Holmes is an aristocratic nihilist and skeptic; Brandeis is a morally earnest social reformer and democrat; and Frankfurter is an intellectual activist, whose notions of self-restraint made him known in his later years as anti-logical anti-activist. The three can be grouped logically in terms of classical distinctions in Medieval logic: Holmes thought and acted in the realm of transcendental principles, albeit his own were skeptical and irrational; Brandeis thought and acted in the realm of universals, with the universal goals of humanity clearly harmonized with scientific action and education, and with groups having a clear political reality as well as individual private men; and finally, Frankfurter, although he accepted the mantle of Holmes and Brandeis, accepted the empiricists' nominalism, rejected Holmes' transcendental values and Brandeis' universals, and found men and traditions in conflict on the level of the immediate and particular. With no faith in the validity of the ideals of Holmes and Brandeis, Frankfurter found that conservatism was the just and proper role of the Court in a democratic society, thus radically reversing the tone of the earlier pragmatic movement. Furthermore, this led to two strange twists in current jurisprudence: (1) Chief Justice Warren, although perhaps basically pragmatically inclined, has found that a formal jurisprudence of rights is more viable for judicial prudence than the petrified and hesitant empiricism of Frankfurter's posture of self-restraint, and (2) Justice Black's formalism of the rights of citizens as deduced from the Fourteenth Amendment now looks like the activist doctrine, the one most concerned with social advance and the one most able to deal with the conservative interests of society in a forthright and courageous way. In the last chapter we will see the current acceptance by the Court of a jurisprudence of rights again, although the Court is also explicitly aware of the problems of the play of powers and the real influences in society which were recognized by the jurisprudence of interests. However, with all these complications, the pioneer work of Justice Holmes must not be neglected or underrated. Holmes denied the force of the tradition of Coke, Locke, and Jefferson. He forms the party of the opposition which, in terms of the open formalism to which this book is dedicated, must be given a full and reasonable hearing.

The transvaluation of all values in constitutional law was initiated by Justice Holmes. Holmes was not a follower of Hobbes or Hegel, since he believed all power came from below, from the force of public opinion, and from the realm of economics, and not from above, as with the totalitarians of sovereignty. And yet he opposed the classic thought of rights and duties and judicial limits on governmental powers on every ground and in every way. Justice Holmes did not believe in rights. Again and again he said they were a false beginning for the law, which instead should be understood in terms of irrational and factual beginnings in history and non-rational and largely unwise goals deemed expedient by most people at whatever time these interests are active. There was no right to life, since the government could ask a citizen to sacrifice his life on the battlefield in war. There was no right to liberty, which Holmes held was a term vastly overexpanded in the law. And "property" was a term which was unrealistic and misleading, a fetish of the socialists on one side and the reactionaries on the other, since the proper analysis of economics was in terms of risk-taking decisions with respect to production and the realities of consumption.

The realities in economics were not the static matters of ownership and title, but the dynamic matters of the stream of goods, policy-making with respect to future needs, which required prophecies about such future needs and the continuing consumption of goods produced, a matter which involved choices as well as simple needs. The processes of production for the future were subject to no science, but were most subservient to public demands when the various forces of production were allowed to struggle and battle in a rough and tumble manner, with various parts disagreeing both as to prophecies of the future and to plans for efficiencies with respect to these prophecies of consumption. These ideas of economic adventures were crucial for Holmes in his transvaluation of values, which reversed the older order between law and economics; *economics* was now the determining science, and *law* was to follow it. The man of the past had been the "black-letter man" of the law books; the man of the future was the man of "economics and statistics." The realities were at the bottom, not at the top.

Justice Holmes was a philosopher, not merely a sociologist of the law, and his outlook on matters of individual life, social life, and "the cosmos" were all consistent with the above, and all the reverse of the older views of Locke, Jefferson, Coke, and Field. To put the matter in its most extreme form, Holmes is the American version of the Nietzschean. But what seemed like screaming and neurotic impotence in the German context was forceful and serious criticism in America; it was "The Revolt against Formalism" of which Professor Morton White has spoken with such favor, and which had such far-reaching consequences in both the thought and the political action of this country. The philosophical background, as delineated in Holmes' comments in his letters, is quite clear: Holmes saw the Kantian morality of law (and all formal legal theory) as not more *real* than the Kantian structures of science, but merely an imposition of a non-real causal and logical order on appearances. The post-Kantian idealistic movement had, in opposition to Kant, insisted on the reality of historical change and intellectual development. Holmes reversed even this idealism, with his "cosmic doubting" that rationality was anything more than those ultimate fictions with which we looked at the cosmos—the universe was irrational, not rational, in its final "bottom." History should be used, but not reversed. Life should be affirmed, since negation assumed a false transcendentalism. Culture and the conventions of language gave social meaning to civilization, and individuals who were conscious of the artificiality of this created fabric over the more basic irrationalities were the truly outstanding men. Constitutional law, in this Holmesian view, was not the particular logical derivations of particular words in a legal document, but was the articulate conclusions from basic instincts which developed along with the irrational development of civilization. Since civilization is largely a matter of language, our law comes from the English-speaking civilization and embodies the "relatively fundamental rules of right as generally understood by all English-speaking communities."[4]

The Fourteenth Amendment did not embody any relatively fundamental rules. Holmes always thought it had been overemphasized: "If the Fourteenth Amendment were before us now for the first time I should think it ought to be construed more narrowly than it has

4. *Otis* v. *Parker,* 187 U.S. 606 (1903).

been construed in the past."[5] The terms were "abstract" and almost "wholly devoid of meaning." Holmes showed no interest in serious study of differences of interpretation of that amendment, since all previous approaches were wrong: both Miller's "clothed with a public interest" and Field's "embodying a public use" were briefly and entirely dismissed as "legal fictions intended to beautify what is disagreeable to the sufferers." Holmes wanted to pierce the veils of the law and see the realities of power: "We fear to grant power and are unwilling to recognize it when it exists. The term 'police power' is used to cover and to apologize for the general power of the legislature to make a part of the community uncomfortable by a change. The truth seems to me to be that the legislature may forbid or restrict any business when it has sufficient force of public opinion behind it." Justice Holmes sometimes manages to suggest also that the law under consideration seemed to him foolish—but this was always in the reverse and through innuendo: "I am far from saying that I think this particular law a wise and rational provision. That is not my affair."[6] Again and again, Holmes states that the function of the judge is to avoid looking through the rose-tinted glasses of the law and stare directly at the brute facts of power, proclaiming aloud that such power is irrational: "I should not think any conciliatory phrase necessary to justify what seems to me one of the incidents of legislative power. I think the police power clearly extends to a law like this, whatever I may think of its wisdom." Granted there does run another strain through the decisions: where reasonable men may disagree, then it is not the part of the judge to take sides. But this extension of the disagreements of reasonable men can go to all limits, when Holmes is so inclined: men can disagree on whether or not the dictatorship of the proletariat is the most beneficial mode of social organization, and if such a social organization is the dominant fashion, then it would be constitutional. The Fourteenth Amendment did not enact Mr. Herbert Spencer's *Social Statics.*

There are two different problems with respect to Holmes' jurisprudence: the first is a study of the consequences of such a philosophy in later jurisprudence, and the second is the evidence for its proper classification as an aspect of romantic irrationalism and a "transvaluation of all values." Brandeis was a great social idealist, a man who was serious about economic reform, while Holmes was

5. *Schlesinger* v. *Wisconsin,* 270 U.S. 230, 241 (1928).
6. *Tyson* v. *Banton,* 273 U.S. 418, 445 (1935).

aloof and disdainful, and yet the jurisprudence of Brandeis would not have had much impact without Holmes. In the search for pragmatic realism, in the tradition of Holmes, the later thinkers disagree: Justice Jackson became absorbed in problems of international law and international conflict; Justice Frankfurter moved to the doctrine of strict "judicial restraint" on the basis of a nominalistic reading of law and social movements; and one of Brandeis' most apt pupils, David Riesman, moved out of the law altogether, into sociology. For Riesman the realities of Holmesian consumption were the artificialities of Veblen's conspicuous consumption for the purposes of conspicuous conformism, and the economic process could only be understood as part of sociology. Justices Douglas and Murphy moved to political action, with the law seen more or less directly as an instrument of liberal political attitudes. Justice Holmes would have identified with none of these, but his jurisprudence was the philosophic explosion which made them viable.

Holmes' affinities to Nietzsche are most obvious in quotations given in Francis Biddle's biography and in his highly praised works: *The Common Law*, "The Path of the Law," and "Ideals and Doubts." Biddle quotes with enthusiasm the romantic irrationalisms of Holmes: "From the beginning, to us, children of the North, life has seemed a place hung about by dark mists, out of which came the pale shine of the dragon's scales, and the cry of fighting men, and the wound of swords. Beowulf, Milton, Durer, Rembrandt, Schopenhauer, Turner, Tennyson, from the first war-song of our race to the stall-fed poetry of the modern English drawing rooms, all have had the same vision." That vision is life, action, and struggle: "On the whole, I am on the side of the unregenerate who affirm the worth of life as an end in itself as against the saints who deny it." "High and dangerous action teaches us to believe as right beyond dispute things for which our doubting minds are slow to find words of proof. Out of heroism grows faith in the worth of heroism." "The rule of joy and the law of duty seem the same to me . . . the end of life is life. Life is action, the use of one's powers."[7]

William James was appalled by the "cold-blooded, conscious egotism and conceit" of Holmes. His philosophy seemed a worship of mere excitement, irresponsible joy for the sake of joy. But Holmes could be the aesthete; in a letter to Laski he complained of the insensitivity of the other justices to his prose style: "I am amused

7. Francis Biddle, *Mr. Justice Holmes* (New York, 1943), pp. 34, 126.

(between ourselves) at some of the changes suggested, when I purposely used short and rather brutal words and, for an antithesis, polysyllables that made them mad. I am pretty accommodating at cutting out thought that I think important, but a man must be allowed his own style."[8] These comments are on a crucial decision of Holmes, concerning the sterilization of the "unfit." Justice Holmes did not believe in socialism since it merely changed external arrangements without bettering the driving spirit within and, furthermore, hurt the weak: "perhaps I am too skeptical as to our ability to do more than shift disagreeable burdens from the shoulders of the stronger to those of the weaker. . . . I believe that wholesale social regeneration which so many now seem to expect, if it can be helped by conscious human effort, cannot be affected appreciably by tinkering with the institution of property, but only by taking in hand life, and trying to build a race." These convictions came to the surface in *Buck* v. *Bell*. In that case the Supreme Court reviewed a Virginia law which allowed the sterilization of women who were institutionalized in hospitals for the feeble-minded. An eighteen-year-old girl, Carrie Buck, protested that the law went against rights in the Fourteenth Amendment. Holmes denied any such rights, and stated:

> We have seen more than once that the public welfare may call upon the best citizens for their lives. It would be strange if it could not call upon those who already sap the strength of the State for these lesser sacrifices [!], often not felt to be such by those concerned, in order to prevent our being swamped with incompetence. It is better for the world, if instead of waiting to execute degenerate offspring for crime, or let them starve for imbecility, society can prevent those who are manifestly unfit from continuing their kind. The principle that sanctions vaccination is broad enough to cover cutting the Fallopian tubes.

The only objection Holmes admitted was that the law did not go far enough: "But, it is said, however it might be if the reasoning were applied generally, it fails when it is confined to the small number who are in the institutions named and is not applied to the multitudes outside. It is the usual last resort of constitutional arguments to point out shortcomings of this sort. But the answer is that the law does all that is needed when it does all that it can, indicates a policy, applies it to all within the lines, and seeks to bring within

8. Holmes to Laski, April 29, 1927, *Holmes-Laski Letters,* ed. Mark de Wolfe Howe (Cambridge, Mass., 1953), II, 939.

the lines all similarly situated, so far as its means allow."[9] In other words, Holmes was sorry the law could not be applied more generally, but something was better than nothing. The race was being improved. And the style of short words and longer polysyllables was not wholly destroyed.

Holmes wrote another letter to Laski, returning to the problems of *Buck* v. *Bell*: "I wrote a decision the other day upholding a state law for sterilizing imbeciles—and felt that I was getting near to the first principles of social reform."[10]

Holmes derided for Laski's benefit what he called "the modern passion for equality." Socialism attempted to avoid the significance of suffering: "Meantime we have learned the doctrine that evil means pain, and the revolt against pain in all its forms has grown more and more marked. From societies for the prevention of cruelty to animals up to socialism, we express in numberless ways the notion that suffering is a wrong which can and ought to be prevented, and a whole literature of sympathy has sprung into being which points out in story and in verse how hard it is to be wounded in the battle of life, how terrible, how unjust that any one should fail." The masses should be indoctrinated with the "truths" of consumption against the functions of ownership, that they consume the preponderant percentage ("fully eighty-five percent," Holmes opined once) of the stream of goods: "When the ignorant are taught to doubt, they do not know safely what they may believe. I do not see so much use in committees on the high cost of living, etc., as I do in bringing home to people a few social and economic truths."

In his first years on the Supreme Court, Holmes actually preferred the companionship of Chief Justice Fuller to that of Justices Harlan and White.[11] For Fuller was an *authentic* legalist, a competent and technical corporation lawyer from Chicago, who never went farther than the law as words; while both Harlan and White puzzled and ruminated over problems of the relation of ongoing constitutional law to economic problems, problems of politics and statesmanship, and problems of proper constitutional interpretation. Holmes thought their opinions were "too long." Better the pure naïve technician than the "serious" men who tried to relate reality to constitutional law, not being "conscious" that the relation was really the

9. *Buck* v. *Bell*, 274 U.S. 200, 207 (1932).
10. Holmes to Laski, May 12, 1927, *Letters*, p. 942.
11. Biddle, *Holmes*, p. 81.

other way around, and that the law should be related to reality. As Holmes stated: "What proximate test of excellence in government can be found, except correspondence to the actual equilibrium of force in the community—that is, conformity to the wishes of the dominant power? Of course, such conformity may lead to destruction, and it is desirable that the dominant power should be wise. But wise or not, the proximate test of good government is that the dominant power has its way." Later, when Brandeis came onto the Court, Holmes admired *his* seriousness, because Brandeis always claimed in agreement with Holmes, that he was adjusting the law to realities and following "the logic of the facts," rather than relating facts to law.

But while Brandeis may have changed Holmes' views on some particular matters of social policy, Holmes remained an advocate of the view that the wise judge remained aware of the movement of social forces, his very recognition tinged with basic skepticism. "The Truth" was recognition of the necessary limitations of the human mind, while "goodness" was a polite cover for the brutalities of force:

> The cosmos is everything I don't know beyond my capacities to predicate, for remember my view that I am in its belly, not the cosmos in mine. These philosophic fellows are forever confusing themselves with the universe. Bradley's cosmos gets its tail in its mouth, and is as self-supporting as a row of men sitting in each others' laps in a circle. Bertrand Russell rebels against his cosmos, which is but to damn the weather, evidence of the fellow's ill adjustment. The business of philosophy is to show we are not fools for doing what we want to do.
>
> I think morality a sort of higher politeness, that stands between us and the ultimate fact—force. A believer in any sort of evolution cannot get a higher formula than organic fitness at the given moment.[12]

Thus there are realities, ameliorations of those realities, and higher levels of human consciousness above these ameliorations. The industrial order for Holmes was the level of man's real operational transformation of the chaotic natural powers below, and thus was an order of reality as "true causes." But civilization was a conscious rising above the industrial order. Holmes could not become a Marxist, because that would be to surrender to a compulsive and unconscious rejection of higher self-consciousness. These views of

12. *Ibid.*, p. 150.

reality and human operations are all condensed in a few remarks in a letter. After remarking on the books he had read in the past year, which, as always, was a formidable list indeed, Holmes stated that the history of human operations is more real than the metaphysical attempts to get beyond human limitations of thought, and yet industrialism is also subject to the negating superiority of the self-conscious vitality of man: "I wonder whether Royce knows any more about the world out of space, time, and causation than I do. . . . I have seen the *verae causae* of events in a little industrial history of England, better worth reading than all the big books. I have rebelled and thanked God that man was an animal capable of denying the industrial order and doing the spontaneous uneconomic thing."

The industrial order was the realm of policy-makers and prophets, but subordinate to the higher order of cultured and self-conscious men: "I mean by the world the few thousand men in the principal cities who as Bourget says constitute the civilized world." These men of the higher consciousness and vitality are not known to the larger group of ordinary conformists: "Decidedly the men who have made life seem large and free would not always be picked out by the crowd." John D. Rockefeller was a great man, because he amassed great power in the form of money, but he lacked the higher order of greatness, because he lacked the higher consciousness—"all your life you have been so busy grubbing and adding and toiling and saving that you never knew what you were doing. You were never conscious of where you were going." The higher thinkers and individuals had a kind of power and, in fact, had much more power than the men of the industrial order. The wealthy men controlled the present, while the more conscious men controlled the future: "Power generally presents itself nowadays in the form of money alone . . . but to an imagination of any scope the most far-reaching form of power is not money, it is the command of ideas."

In the famous essay "The Path of the Law,"[13] Holmes not only stated his famous definition of the law as prophecy as to what the courts will do, but stated it from the "realistic viewpoint." This viewpoint was that of the "bad man": "If you want to know the law and nothing else, you must look at it as a bad man, who cares only for the material consequences which such knowledge enables him to predict, and not as a good one, who finds his reasons for conduct in conscience." The good man mixes law and morals, while the bad

13. 10 Harvard Law Review 61 (1896).

man sees the law as consequences of public force. There is no logic in the law, for "you can give any conclusion a logical form." There is no permanent stability in the law, and "we do not realize how large a part of our law is open to reconsideration upon a slight change in the habit of the public mind." The law as it stood at the time, according to Holmes, was nothing but the economics of fifty years before that time.

The cure for dated legal rules, for Holmes, was knowledge of historical origins and articulation of the ends of the law, and the grounds for the ends. These ends do not have to be rational or reasonable but should be conscious.

Holmes gave a striking example of the old and the new in law and the lack of conscious reformulation of the law. The ancient law of torts arose through several particular writs allowing legal action. These writs were meant to stop local violence in early feudal days and to overcome the laws of vengeance with laws of legal injury and redress. But *new* tort law is largely concerned with accidents in modern industry and transportation. The question of how society should shoulder the burden of these accidents, which are so widespread that they are a matter of statistical prediction, is ignored because of the confusion of the pluralistic terminologies of privity, negligence, master and servant law, etc., inherited without revision from the past. Thus the study of the history of the law is "a first step toward an enlightened skepticism, that is, toward a deliberative reconsideration of the worth of these rules."

From this example the generalization is made that most law is similarly irrational and out of touch with the times. It was quite common in our historiography of the 1890's to find our freedoms came from "the forests of Germany" but Holmes believed nothing of the kind; rather our stupidities come from blind acceptance of power relations developed in the forests of Germany: "If we want to know why a rule of law exists, we go to tradition. We follow it into the Year Books, and perhaps beyond them to the customs of the Salian Franks, and somewhere in the past, in the German forests, in the assumptions of a dominant class, in the absence of generalized ideas, we find out the practical motive for what now is best justified by the mere fact of its acceptance and that men are accustomed to it."[14]

If lawyers want to look for acceptable reasons for rules of law,

14. Oliver Wendell Holmes, Jr., *The Common Law* (Boston, 1937), p. 17.

they should look to the realities of consumption, not to the problems of freedom: "Every lawyer ought to seek an understanding of economics." The minutiae of early legal history that Holmes can cite in his historical study of modern law tends to overwhelm the imagination of the reader, and make him forget some other basic events in the history of the common law completely ignored by Holmes.

Holmes ignored the respect accorded to existing law and customs by the Norman conquerors: the acceptance of law by the new rulers, rather than the "imposing of ideas by a dominant class."

Holmes ignored Magna Carta completely.

Holmes ignored Coke's great restatement of the common law, de-emphasizing the feudal elements in the *Institutes.* He ignored all the struggles for constitutional rights at the time of the Stuart accession and the Restoration.

Holmes ignored the Parliamentary Revolution of 1688, with the correlative establishment of the permanent right to legislation by representatives of the electorate, the establishment of the supremacy of law over the executive power, and the recognition that legislation was a legitimate and basic way to change the law.

Holmes ignored the Declaration of Independence, the adoption of the American Constitution, the Bill of Rights, the development of code pleading in most American state jurisdictions (replacing the older emphasis on procedure at the expense of substance), and the adoption of the Thirteenth, Fourteenth, and Fifteenth Amendments. Parliament, Congress, and state legislatures are never mentioned as crucial institutions in the development of Anglo-American jurisprudence. Holmes found the common law irrational, because he ignored all the more reasonable aspects of that law, with respect to discussion, deliberation, rights, control over arbitrary power, the acceptance of legislative revisions, with constitutional controls even over modern legislative powers.

The move back to the Salian Franks and the mythic German woods, in Holmes' history of the law, allowed the irrationalities to become paramount, and the more complex structures of deliberation and discussion developed in the last few six or seven centuries tended to disappear before the "sophisticated" historical sense of the present. The presentation is exactly the same in the larger work *The Common Law.* It is not Magna Carta, nor the Petition of Right, nor Coke, nor Locke, nor modern powers of legislation, nor checks and balances, nor the development of political parties, that receive attention, but rather the relation of old writs of procedure to jurisdictional powers in feudal times. The law is found to be illogical, because all the larger and more reasonable and logical parts are suppressed. The very few English philosophers of law that Holmes does mention are the authoritarians, those who wished to reduce the rule of sovereign power to a science: Hobbes, Bentham, and Austin. These few were wrong because they saw real power as coming from the top, whereas Holmes saw real power as coming from *below*. But Locke is never mentioned, nor Madison, nor, for that matter, conservatives such as Hamilton, Burke, Hume, and Webster: all these thinkers and all their debates and discussions and differences are out the window, in a philosophy of law which jumps from medieval anthropology to self-consciousness about the struggles in the modern economic world.

There is a qualification on this, but the qualification is not a legal restriction in the ordinary sense. What has developed from the days of the Salian Franks is *civilization*. The rules of law are the articulations of the deepest instincts of modern civilized man. The basic premises can never be made fully explicit, but they are the expressions of culture. Such culture is not absolute, but rather "experimental," yet it is the expression of basic developed policy.

Thus the anecdote Holmes told again and again, that he didn't mind paying his taxes, because with these taxes he bought "civilization." The particular problems of policy and budget, or, as Holmes put it, "whether the money was spent well or ill," did not matter to Holmes in comparison with the general evolutionary result of the progress of culture. Thus the old literal notions of constitutional limitations, as stated by such men as Justice Story or Judge Cooley, were ignored by Holmes as quaint fictions of legalistic terminology. Holmes' view has had its effect in the later history of what still remains basic in constitutional law, due process. After Holmes, due process has been defined in terms of "those canons of decency and fairness developed by the English-speaking peoples."[15] Where Justice Field thought that the Declaration of Independence was the basic preamble to American constitutional law, Justice Holmes thought that the inherent evolutionary norms of English-speaking civilizations were the foundation of jurisprudence. These inherent norms were also the rules of interpretation of laws and precedents. The Declaration of Independence was but the expression of a stage in

15. *Twining* v. *New Jersey,* 211 U.S. 78 (1908); *Malinski* v. *New York,* 324 U.S. 401 (1945).

the development of modern norms. For Holmes, culture was the true foundation of legal judgment. The vast lists of books that he read every year were better aids to the development of sensitivities to the ultimate foundations of the law than the precedents embodied in the formal law reports.

For Justice Holmes, the activities and pursuits of civilization were experimental attempts to discover values in a universe that was beyond the reach of rationality. The norms of the law are but one example of such experimentation. Holmes has been derided for constantly returning to the notions of the gambler and the soldier to explain his views, but such themes were basic to his philosophy and not mere reflections of an outdated leisure-class background. An expression of values is an expression of faith, in a universe that, in one way or another, may be hostile to such expression, or at best is not friendly. Therefore an element of courage and endurance is a necessary part of the life of meaning, whether on the individual level or on the level of economic activity or political organization. Holmes felt that war was the great test for finding the value of human life and consequently took patriotism in war as an ultimate virtue. Although he supposedly authored a "liberal" doctrine of freedom of speech in wartime, in his opinions on radical dissent and the "clear and present danger" concept, any close examination discovers that most of the defendants were sent to prison, since they *did* constitute a clear and present danger to the country at war. In an early Colorado case, Holmes justified the imprisonment of a newspaper editor during civil commotions, on the grounds that the Governor could have done anything to maintain the civil order, and since he was justified in shooting the editor, the lesser punishment of imprisonment was also legal. Furthermore, since any choice of values meant the rejection of other values, life was a gamble, not a science. Thus the famous description of the various states as "insulated chambers for experiments" did not mean experiment in the scientific sense, involving measures and controls and counter-experiments and the like, but experiments in the ultimate sense of basic risk-taking, of embarking on one general course of policies when alternative possibilities beckon but are rejected.

The struggle among various values was to Holmes both inevitable and healthy. In evolutionary terms it might even be beneficial to society at large (although Holmes could be skeptical about that). Justice Holmes was appointed to the Supreme Court by the reformer

Theodore Roosevelt because he had decided in favor of labor organization when Chief Justice of the Supreme Court of Massachusetts. In *Vegelahn* v. *Gunter*,[16] Holmes had said: "Combination on the side of capital is patent and powerful. Combination on the side of labor is the necessary and desirable counterpart, if the battle is to be carried on in a fair and equal way." But Holmes was *also* for the combinations of capital. When Roosevelt decided to make his first major attack on the trusts in prosecuting J. P. Morgan and James J. Hill in the *Northern Securities* case, Holmes cast his opinion for Hill and Morgan and against Roosevelt and the Sherman Act. In private letters Holmes stated that he despised the Sherman Act, and that attempts to break up the large combinations of capital were foolish, detestable, and short-sighted. The big capitalists served social interests in their investments, since most large wealth was placed in investments and productive enterprises. The profits obtained by large combinations were signs of their social usefulness, and the brilliant capitalists were not only "the best prophets we could buy," but were motivated, by the prospect of returns, to give a "poignant scrutiny to future risks" which socialist planners did not do. Capitalism meant a process of decentralized decision-making about production, and efficient prophets and producers should be rewarded, not punished, in Holmes' view, for the benefits of "the acute talents of the industrialists" flowed to all of society. Holmes' views about economics are not primitive. They are not a throwback to the "limited wages fund" doctrine of J. S. Mill, and he did not stop thinking about economics when he was about twenty-five, as his critics have insisted. At the present time, in both America and in socialist countries, problems of economics are approached in terms of centralized versus decentralized decision-making, risk-taking with respect to future consumption needs, and the flow of goods in production, distribution, and consumption, just as Holmes did. Holmes did not talk in quantitative terms about his theories, as current scientific economists do, and his quantitative guesses are literary rather than scientific in nature. But his conception of the principles of economic analysis are not naïve or dated, and they allowed him to view the economic process as an example of the general process of organized risk-taking.

Total monopolies were simply inconceivable to Holmes, but the partial monopolies reached by combination were justified as experiments in the realm of total life-activities. All life is a gamble, and

16. *Vegelahn* v. *Gunter*, 167 Mass. 92 (1897).

the big combinations were simply gambling on a magnificent scale. The puny and artificial rationalities of classical economics were hardly reason enough to cut the great combinations down, in Holmes' view. In major labor cases on the Supreme Court, Holmes defended the jurisdictional strike, the sympathy strike, the refusal to use non-union materials, and picketing, as effective means to reach the imagined ends of labor organization. Where Holmes had earlier indicated that labor organization and power were called for to balance capital organization and power and to reach an "equality" in bargaining positions, he later expressed doubts that labor could raise wages significantly in that way or could do more than change the rates of one sort of labor in comparison with other sorts. But these doubts did not lead him to modify his views that such organizations should be allowed to *experiment* with their ventures and beliefs. His views are directly opposed to Field's views. Field had strenuously objected to any legally established monopoly since such monopolies violated basic individual rights, while Holmes extended judicial toleration to the various partial monopolies of labor and capital, derided any so-called "rights" of individuals involved as "legal fictions" and "false absolutes," and assumed that the struggle between such partial monopolies was an inevitable clash of basic attitudes and values, legitimated by public opinion and by possible benefits to society in terms of increased consumption. Holmes was for Big Power on the industrial level, and he thought that the antitrust actions of the government simply attempted foolishly to legislate against the realities of operational success. Unlike Brandeis, Holmes saw no curse to bigness. The possibility of an industrial oligarchy dawned on Holmes, and from his philosophical view it was impossible: the men who chased money as power were too stupid and unself-conscious to realize that ideas and cultural norms were a vastly more extensive form of power, and thus these men were no threat at all.

To sum up, Holmes developed his legal thought within the scope of an operational view of human life, based on primitive notions of power, vitality, risk, and struggle as the true realities of existence which arose from the irrational and animal order. The modern industrial and commercial order was primary and basic in civilization, law, and life itself, and the only proper "reform" of that order was to increase the inner vitality of men and organizations involved. Socialism and communism, the Sherman Act and labor injunctions merely dealt with externals and effected no basic changes. Such changes could only be effected by the courageous facing of the realities of power and force on the industrial level by spirited men gifted with hope and endurance and prophetic powers, who lopped off the imbeciles and the dispirited through sterilization. At the second level, above the level of practical commercial realities, was the organization of ideas of law and culture. Such law and culture should relate to the processes of power, rather than attempting to force these processes into verbal molds or ignoring these processes altogether in a sterile logical legalism. The law as properly understood would replace the study of legal forms with a study of history and the future. Assuming that economic realities are understood, the higher cultural realities are those of historical development and change: "I can imagine a book on the law, getting rid of all talk of duties and rights. . . ." The proper sciences of the law are those of history and prophecy, with the behavioristic facts of what the courts will do reasoned in terms of developing and instinctual civilized norms which never get full articulation. On the higher level, above even these norms, is the place of the lonely thinker, aware of the complacencies of both the masses and the proper classes in ongoing society, and aware of the impossibility of "getting the universe by the tail" through the devices of predication, realizing that "the chief end of man is to form general propositions, and that no general proposition is worth a damn."

Thus the dissents of Holmes were more powerful than his assents, for the dissents were the achievement of the lonely thinker, while the concurrences were the acceptances of the civilized organization man. As Holmes stated his own feelings, "Only when you have worked alone—when you have felt around you the black gulf of solitude, and in hope and in despair you have trusted your own unshaken will— then only will you have achieved, then only can you gain the secret isolated joy of the thinker—the subtle rapture of postponed power, which to his prophetic vision is more real than that which commands an army."[17] It was on this level that Holmes operated in his dissents on the Supreme Court.

When Holmes left the Supreme Court in 1932, at age 92 (and only then because of the embarrassed urgings of Chief Justice Hughes), none of his views had swayed the majority of the Court. His peculiar relations with Justice Brandeis made his dissents more forceful, but

17. Biddle, *Holmes*, p. 81.

nonetheless not acceptable. It can be properly questioned whether Holmes *meant* to have his dissents taken seriously as bases for changing the law; the scholar Konevsky thinks they were meant to be dissents for their own sake, while Brandeis wrote his as "educational briefs" to show why the law should soon be changed. But Holmes' views did have power, and did lead to changes which, as he said, were more fundamental than the power which commands armies.

Various aspects of Holmes' thought became central in the jurisprudence of later men. Holmes' crucial idea of the reversal of the relation of law and economics was taken up by Brandeis. The notion of judicial self-restraint was another idea of Holmes, taken up by Justice Frankfurter. The struggle for values and the power of large organizations to promote values was taken up by Justice Robert Jackson. The basic realities of the processes of consumption have been studied by David Riesman, and the realities of production by James Burnham. Mr. Justice Holmes suggested all these ideas from the point of view of romantic and irrational vitalism, coupled with amused detachment, but the ideas became separated from this "Olympian" Nietzschean plane and grew in the soil of prosaic politics, economics, and law.

Justice Brandeis was appointed to the Supreme Court in 1916, in a storm of protest from conservatives, for he had previously exhibited no qualms about speaking forth on matters of policy which his opponents regarded as within the domain of private business. Brandeis had been active as a labor lawyer, and in labor disputes he had assumed the function of arbiter, attempting to persuade each side to see the proper claims of the other side. He had published an exposé of banking practices, called *Other People's Money,* had been involved in disputes over the efficiency of railroad operations, and had campaigned for reforms in workmen's insurance. His study of costs of collection and administration with respect to workmen's insurance was the first public step toward the old-age insurance programs that now exist as the Social Security laws.

Brandeis was for the organization of labor, something thought radical in his day, but for the reason that such organization would allow negotiations between labor and management to be workably handled. He never thought that organization of labor in itself would raise the workers' real wages, for that, he believed, could only come about through increased production and efficiencies of cost-handling; such things could only be achieved through the cooperation of labor and management and the self-discipline of both groups. "Industrial Democracy," a favorite phrase of Brandeis', meant simply the recognition of organized labor by management; it did not mean profit-sharing or control-sharing. However, Brandeis did think some corporations were simply too big. There was a separation of ownership from control and a separation of management from work and production, and therefore the needed recognition of the persons involved as real human beings was impossible. Unlike Holmes, Brandeis was *for* the anti-trust legislation and wanted a condition he called "regulated competition," i.e., large trusts would be broken into smaller competitive enterprises, but sharing of information and limitations of entry into the industry would prevent the situation from becoming "dog-eat-dog" competition, with no security and no stable long-range planning possible by any company involved. For instance, on the Court he was for trade associations.

The essence of political democracy, for Brandeis, was government by discussion. He did not think that such was fully the case in the United States but believed that we were approaching this ideal. This involved responsibilities on the part of the citizen, not just the administrative rulers or power holders: "That public discussion is a public duty,—this should be the fundamental principle of the American Government." However, the emphasis on governmental processes is *administrative;* good government is essentially the arbitration of various claims made by the several groups that make up society. The growth of democracy is based on the developing recognition of the claims of the previously downtrodden and abused; these claims do not overwhelm all other claims, but they must be balanced with the others. But Brandeis assumed there was a "science of administration," and that professional arbiters could satisfactorily settle such problems of competing claims on a disinterested and objective level. Brandeis was an early proponent of the various administrative agencies which developed in the New Deal era as the solution to problems of transportation, communication, labor, etc.

Brandeis had a different notion of property from that of either Field or Holmes. For Brandeis, property is power, and power is property. Stock ownership is not necessarily property, in this view, for it no longer gives any control over the enterprise in which the investment is made. Selling stock can be viewed simply as a way on the part of management of raising capital funds in order to continue a corporate enterprise; thus the real power is held by the directors and officers, not the stockholders. Even knowledge may be viewed as a kind of property, if it gives any sort of control over men and things or leads to increased efficiencies in any one business. On a larger and more general level, the growing total of human experience in public affairs is a great fund of common property and can lead to the further development of vital democratic institutions.

The reader has noticed that Brandeis shares with Holmes the basic assumption that all values need to be transvalued, that the law should follow the facts, rather than determine situations, that economics is the realm of ultimate policy determinations, and that law is recognition of operational achievements in that "more real" sphere. Brandeis rejected formal legalism and understood the "logic of facts" as leading to arbitration of disputes, rather than leading to judicial aloofness, as with Holmes. For Brandeis, there was no particular dividing line between the methods of public discussion, the methods of proper arbitration of a dispute, the methods of a lawyer engaged in counseling one side in a dispute, and the methods of a judge listening to a case in court. They all should follow "the logic of facts."

Brandeis was quite explicit about this method. Practical reasoning should begin with the recognition of some particular problem. Then such reasoning should proceed to a consideration of various remedies. This is an empirical research into all the opinions about the matter from relevant and competent authorities and a compilation of laws which are or have been used. For all this, a decision as to the proper remedy can only be made with full consideration of the conditions in the place where the problem exists now.[18] It might be said that the principle of this method is the recognition and coordination of opinions with respect to practical public problems. The genius of Brandeis was to discover from all the data he collected some acceptable policy, some acceptable direction.

The difficulties of Brandeis' position are several. First, there is some basic theoretical problem as to how facts can ever give rise to policies, even granted objective and disinterested administrators. But more than that, there were practical problems. Brandeis never in fact convinced other significant policy-makers that his views were the "factual" ones. Wilson appointed Brandeis to the Supreme Court but rarely if ever listened to his advice on the crucial policies of the day; Brandeis could never see him. The same thing happened in the

18. *Adams* v. *Tanner*, 244 U.S. 590 (1925).

early days of the New Deal. Brandeis was not taken into the high councils of policy-making, and in fact all the legalized monopolies that the New Deal instigated under the Wall Street conservative Hugh Johnson and the National Recovery Administration were exactly the opposite of what Brandeis thought would be best. Brandeis was in a minority position on the Supreme Court just as much as Holmes; the logic of the facts was not persuasive to Chief Justice Taft, or to Chief Justice Charles Evans Hughes, or to a majority of the Court. And finally, when *other* people have tried to follow Brandeis' "logic of the facts," they get no clear results: when others compiled all the various opinions and all the various laws on a problem, they discovered experts and jurisdictions marching in all different directions. But Brandeis was always able to discover some common direction of change.

All this is typified in *Burns Baking* v. *Bryan*.[19] The Court had declared unconstitutional a Nebraska law which governed the weight of bread. The law made it illegal to sell loaves of less than standard weight and also made it illegal to sell loaves of *more* than standard weight. This was held by the Court to be arbitrary and unreasonable. Brandeis dissented. The dissent is a long study of the history of breadmaking, which is vastly more detailed than anything presented in the briefs of counsel, and then a study of legislation with respect to minimum and maximum weights. In this realm Brandeis found that some jurisdictions did have laws about maximum standard weights for products, and other jurisdictions did not have such laws, and thus the empirical evidence went various ways. But from that Brandeis thought that the law should be declared constitutional, since it was "not entirely unreasonable" on the basis of experience, and the court should not infringe on basic policy-making powers of the states unless absolutely necessary.

This last point is the constant dilemma of those who maintain the transvaluation of values and the subordination of law to facts. Brandeis is more deeply concerned about the bread industry than the lawyers hired by that industry, and yet he counsels that the Supreme Court should refrain from judgments about the state laws concerning the bread industry. The Court should investigate all the facts, since the law should follow facts, and on the other hand the Court could be the basic fact in the situation. Lesser laws, like the Nebraska law, can determine situations, but not the opinions of the Supreme

19. *Burns Baking* v. *Bryan*, 264 U.S. 504 (1927).

Court. If the Court determines things, then what has happened to the transvaluation of values and the priority of economic processes? Thus the Court should *avoid* using its power to determine things, which it doesn't have anyway if the logic of the facts is followed.

The Brandeis brief was the weapon by which Brandeis the lawyer persuaded the Supreme Court that it could, indeed, allow state legislatures to pass laws concerning conditions of work in industry, maximum hours, and minimum wages. It should be granted that the Supreme Court had become bound by its own doctrine of "liberty of contract" to such an extent that *no laws* regulating industrial conditions could be passed by the appropriate state governments. Brandeis offered a way out. Rather than recognizing the *lawful province* of legislative powers, the Court turned to the Brandeis distinction of "law" versus "the truth." Thus in the first case, *Muller v. Oregon*,[20] Justice Brewer thanked Brandeis for his brief in the opinion giving the decision for the case. Brewer followed Brandeis' suggestions, and distinguished law from fact: even though women are now "legally and formally" on an absolutely equal plane with men, "It would still be true that she is so constituted that she will rest upon him and look to him for protection; that her physical structure and a proper discharge of her maternal functions—having in view not only her own health, but the well-being of the race—justify legislation to protect her from the greed as well as the passion of man." The *truth* that women were physically weaker than men had to be distinguished from the *law* that women were equal with men. Obviously all this was part of the law, but apparently the Court was unable to distinguish the equality of women *with respect* to voting rights, jury duty, and the like political capacities, from inequalities in other *legal* respects, such as with respect to permissible hours of factory work. So the distinction had to be made between legal equality, entire and absolute, and factual inequality, which could be legally recognized. The same peculiar distinction was later made with respect to reviewing state legislation. Judging that such state legislation was *constitutional* was "recognition of facts" and an exercise in "judicial self-restraint," while judging that state legislation was *unconstitutional* was "legalism" and "judicial legislation."

When Justice Brandeis was on the Court, he continued his practice of researching all relevant opinions on a case involving social problems and presenting the data in heavily footnoted dissents.

20. *Muller v. Oregon*, 208 U.S. 412 (1908).

These opinions were directed at particular social policies. While Brandeis reasoned that the Court should adopt policies of judicial self-restraint with respect to the examination of state legislation, he also held that the Supreme Court was an agency for forwarding proper public policies, just as much as any other public agency. Brandeis managed to advocate both judicial self-restraint and judicial activism, if not at exactly the same time, at least over a period of time. But in both positions he maintained that facts and administrative policies were more fundamental than judicial determinations of law.

However, Brandeis was in *no* sense a relativist, when basic moral values were considered. Unlike most other pragmatic thinkers, he did not use such terms as "maladjustment" or "unresolved tensions" to describe things he thought were wrong—he used "evil." Long working hours for women were "evil." Practices of private employment agencies were "evil." The social consequences of using some vague criterion of "common understanding" rather than scientific investigation in matters of public concern were "evil." Brandeis did not, like Holmes, view the process of valuation as a gambler's choice among alternatives or a courageous stand in a bewildering universe; evils were evils, and the object of public administration and law was to ameliorate these evils. Furthermore, such evils *could* be ameliorated through the use of fact-finding methods and through the gradual development of cooperation among groups, rather than cutthroat competition. Brandeis did not believe that some sort of Darwinian struggle among economic forces was for the ultimate good of society: "Unfettered individual competition is not a principle to which the regulation of industry may be trusted."

Justice Holmes replaced the priority of legal rights with a priority of history and expediency; Brandeis replaced legal determinations with *moral* determinations concerning human welfare in modern industrial conditions. This was not an empty moralism, but a moralism fully aware of business conditions, economic laws, accounting procedures, and sociological conditioning, a moralism aware of the need for public propagandizing with respect to important new policies and the need for proper legal techniques of argumentation in courts. But *force* was not the ultimate basis, as with Holmes, but rather *protection* against evils. Thus, in *New State Ice Company* v. *Liebmann*,[21] Justice Brandeis rejected both Miller's and Field's notions

21. *New State Ice Company* v. *Leibmann*, 285 U.S. 262 (1935).

of the legal limits of the public interest: "The notion of a distinct category of business affected with a public interest, employing property devoted to a public use, rests upon a historical error." In its place Brandeis used a notion of *protection*: "The true principle is that the state's power extends to every regulation of any business reasonably required and appropriate for the public protection." The whole debate between Justices Waite and Field over public interest versus public use as the proper determinant is dismissed by Brandeis as wrongheaded, and his own term, taken from another philosophical orientation altogether, replaces it. That term is "protection." The various criteria for capital evaluation in rate cases, stated in *Smyth* v. *Ames*, were adjudged to be wrong by Brandeis, because they have "failed to give adequate protection either to capital or to the public." It is the duty of the Supreme Court "to give to capital embarked in public utilities *the protection* guaranteed by the Constitution."[22] The exercise of free speech and assembly may be restricted "in order to *protect* the state from destruction or from serious injury, political, economic, or moral." Brandeis searched through hundreds of pages of accounting estimates and income statements, but what he was looking for was primarily a moral matter, what Professor Jaffe has called "an intuitive judgment of what will be just."

Thus Brandeis could not separate moral issues from economic, political, and legal issues, as Holmes could; they were all on the same level for Brandeis. He believed that corporations were a threat to individual humans and to the American political system: "The typical corporation of the last century, owned by a few men, is being supplanted by a huge concern in which the lives of hundreds of thousands of employees and the property of hundreds of thousands of investors are subjected, through the corporate mechanism, to the control of a few men. The changes wrought are so fundamental and so far reaching as to lead scholars to compare the evolving 'corporate system' with the feudal system; and to lead other men of insight and experience to assert that this 'master institution of civilized life' is committing it to the rule of a plutocracy." This economic development was immediately connected with moral and political issues by Brandeis:

> There is widespread belief that existing unemployment is the result of inequality in the distribution of wealth which the giant

22. *Southwest Bell* v. *Public Service Commission*, 262 U.S. 276 (1926).

corporations have fostered; that by the control which the few have exerted through corporations, individual effort and initiative are being paralysed; creative power impaired and human happiness lessened, that the true prosperity of our past came not from big business, but through the courage and energy of small men . . . only through participation by the many in the responsibilities and determinations of business, can America secure the intellectual and moral development which is essential to the maintenance of liberty.[23]

The "logic of the facts" in this more complicated reasoning involves the realization of the complex interrelation of industrial and financial organization with political liberty and moral creativity and determination. The wealthy few could take over the political power of the country in the view of Brandeis, and this would result in the stifling of individual initiative, which in turn would affect the economic prosperity of the nation, and so on. The best remedy for this was responsible awareness of the situation and control of the large corporations. Brandeis never suggested *national* incorporations, however, preferring to give broader powers of control to state legislatures. National incorporation laws would sound too much like a return to the "logic of law," and a rejection of the "logic of facts." All that Brandeis was advocating with the above opinion was the right of the State of Pennsylvania to prevent Liggett Drugs from buying any more drug stores in that state. But Brandeis' dissents were meant to educate the reader to the broader evils.

Unlike Holmes, Brandeis did not see the history of the law as a history of irrational customs. Basic law was made by intelligent and moral men at the time of the Constitution. The historical appeal is to the Founding Fathers, not to Franks and Visigoths:

> Those who won our independence believed that the final end of the state was to make men free to develop their faculties, and that in its government the deliberative forces should predominate over the arbitrary. They value liberty both as an end and a means. They believed liberty to be the secret of happiness and courage to be the secret of liberty. They believed that freedom to think as you will and speak as you think are means indispensable to the discovery and spread of political truth; that without free speech and assembly discussion would be futile; that with them, discussion affords ordinarily adequate protection against

23. *Liggett* v. *Lee,* 288 U.S. 517 (1932).

the dissemination of noxious doctrines; that the greatest menace to freedom is an inert people; that public discussion is a public duty; and that this should be a fundamental principle of the American government.[24]

Thus, when Brandeis substituted the "logic of the facts" for the "logic of the law," he included moral realities and politics by discussion within the realm of the facts.

A final unique quality of Brandeis' "logic of the facts" is his inclusion of the *reality* of *groups* as part of the facts of political and legal life. The twentieth-century liberal, Brandeis stated, must seek for groups the rights sought for *persons* in the eighteenth and nineteenth centuries. The individual must be seen as conditioned by his group and existing in a group context: "This right of development on the part of the group is essential to the full development of rights by the individual. For the individual is dependent for his development and his happiness in large part on the group of which he forms a part." Brandeis thought that problems of prejudice against minorities could not be solved unless the minority groups were recognized as groups: "Why is it that liberalism has failed to eliminate prejudice? It is because the liberal movement has not yet brought *full* liberty. Enlightened countries grant to the individual equality before the law; but they fail still to recognize the equality of whole peoples. We seek to protect as individuals those constituting a minority; but we fail to recognize that protection cannot be complete unless group equality also is recognized."

Certain quotations would make Brandeis an advocate of much recent Black separatism: "The misnamed cosmopolitanism which seeks the obliteration of peoples is unattainable. The new nationalism proclaims that each race or people, like each individual, has a right and duty to develop, and that only through such differentiated development will high civilization be attained. Not until these principles, like those of democracy, are completely accepted, will liberty be fully attained, and minorities secure in their rights."[25]

The role of the Supreme Court for Brandeis was not to hold aloof over the various legislative experiments in economics and state politics, as with Holmes, but rather to re-establish contact with the moral, political, and economic needs of the society of today, a society

24. *Whitney* v. *California,* 274 U.S. 357 (1927).
25. Lewis Dembitz Brandeis, *The Curse of Bigness,* ed. Osmond Fraenkel (New York, 1935), part 5.

which has undergone revolutionary transformations in the last fifty years. But within the sophisticated study of the operations of this society, the notions of basic moral good and basic moral evil remain, to prevent the law from becoming a mere index of success or strength or current fashion. But past law, as literal words which determine precedents and as statements of fundamental rights and duties paramount in a free society, was rejected by Brandeis. Like Holmes, he refused to distinguish between the views of Justice Miller and Justice Field; in the new age devoted to facts and economics, both are condemned as "legalists." Justice Brandeis saw that the various groups of modern society could achieve self-realization in their common and mutual recognition and that progress toward such a goal was a genuine good, just as various exploitations and repressions were genuine evils. Government and law were basic public instruments of moral and social progress. Thus Brandeis managed to reverse Holmes' separation of law and morality, Holmes' separation of legislative policy-making and judicial aloofness, Holmes' separation of action and philosophic skepticism, and yet still remain within the transvaluation of values implied in "the logic of the facts." Law remained subordinate and instrumental, not to man's follies and fashions, but rather, in Brandeis' view, to growing democratic moral ideals.

It is impossible to shorten or summarize many of Justice Brandeis' fifty- and sixty-page opinions, heavily footnoted and laden with statistical data, for the reason that the very essence of these opinions lies in their length and in the detail with which the questions are pursued and examined. But in these dissents and concurring opinions two other factors are significant, which are questioned in the jurisprudence of Felix Frankfurter, the third justice in the great triumvirate of "factualists" and transvaluators. Justice Frankfurter questioned the obviousness of the moral progress of mankind through the accumulation of experience, which is basic in Brandeis' optimism and moral earnestness, and, along with this, Justice Frankfurter also questioned the supposed identity of his own personal feelings about moral and political issues with the objective moral values of civilization.

Justice Frankfurter came to the Supreme Court at a time when two things had happened. First, the lonely pleas in dissent of Brandeis and Holmes, for a "logic of the facts," had finally triumphed in the Court, through the death of the earlier members and their replacement by Franklin Roosevelt; and thus positive burdens were put on a jurisprudence which had enjoyed the position of critic. And second, totalitarian systems had arisen in Europe which threatened the democracies and also dampened the optimism of those who had thought history led ever upwards and onwards. Where earlier liberalism could view its opponents as simply being fifty years behind the times, it was now challenged on both the right and the left by political organizations which also claimed to have history on their side. Holmes and Brandeis had somehow managed to agree on almost every major constitutional case, although Holmes based his views on the perspective of an Olympian Mephistopheles, amused at the dialectical clash of economic forces and experimental policies beneath him, while Brandeis based his examinations on the perspective of an earnest professional mediator and guide of harmonizing and cooperating human beings. But now that "the logic of facts" dominated, problems arose of choices for constructive action. The choice between alternatives was difficult; the situation was more ambiguous, and the *logic* of the problem was no longer clear.

Now, it should be said, that although Holmes and Brandeis both decried ordinary logic as irrelevant and useless to the "living law," both were magnificent logicians when it came to writing their own legal opinions. That is, basic formal logic can start in the law with the formulation of the issue. When the issue is formulated, then it can be decided by recourse to some one or more governing concepts. If there is *just one* governing concept or crucial middle term, then the answer proceeds clearly *and deductively* from the statement of the issue and the statement of the governing concept. Now in all of Holmes' and Brandeis' major opinions, this ordinary classical logical pattern is followed. Neither Holmes nor Brandeis ever indicates any doubt as to what the issue is in the case at hand, and they always state the issue clearly at the beginning of their opinion, and in legal terminology. Then, no matter how much they attacked legalism, formalism, precedent, the outdated economic views of their fellow judges, the strait-jacket of eighteenth-century words, and the uselessness of logic and reason to solve practical problems, they both usually arrived at a governing, single, legal, logical, consideration with respect to the issue. In Holmes' famous dissent in *Lochner* v. *New York*, for instance, he immediately stated the issue: should the court declare legislation unconstitutional because it is not in accord with the economic theories of the justices? He then turned to the dominant consideration, the vast difference between what legislators do in passing laws and what the Supreme Court should do in reviewing legislation. The Supreme Court should concern itself only with fundamental constitutional principles and not with particular economic theories, and state legislators may regulate social and economic life in many ways not germane to fundamental law. Holmes having made this clear distinction between legislation and guarding fundamental law, and having placed the New York baking law under the former classification, then his conclusion followed clearly and deductively from the argument. It is a masterpiece of old-fashioned legal logic, with clear distinctions and clear classifications and clear deductions explicitly and articulately made.

The majority opinion of Chief Justice Peckham seems weaker, not because of "the facts," but because Peckham could find *no governing consideration* with respect to the case, since he found that *both* the right of the state to make laws, *and* the right of the citizen to make contracts, had some claim to govern the case. He was then forced to "weigh" and "balance" the claims, admitting much that could be said on the other side, and buttressing his final decision with a number of external arguments, some of which admittedly were drawn from the non-legal sphere of economic theory. All of this follows from the logic of having two competing middle terms—the formal argument is weak, and the conclusion cannot have rational force, but only persuasive authority, and that not from purely legal sources.

The same logical and legal clarity found in Holmes' thought was found in that of Brandeis. In his brief in *Muller* v. *Oregon*, the question was stated by Brandeis immediately: "Is there reasonable ground for holding that to permit women in Oregon to work more than ten hours a day in a factory is dangerous to the public health, safety, morals, or welfare?" The governing considerations are twofold, but both prove the point: (1) both foreign and American legislation has restricted the hours of labor for women, and (2) the world's experience has shown that the health and morals of women are impaired by the fatigue of long hours of factory work. The power of the state is defined in terms of "the duty and the function of the legislature to discern and detect evils and obstacles to a greater public welfare" and then to remedy these conditions. The evil is the menace to vitality caused by fatigue in industrial work. From all this the conclusion follows *logically* and *legally*. The factual information and the opinions from experts are part of a clear deductive syllogism. The entire argument is a legal one, concerning the proper legal definition of the range and extent of the police powers of a state legislature.

Holmes may have talked a great deal about "inarticulate major premises," and "general propositions do not decide concrete cases," and "the life of the law has not been logic, it has been experience," but his own major premises are articulate. He does decide concrete cases from general propositions, and his opinions do not avoid logic, but rather are exemplary instances of it. The case is the same for Justice Brandeis. But this clear use of logic was rejected by Frankfurter. Justice Frankfurter thought himself, more than any of the other admirers of Holmes and Brandeis, their true heir. He tried to practice what they preached, namely that the life of the law was not logic. This led Justice Frankfurter into areas where the earlier angels of transvaluation had never trod: conflicting logical considerations and non-legal definitions of terms.

Thus in an early controversial case, *Minersville School District* v. *Gobitis*,[26] Frankfurter posed the issue so that there were *two* governing considerations. The Gobitis children, Jehovah's Witnesses, refused to salute the flag, as required by the school board. Frankfurter stated the issue as a conflict between (1) the Court's self-restraint in reviewing local legislative policies, and (2) religious freedom under the First Amendment. Since the two considerations had to be "balanced," Frankfurter went into the factual considerations: the Gobitis children could simply take the consequences of not saluting the flag and be labeled as delinquents subjecting their parents to certain fines, or their parents could send them to private schools. Furthermore, there were democratic processes by which the school board decision could be reversed, i.e., by voting out the school board. To impose a solution "from above" would take away local liberty: "When all the effective means for inducing political changes are left free from interference, education in the abandonment of foolish legislation is itself a training in liberty." And furthermore, the whole matter of coercion and compulsion in relation to freedom was a matter of degree.

The final consideration deciding between the basic legal issues was a highly questionable and certainly non-legal notion of "sentimental bonds." The rejection of logic led to the acceptance of irrational symbols: "The ultimate foundation of a free society is the binding tie of cohesive sentiment. Such a sentiment is fostered by all

26. *Minersville School District* v. *Gobitis*, 298 U.S. 38 (1936).

those agencies of the mind and spirit which may serve to gather up the traditions of a people, transmit them from generation to generation, and thereby create that continuity of a treasured life which constitutes a civilization. We live by symbols."

Nowhere in constitutional law is there reference to the foundational character of sentimental symbolism, except now in this opinion. Justice Frankfurter may have been following the jurisprudence of Thurman Arnold, who had satirized all rational jurisprudence, but also all irrational jurisprudence in his *Symbols of Government*, but he was criticized for not distinguishing his views on emotional symbols from the Nazi view. Frankfurter stated that they were different symbols and represented different things: "We are told that symbolism is a dramatic but primitive way of communicating ideas. Symbolism is inescapable. Even the most sophisticated live by symbols. But it is not for this Court to make psychological judgments as to the effectiveness of a particular symbol in inculcating concededly indispensable feelings, particularly if the state happens to see fit to utilize the symbol that represents our heritage and our hopes . . . the significance of a symbol lies in what it represents. To reject the swastika does not imply rejection of the cross."

But Frankfurter was unable, on the level of symbol or on the level of sentimental bonds, to distinguish "free societies" from totalitarian societies, and the *Minersville* decision was soon overthrown. Chief Justice Stone, in his dissent, had stated that there was but one governing consideration, the individual freedoms protected under the First Amendment. Logic and law were on his side because of the way in which he stated the issue. In a peculiar note Justice Frankfurter wrote to Stone, the paradoxes of the Frankfurter version of the logic of the facts, taken literally, are even more striking, for in the note he stated that his "private notions of liberty and toleration and good sense" were on the side of the Gobitis children and their parents, but that he could not bring them to bear on the case, since "we are not the primary resolvers of the clash; we are not exercising an independent judgment." Frankfurter restated the bind he was in: "Here we have an illustration of what the Greeks thousands of years ago recognized as a tragic issue, namely the clash of rights, not the clash of wrongs. For resolving such a clash we have no calculus."

Thus the wonderful thing about Justice Frankfurter was that with the relentlessness of his intelligence and with his lifelong idolization of the activities of the Supreme Court, he was driving the "logic of the facts" and the transvaluations of values to their inherent conclusions: fundamental considerations deciding between inherently conflicting claims would be irrational rather than rational, non-legal rather than legal. And since the function of the Court was limited to *recognition* of the democratic processes going on in the country, the Court might as well not exist. (Indeed, for a while the Learned Hand–Frankfurter position seemed to be just that—judicial review should cease altogether.)

With respect to rate hearings and review in utility cases, for instance, the three justices can easily be contrasted. Holmes hated the cases: "another damned rate hearing next week," while Brandeis loved them, and enjoyed matching wits with Charles Evans Hughes, going through hundreds of pages of data and evidence to justify commission findings or to call for a review of all investments and evaluations in terms of a notion of "prudent investment" that Brandeis held to be objective in nature.[27] Justice Frankfurter could not see why the Supreme Court should review commission findings at all, since he could not see any legal issues involved: "The determination of utility rates does not present questions of an essentially legal nature. . . . The real issue is whether the courts, or commissioners and legislators, are the ultimate arbiters of utility rates." (And Frankfurter stated it was the latter.)[28]

Again and again, Justice Frankfurter became involved in the peculiar situation; the issues of the case were stated as conflicting basic rights, and "judicial restraint" required that the opinion of the Court should go the *opposite* way from personal or moral feelings. In *Galvan* v. *Press,* Frankfurter posed the issue as one of the rights of persons versus the power of Congress. The basic considerations in the issue were two, and they conflicted: notions of due process in the Fourteenth Amendment, and the traditional exercise of power over aliens by Congress. Everything leans toward the rights of aliens, except the final conclusion: "Since he is a 'person,' an alien has the same rights as a citizen under the due process clause, and deportation . . . strikes one with a harsh sense of incongruity. If due process bars Congress from enactments that shock the sense of fair play, is it not beyond the powers of Congress to deport an alien who was duped into joining the Communist Party?" Frankfurter says there is no doubt the rights of the person would be para-

27. *Driscoll* v. *Edison Light and Power Company,* 307 U.S. 107 (1938).
28. *Galvan* v. *Press,* 347 U.S. 522 (1953).

mount, "were we writing on a clean slate." But he is forced to recognize that it is a dirty slate: "But the slate is not clean . . . that the formulation of policies respecting aliens is exclusively entrusted to Congress has become about as firmly embedded in the legislative and judicial tissue of our body politics as any aspect of our government."[29]

In the case of *Haley* v. *Ohio,* Frankfurter found that he could come out on the right side, but not because he, Justice Frankfurter, thought it was the right side. A fifteen-year-old Negro boy had confessed to a murder after hours of police interrogation, and the confession had been used to convict him and sentence him to death. Frankfurter spent a great deal of time in his separate opinion, worrying about the fact that he personally was against capital punishment, that he was against treating minors as if they were adults with respect to criminal charges. He wished to avoid the fact that "like other mortals, judges, though unaware, may be in the grip of prepossessions." Having cleansed himself, Frankfurter found that the legal terms in the Fourteenth Amendment were too vague and abstract to cover the situation in determinate fashion. The ultimate consideration covering the conflicting legal claims is non-rational and non-legal: "The pervasive feelings of society." As in the *Minersville* case, it is sentiment that decides crucial constitutional conflicts: "Detention for purposes of eliciting confessions through secret, long continued interrogation violates sentiments deeply embedded in the feelings of our people."[30] The judge must psychoanalyze society, after having done the same for himself: "Essentially it invites psychological judgment that reflects deep, even if inarticulate, feelings of our society. Judges must divine that feeling as best they can from all the relevant evidence and light which they can bring to bear for a confident judgment of such an issue, and with every effort to detach themselves from their merely private views."[31]

Holmes and Brandeis had pleaded that the justices of the Court did not necessarily have to think that legislation being reviewed was wise in order to allow it to be constitutional. Frankfurter went one step further: the constitutional judgment did not have to be wise. In fact, constitutionality and wisdom were two entirely separate things: "It must never be forgotten that our constant preoccupation with the constitutionality of legislation rather than with its wisdom tends

29. *Haley* v. *Ohio,* 332 U.S. 596 (1948).   30. *Ibid.,* p. 603.
31. *Dennis* v. *United States,* 341 U.S. 494, 556 (1951).

to a false value: even the most rampant worshipper of judicial supremacy admits that wisdom and justice are not the basis of constitutionality." And "preoccupation by our people with constitutionality, instead of with the wisdom, of legislative or executive action is preoccupation with a false value."[32]

When Justice Holmes discussed the ultimate irrationalities of the universe, it was a guard against taking his own *ratio* as cosmic, but he did not abandon human conceptions of limited truth and limited exploration of articulate values. Justice Frankfurter wished to probe beyond these limits of "can't helps" in Holmes and derive law from the irrationalities themselves, rather than live with the Nietzschean illusions and civilized fictions. In a speech at a Tanglewood Festival, that may or may not be taken as fundamental in Frankfurter's views, he declared that *music* was the fundamental medium of communication, and the only way the community of humanity could be established. Rational concepts are divisive, while sentiments and feelings and musical moods bind together.

The peculiar paradox of Frankfurter was that he was intellectual enough to face legal issues, and his academic background as a professor of law at Harvard was precise enough so that he never wished to avoid questions of the literal wording of the law or the literal force of precedents, matters frequently ignored by Holmes and Brandeis, but at the same time he wanted to interpret these constitutional words and phrases in "factual" and "progressive" ways which led him from the law to irrational concepts. Holmes and Brandeis never came close to meeting the other justices of the Court on the matter of the legal issues involved, but Frankfurter did. He argued with Chief Justice Stone about the precise weight to be given to the First Amendment in relation to the Tenth. He argued with Justice Black about the purpose and significance of the three parallel clauses in the first section of the Fourteenth Amendment. But, having joined on legal issues, Frankfurter would then dive to his logic of the facts. This was always for the sake of precision, for concepts meant nothing more than the facts they contained, and "due process" and "equal protection" were too vague and indeterminate when left on abstract verbal levels. Granted that there would be differences of opinion, the only proper recourse was to factual recognition of feelings. The problems of such "objective" consideration of feelings are found most clearly in his *Malinski* opinion:

32. *Malinski* v. *New York,* 324 U.S. 401, 416 (1945).

Judicial review inescapably imposes upon this Court an exercise of judgment upon the whole course of the proceedings in order to ascertain whether they offend those canons of decency and fairness which express the notions of justice of English-speaking peoples even toward those charged with the most heinous offenses. These standards of justice are not authoritatively formulated anywhere as though they were prescriptions in a pharmacopeia. But neither does the application of the Due Process Clause imply that judges are wholly at large. The judicial judgment in applying the Due Process Clause must move within the limits of accepted notions of justice and is not to be based upon idiosyncracies of a purely personal judgment. The fact that judges may differ among themselves whether in a particular case a trial offends accepted notions of justice is not disproof that general rather than idiosyncratic standards are applied.[33]

Since conceptual definitions would be abstract and false, Frankfurter refused to make them in crucial cases. The most important of such cases had to do with the application of the due process guarantees to criminal trials. In *Wolf* v. *Colorado*,[34] Frankfurter stated that evidence taken in an illegal search was admissible in the state court, although he personally felt it was wrong to admit it and although such evidence could not have been used in a Federal Court. In *Irvine* v. *California*,[35] Frankfurter stated that evidence illegally obtained through planted microphones was *not* admissible. What was the difference? Frankfurter replied that there was no conceptual difference and that the application of due process could only be understood as a gradual process of inclusion and exclusion of particular instances. Some cases would be beyond the feelings of justice held by English-speaking peoples, and other cases would not. It would be wrong to define the matter, for "basic rights do not become petrified at any one time." To continued criticism, Frankfurter made the famous distinction-without-a-difference, the distinction between "empiricism," which Frankfurter followed and which was proper, and "ad hocness," which was too particular and non-continuous, and was wrong: "Empiricism implies judgment upon variant situations by the wisdom of experience. Ad hocness in adjudication means treating a particular case by itself and not in relation

33. *Wolf* v. *Colorado*, 338 U.S. 25 (1949).
34. *Irvine* v. *California*, 347 U.S. 128 (1954).
35. *Ibid.*, p. 147.

to the meaning of a course of decisions and the guides they serve for the future. There is all the difference in the world between disposing of a case as though it were a discrete instance, and recognizing it as part of the process of judgment, taking its place in relation to what went before and further cutting a channel for what is to come."[36]

The revolt against formalism demands that no definitions be given, for otherwise "alternative modes are frozen." The empirical method keeps to the non-rational but factual "feelings": "In applying such a large, untechnical concept as 'due process,' the Court enforces those permanent and pervasive feelings of our society as to which there is compelling evidence."[37] Definitions would be "mechanical": "Since due process is not a mechanical yardstick, it does not afford mechanical answers. In applying the Due Process Clause judicial judgment is involved in an empirical process in the sense that results are not predetermined or mechanically ascertainable." Thus, in order to predict what the Court might do next, one must look, not at definitions, but at the permanent and pervasive feelings of society.

Now, let us say, we did a public opinion poll on the West Side of Chicago in order to discover the "permanent and pervasive feelings of justice" that would be discovered there with compelling evidence. This would be the wrong place. The proper place to discover these feelings is in England. The feelings are more pervasive there, and they are not affected by the artificial formalities of Constitution and Supreme Court: "The liberties that are defined by our Bill of Rights are, on the whole, more living realities in the daily lives of Englishmen without any formal constitution, because they are part of the national habit, they are in the marrow of the bones of the people."[38] In this country, the feelings may actually be wrong, and then a certain education in right feelings may be the task of the formal law, as in the community of Little Rock, Arkansas: "Violent resistance to law cannot be made a legal reason for its suspension without loosening the fabric of our society . . . experience attests that such local habits and feelings, will yield, gradually though this may be, to law and education."[39]

Justice Frankfurter even goes so far as to qualify Justice Holmes'

36. 339 U.S. 9 (1950).
37. Felix Frankfurter, *Mr. Justice Holmes and the Supreme Court* (Cambridge, Mass., 1938), p. 63.
38. *Cooper* v. *Aaron*, 358 U.S. 20, 22, 25 (1958).
39. *Harris* v. *United States*, 331 U.S. 145 (1947).

dictum that general propositions do not decide concrete cases. They do, if it is added that people may *feel strongly* about these propositions. The feelings are the middle term in the syllogism, again, although generalities are admitted to have a kind of existence: "I am not unmindful of Mr. Justice Holmes' caution that 'general propositions do not decide concrete cases.' Whether they do or not often depends on the strength of conviction with which such 'general propositions' are held. A principle may be accepted in principle, but the impact of an immediate situation may lead to a deviation from the principle. Or, while accepted in principle, a competing principle may seem more important. Thus, a decision may turn on whether one gives the Fourth Amendment a place second to none in the Bill of Rights, or considers it on the whole a kind of nuisance in the war against crime."[40] Even the abstractions of the Supreme Court may have had an effect on the realities of empirical life. "The raw material of modern government is business," but the Supreme Court has influenced business: "It cannot be denied that the Supreme Court has enormously furthered corporate growth. By devising facilities for business, the decisions of the Court themselves have operated as economic factors."[41]

But larger or higher principles can never have final and comprehensive influence in jurisprudence because they always conflict. In this conflict of principles, the logic of facts always returns to the "empiricism" of a line of particular decisions, with the gradual process of inclusions and exclusions proceeding in terms of basic feelings: "The core of the difficulty is that there is hardly a question of any real difficulty before the Court that does not entail more than one so-called principle. Anybody can decide a question if only a single principle is in controversy. Partisans and advocates often cast a question in that form, but the form is deceptive." Because the general principles conflict, the problem for the Court is always the problem of drawing the line: "The boundary at which the conflicting interests balance cannot be determined by any general formula in advance, but points in the line, or helping to establish it, are fixed by decisions that this or that concrete case falls on the nearer or the farther side."[42] Justice Frankfurter seemed unaware that the earlier warriors for "the logic of the facts" also employed old-fash-

40. Frankfurter, *Holmes and the Court,* p. 8.
41. *Hudson* v. *McCarter,* 309 U.S. 349 (1941).
42. *Missouri* v. *Holland,* 252 U.S. 416 (1920).

ioned logic as a weapon and never found themselves "balancing" opposite principles or slowly drawing difficult lines by some non-mathematical extrapolation from individual point-cases. However, Frankfurter is the logical result and pragmatic culmination of the jurisprudence started by Holmes.

Unlike Holmes, Frankfurter took seriously the literal words of the Constitution and later precedents. Justice Holmes started his trans-valuating jurisprudence of experience with the view that the formalities of the law had to be seen as irrational habits, enduring from earlier ages, to be revised in the self-conscious sophistication of modern philosophic skepticism in terms of the expediencies of the future. Legislation was subordinated to the higher realm of judicial control, but such legislation was viewed usually with thinly disguised amusement and contempt, as more or less blind experimentation, while judicial interpretation was the key to ultimate control. The entire Constitution was a more or less minor incident in this grand process of legal insight into civilized development: "When we are dealing with words that are a constituent act, like the Constitution of the United States, we must realize that they have called into life a being the development of which could not have been foreseen completely by the most gifted of its begetters. It was enough for them to hope that they had created an organism; it has taken a century, and has cost their successors much sweat and blood to prove that they created a nation. The case before us must be considered in the light of our whole experience and not merely in that of what was said a hundred years ago."[43]

Justice Frankfurter's view of constitutional interpretation was also in terms of the words as "living law," but he did consider the literal words and phrases and not just discussion of the grand experience of a hundred years. His discussions of the peculiar role of the due process clause in the Fourteenth Amendment, in relation to the rest of the Constitution and in relation to application to various sorts of concrete cases, are disputable but nonetheless classic. Holmes grandly wished to ignore the whole Fourteenth Amendment; that could hardly be done once the "logic of the facts" captured a majority in the Court, and Frankfurter related legal terms literally to problems of changing norms.

Brandeis had assumed an idealism in the march of experience and had personally crusaded for his vision of social welfare, on the Court

43. *Brown* v. *Topeka Board of Education*, 347 U.S. 483, 489, 494, 495 (1953).

and off, always assuming that his vision was the vision of history, America, and mankind, and usually assuming that judgments about social evils were as objective as any empirical date in the social process. Frankfurter had no such faith and states a sophisticated skepticism as to whether his judgment was the same as the judgment of the people and of history.

Unlike Holmes, Frankfurter usually met the "legal" interpreters of constitutional law head-on, term for term and clause for clause. Unlike Brandeis, Frankfurter did this without any absolute faith either in the constitutional process, or in his own moral judgments and feelings, or in the march of progress and the basic harmonization of all classes and groups. Frankfurter's friends urged him to activism, in which the law could be said to determine facts and situations, rather than merely recognizing in "self-restraint" existing trends and historical movements. The critics of Holmes and Brandeis had been political conservatives who stormed and fumed at the transvalued logic; Frankfurter's critics were the liberals. If Frankfurter admitted that the law could and did determine situations, he went on to hold that it *should not*; and therefore the "logic of the facts," insisting that situations and history determined the law, became the logic of "self-restraint" in a most paradoxical form: the law could determine situations, but the law should, in the name of democracy, avoid doing so. And in Frankfurter's jurisprudence this emphasis on legislative processes as *more fundamental* than judicial processes, and more rational, became stressed, in complete opposition to Holmes' ignoring of such legislative structures and changes in basic law.

The process of electing legislators, and either re-electing them or electing different ones because of laws passed or not passed, impressed Frankfurter more and more as the heart of the free democratic process. Holmes had always viewed such law-making as far *below* the judicial area and had understood elections as a way of applying the force of a temporarily dominant class or opinion. Dominant public opinion might elect a legislature that passed laws in accordance with it, but Justice Holmes never believed that such movements in the winds of fashion were more important than constitutional interpretation. For Holmes the justices were above such partisan debates and political movements, even if these went from laissez-faire to socialism and back; in fact it was the duty of the justices to stay above such whimsical and more or less foolish and arbitrary moves. But for Justice Frankfurter, it became increasingly more difficult to see why a "logic of the facts" would allow the law to impose its structures on the facts of the democratic process at any time or in any way. If all interpretation of law was a sort of legislation, why not leave it to the legislators? Even when a minority seemed to have a majority hamstrung, as in the reapportionment cases, Frankfurter was worried about judicial impositions on the processes of democratic life. In the jurisprudence of Justice Holmes, the realization that reasonable men could disagree led to the superiority of the judges who could rise above such oppositions; in the jurisprudence of Frankfurter, since he saw that even realistic pragmatic judges could disagree, and that as a man he frequently disagreed with himself as a judge, the movement was toward the irrational binding forces of symbol and sentiment, tradition and feeling. And in terms of the logical consequences of an attack on logic and legal formalism, Frankfurter was more thoroughgoing in his position. (It may be granted that even more thorough transvaluations would cause one to leave law and jurisprudence altogether, as David Riesman, one of Brandeis' most brilliant law clerks, left legal studies for the "more real" field of sociology, or as Jackson or Arthur Goldberg left for the "more real" field of international politics.)

In this study of the transvaluation of values in the law, there is one final stage beyond the developments of jurisprudence of Mr. Justice Frankfurter, which is both the culmination and the reversal of the original inspiration. Because of basic pragmatic considerations, Holmes wanted to subordinate the law to the ongoing processes of society and civilization. As applied literally and prosaically by Justice Frankfurter, this meant that the Courts should not impose their notions of justice on disputants. If legislative remedies were at all possible they should be used. When absolutely necessary to impose adjudicated determinations, as in the due process cases, the judicial remedies should be in terms of objective but non-legal standards. The Holmesian reversal implied that the reasons of the law stemmed ultimately from non-rational developments; in the last analysis, as made by Justice Frankfurter, this meant that the basic considerations in crucial constitutional cases were matters of the "feelings" of the citizenry. The Holmesian reversal had never prevented Holmes from arguing with simple and direct logical force; Justice Frankfurter held that such logic was "one-sided" and "partisan," and he always found that there were too many considerations, which were also too complex, to allow orthodox logic to be employed. Justice Frankfurter's intellectual nominalism and universal pragmatism led him to debate the views of Mr. Justice Hugo Black on the bench, for Black stated his views in terms of a logical formalism and a direct legalism, depending on a "proper reading" of the words of the Constitution. But that dispute was a standoff, merely an example of the perennial dispute between formal logicians and pragmatists, and it generated more anger than constructive result.

In the midst of these disputations, a new Chief Justice came on the scene, with a pragmatic outlook which was more comprehensive than Frankfurter's and this outlook was able to reverse the direction of the Holmesian thought. For there is nothing wrong with form and law and logic in a broad pragmatic approach to practical problems. Charles Peirce saw form and logic as intrinsic to his pragmatic views; John Dewey developed a theory of inquiry in which logic and formal relationships stood at the very heart of the subject; Northrop developed a theory of civilizations, pragmatic in outlook, in which formal logic and structured reasoning stood paramount in the outlook of Western civilization. The pragmatic approach to law does not require the psychoanalytic searches, the resistance to all definitions and classifications, or the reliance on irrational feelings and emotional symbols that seemed the culmination of the transvaluation of law and experience in the developed Holmesian jurisprudence. And this was all understood, whether with self-conscious sophistication or not, by Chief Justice Warren. Warren's pragmatism included the law as a determinant, and not simply a mirror, of the processes of society. Warren's pragmatism included logic as part of the "life of the law." Justice Warren recognized the proper formalities of the law as part of the "realities" of social existence, and he recognized the institutionalized power of the Supreme Court in the American experience; the law *as law* does not have to be rejected as unreal, as a "strait-jacket" of definitions, as a deepfreeze of meanings. "Experience can follow the law's ideals," said Warren, and the transvaluation was reversed.

Chief Justice Warren's pragmatic acceptance of the law as a determining factor in democratic civilization can be seen in a shift of emphasis in two crucial constitutional decisions. In 1953, in *Brown* v. *Topeka,* Warren argued logically, but all the emphasis was on the minor, or factual, premise, and the basic consideration was in line with the psychological jurisprudence of Frankfurter's "feelings of inferiority." But by 1958, in *Cooper* v. *Aaron,* the entire argument is *legal* and *logical,* a matter of deductions from statements in the Constitution and precedents of long standing. Formalism has been understood as *necessary* and *sufficient* in the broader pragmatic jurisprudence.

In more detail: in the *Brown* case, Chief Justice Warren assumed that words can only be understood in their "living contexts" and that the Fourteenth Amendment must be understood in terms of the developments in American education. It is the current meaning of the Fourteenth Amendment that matters and not earlier meanings. That these meanings change as society changes is more or less straight Frankfurter-analysis, accepted by Warren at the time:

> Reargument was largely devoted to the circumstances surrounding the adoption of the Fourteenth Amendment in 1868. It covered exhaustively consideration of the Amendment in Congress, ratification by the states, then existing practices in racial segregation, and the views of proponents, and opponents of the Amendment. This discussion and our own investigation convince us that although these sources cast some light, it is not enough to resolve the problem with which we are faced. At best, they are inconclusive. . . . In approaching this problem, we cannot turn the clock back to 1868 when the Amendment was adopted, or even to 1896 when *Plessy* v. *Ferguson* was written. We must consider public education in the light of its full development and in its present place in American life throughout the nation.[44]

The "separate-but-equal" doctrine is unconstitutional, because it ignores the ultimate factor of feelings: "To separate them from others of similar age and qualifications solely because of their race generates a feeling of inferiority as to their status in the community, that may affect their hearts and minds in a way ever unlikely to be undone."

In the *Brown* case, constitutional law ends, as with Frankfurter, in psychology, but Warren is not content to follow his own judgments here and relies on writings of authorities, given in a famous footnote to the statement that the psychological bases are a matter of knowledge: "Whatever may have been the extent of psychological knowledge at the time of *Plessy* v. *Ferguson,* this finding is amply supported by modern authority. (note:) 1. K. B. Clark: *The Effect*

44. *Ibid.*

of Prejudice and Discrimination on Personality Development; Witmer and Kotinsky: *Personality in the Making*, c VI.; Deutscher and Chein: *The Psychological Effects of Enforced Segregation*; . . . Frazier: *The Negro in the United States*; and see generally Myrdal: *An American Dilemma*."

From these studies of the development of American education and the nature of psychological development, Chief Justice Warren could phrase the minor premise of his syllogism, which as the premise closer to the facts, became the important premise. The equal protection clause of the Fourteenth Amendment is the ambiguous but governing term in the abstract major premise: "Separate educational facilities are inherently unequal. Therefore plaintiffs are deprived of the equal protection of the laws guaranteed by the Fourteenth Amendment."

All the reasoning is different in *Cooper* v. *Aaron*, five years later. The Little Rock, Arkansas, School Board had closed the city schools, in order to prevent the violence that had ensued when integration had begun. Chief Justice Warren argued that the law is clear, and the experience of the community must follow the law. The Constitution is clear; there are no longer any doubts or ambiguities about the Fourteenth Amendment. The law is *command*, not reflection of social experience:

> The constitutional rights of respondents are not to be sacrificed or yielded to violence and disorder. . . . The controlling legal principles are plain. The command of the Fourteenth Amendment is that No State shall deny to any person within its jurisdiction the equal protection of the laws. . . . Article VI of the Constitution makes the Constitution the 'Supreme Law of the Land.' A basic principle is that the federal judiciary is supreme in the exposition of the law of the Constitution. [Marshall's *Marbury* v. *Madison* is cited.] It follows that the interpretation of the Fourteenth Amendment enunciated by this court in *Brown* v. *Topeka* is the Supreme Law of the Land.[45]

Chief Justice Warren turned from explorations of education and psychology in *Brown* v. *Topeka* to straight formal analysis of law as ultimate determination in *Cooper* v. *Aaron*. This is not to say that Warren changed his ultimate views of jurisprudence from the *Brown* case to the *Cooper* v. *Aaron* case, but rather that the pragmatic prob-

---

45. *Cooper* v. *Aaron*, 358 U.S. 20 (1958).

lem of interpreting the law where public opinion was divided led to a reassertion of the significance of the intrinsic meaning of the Constitution, the properly legal powers of the Supreme Court, and the ability of words to lead actions and to determine values, rather than the other way around: "The Constitution created a government dedicated to equal justice under law. The Fourteenth Amendment embodied and emphasised that ideal. . . . The principles announced in the *Brown* decision and the obedience of the States to them, according to the command of the Constitution, are indispensable for the protection of the freedoms guaranteed by our fundamental charter for all of us. Our constitutional ideal of equal justice under law is thus made a living truth." This last statement is vital in seeing the pragmatic transformation of the Holmesian jurisprudence. Justice Holmes had insisted that proper judgment went from social truths to a living and developing law. Chief Justice Warren now insists that progress is achieved when society goes from the ideals of the law to living truths.

The swing away from Frankfurter's jurisprudence of feelings and experience is marked in the *Cooper* case by the fact that Justice Frankfurter felt called upon to write a separate opinion, distinguishing his views from those of the Court, even though the opinion of the Court was unanimous. Frankfurter appealed to notions of compromise and mutual adjustment, apart from the law: "By working together, men of different minds and tempers, even if they do not reach agreement, acquire understanding and thereby tolerance of their differences." Frankfurter tried to separate law and force, again assuming compromise to be better than ordinary adjudication (and somehow overlooking the fact that policemen have always been an aspect of our law): "The use of force to further obedience to law is in any event a last resort and one not congenial to the spirit of our nation." The basic consideration for Frankfurter remained considerations of feeling and experience: "Deep emotions have, no doubt, been stirred. They will not be calmed by letting violence loose . . . nor by submitting to it under whatever guise employed. Only the constructive use of time will achieve what an advanced civilization demands and the Constitution confirms."

Civilization still is prior to the formal Constitution in Frankfurter's thought; words follow emotions, and not vice-versa. The emotions in Little Rock were violent, therefore Frankfurter made appeal to other cities and their experience, rather than to formal law: "That the responsibility of those who exercise power in a democratic government is not to reflect inflamed public feeling, but to help form its understanding, is especially true when they are confronted with a problem like a racially discriminating public school system. This is the lesson to be drawn from the heartening experience in [northern cities]."

The final appeal, in the peroration of the opinion, is to "our moral heritage," which derives especially from Lincoln's speeches and the blood shed in the Civil War, rather than from formal precedent: "Lincoln's appeal to 'the better angels of our nature' failed to avert a fratricidal war. But the compassionate wisdom of Lincoln's First and Second Inaugurals bequeathed to the Union, cemented with blood, a moral heritage which, when drawn upon in times of stress and strife, is sure to find specific ways and means to surmount difficulties that may appear to be insurmountable."

But by the time of *Cooper* v. *Aaron* the insistence that law be based on non-law, on the feelings of society and the march of civilization and inarticulate notions of decency and fair play, no longer had the practical power to carry the assent of the nation, to shock the bar, the press, and the complacent classes out of their torpor. It was the querulous opinion of an isolated individual, trying to avoid recognizing the law as basic, when such simple recognition was the obvious factor required in the pragmatic situation. But a lifetime of scholarship and polemic had been devoted to proving that Holmes' and Brandeis' derivation of law from facts was the proper founding of the law. What for Chief Justice Warren was an easy matter of moving to formal legal considerations, when such were called for, was no longer possible for Frankfurter. If constitutional law could stand on its own, determining facts rather than being determined, if the Court could announce that its interpretations were final and ultimate, and that it alone was the proper source of the "Supreme Law of the Land," then the comprehensive philosophy of the "logic of experience" was no longer the crest of the advancing wave of civilization, but simply another approach among the many positions held and proposed by the various justices of the Court.

Warren's pragmatism was able to include Frankfurter's concepts of basic feelings and civilized notions of decency, and also legal and formal constitutional reasonings of the sort common to Justice Black and the earlier Justice Field. In the famous *Miranda* case, limiting the use of pre-trial confessions, Warren may have used Frankfurter's

notions of advancing civilization, but he insisted that he was following formal notions of basic constitutional rights: "We start here with
the premise that our holding is not an innovation in our jurisprudence, but an application of principles long recognized and applied
in other settings. The Escobedo case was but an explication of basic
rights that are enshrined in our Constitution."[46]

However, Chief Justice Warren also held to Frankfurter's notion
of the indefinability of due process with respect to applications of
admission of evidence in criminal trials. Frankfurter's great statement of due process as the feelings of decency and fairness in English-
speaking peoples came in the *Rochin* case; Warren constantly referred to that opinion, ignoring Justice Black's long and constant
tirades against it. Thus in *Breithaupt* v. *Abram*, Warren stated, "The
judgment in this case should be reversed if *Rochin* v. *California* is
to retain its vitality."[47] In later cases Warren has referred to his
opinion in the *Breithaupt* case. Warren avoided any logical tangles,
such as Justice Brennan developed in presenting *his* attempted union
of pragmatism and legal form, in *Stovall* v. *Denno*[48] where the rights
of citizens with respect to pre-trial procedures were held to apply
prospectively, but not retroactively. The Court as declarer of rights,
and the Court as legislator of "new standards," became hopelessly
confused in the Brennan's *Stovall* opinion; but such was never the
case in Warren's presentations or in his comprehensive jurisprudence. His pragmatic view always insisted that law and rights are
basic, not derivative. It reached to such legal depths, that some of his
opinions have the same general style of argumentation as Justice
Field's. Instead of the "inherent rights" of Justice Field, there are the
"vital personal rights" and the "basic civil rights of man" of Chief
Justice Warren. These rights are derived from the Constitution, and
from the pursuit of happiness of free men. In *Loving* v. *Virginia*[49]
the Chief Justice stated that "This case presents a constitutional
question never addressed by this Court." The problem of marriage
is found by Warren to be a Federal question under the Fourteenth
Amendment, and not a matter left to the discretion of the states,
because "Marriage is one of the basic civil rights of man fundamental
to our very existence and survival," and "The freedom to marry has

46. *Miranda* v. *Arizona*, 384 U.S. 436 (1967).
47. *Breithaupt* v. *Abram*, 352 U.S. 432, 440 (1956).
48. *Stovall* v. *Denno*, 358 U.S. 293 (1966).
49. *Loving* v. *Virginia*, 338 U.S. 1 (1968).

long been recognized as one of the vital personal rights essential to the orderly pursuit of happiness by free men." The Chief Justice had returned to explication of the notions of life, liberty, and the pursuit of happiness.

As we said, the ultimate purpose of this chapter has been to illustrate the comprehensive largeness of the method of argumentation through seriatim opinions practiced as fundamental for our constitutional law by the justices of the Supreme Court. The jurisprudence of Mr. Justice Holmes was a brilliant philosophical opposition to what he took to be all previous legalism in the Court's constitutional interpretations. The oppositions between Justice Field and Justice Miller, or Field and Waite, pale into insignificance in comparison with the transvaluations of Holmes. Law is to follow and recognize social currents and experiments, not limit and judge them. Experience is the life of the law, not logical deduction from earlier or supreme law. Words and basic constitutional documents are but signs of truly significant developments and movements in civilization. Or, more fundamentally, for Holmes the irrational was more real than the rational; the moving, the experimental, and the adventurous was more significant than the unchanging definition, the accepted political or legal procedure, the literal and prosaic reading of the sentences of precedent. The procedures of our basic legal institution were open enough to include Holmes' forceful strictures for almost thirty years; they were large enough to include the combined battery of the Olympian skepticism of Holmes and the social idealism of Justice Brandeis. The law was flexible enough to allow the new jurisprudence to assume command of argument and majority policy, with the new appointees to the Supreme Bench in 1938 and 1939. The accession to power of those who believed in the logic of experience did not stop the dialogue of dissent on the Court, but in fact increased it, with different justices reading the facts in different ways. Justice Frankfurter may be taken as the scholarly and brilliant paradigm of this development of Holmes' views, and as the prosaic culmination of Holmes' poetic Nietzschean flights. Frankfurter developed the theses that law is derived from feelings, and that the Constitution is interpreted through the development of English-speaking people's notions of decency. Justice Black had argued for a return to formalism and to classic notions of the Constitution as basic law since certain opinions expressed in the later thirties, but the true delimitation of Holmes' transvaluation of reasonings and values in the law came with Chief Justice Warren's comprehensive acceptance of formalism and a jurisprudence of basic rights and constitutional interpretation within the confines of the very sort of pragmatic philosophy that had earlier preached the necessary rejection of formalism.

The processes of our basic law include all these different philosophic positions and oppositions and developments without any serious strain; in fact the law is healthier for the ability it exhibits to include such different theories of law and bases for evaluation and yet maintain stability and authority at the same time. The law, as the process of reasonable settlement of disputes, or the law as the establishment or recognition of basic norms, is reason, in that oppositions can peacefully be maintained, revolutions in jurisprudence can occur and be followed by counter-revolutions, and the openness to argumentation and the power to decide particular cases stand firm.

6

Change, Reason, and the Law

THE PRINCIPLES of constitutional law in America are no fixed set of premises or opinions, but rather the acceptance of different arguments from different basic perspectives in majority argument and in dissent on the Supreme Court. Thus the dominance of reason in the rule of law does not mean the sterile maintenance of a mechanical jurisprudence or the imposition of one biased set of political values, but rather the ability to change the bases of the law to allow for continued practical determination of affairs in new circumstances and, at the same time, allow for continued argument about these bases, at any one time and at all times. The rule of law is the action and interaction among differing free and reasonable men. The rule of law is not the opposite of the rule of men, for it is always men who rule. If they rule giving reasons for what they do, accepting the reasons of those who dissent, and if they in time move to the dissenting position, and the previous dissenters become the new majority or dominant power, then the rule of law obtains. Change is necessary, therefore, to have the rule of law. In particular, this country is more under the rule of law because we have gone from a jurisprudence of rights to a jurisprudence of interests and their current confrontation, than if we had always maintained one philosophic theory of law, allowing no contrary or opposite position to develop or have ruling power. Thus reason not only allows for change, reason demands change on the level of independent determinants in practical action,

212

and not just on the level of obviously changing situations and environments.

Reason is properly understood in practical affairs as significant argument, and argument in its full sense means controversy between men and between positions, as well as the full ordered structuring of any one view. The procedures of hearing and deciding cases and of reporting all the opinions of the justices in seriatim form, followed by the Supreme Court, are paradigmatic of the rule of reason in American society. Oppositions are peacefully resolved, not only between disputants coming as pleaders to the Court, but among the factions on the Court itself. The Court has made itself independent and self-directing, the personification of self-directing reason. In a society threatened by conformism, image-making, manipulations of opinion, fashionable impulses, and violent spasms, the Supreme Court stands for autonomous freedom.

The arguments of both Hamilton and Madison in the *Federalist Papers* developed conceptions of the new government not merely as a democracy, but as a reasonable democracy. Passions and interests and biases were to be restrained by time, distance, and rehearings. Checks and balances were to stabilize forces within the national government, between national and state governments, and between all governments and the people. The government was reasonably to direct and effectuate popular will, and the people were reasonably to restrain the government. As noted in Chapter Three, Hamilton and Madison did not agree on what constituted good government and what constituted immediate and harmful political passion, but this makes their combined essays all the more remarkable. There are peaceful rational arguments within the general open form of reasonable analysis, and they give an example of open acceptance and tolerance of opposition as opposed to the imposition of some dominant whim. The *Federalist Papers* were not reactionary and "against change," but in fact advocated a revolutionary change from the Articles of the Confederation to the new stronger and more effective Constitution. And the Constitution was in turn a mode of providing for more open and accepted changes, such as the radical change to Jeffersonian policies in 1800 and the radical change when the Supreme Court, the guardian of the Constitution after *Marbury* v. *Madison*, began to admit argument and difference, change and reason, within its confines.

The acceptance of the Supreme Court and its arguments demands more than mere democracy—such acceptance demands reasonable democracy. The Supreme Court operates as an argued and reasonable restraint on the dominance of mere power and mere fashion in society. Such reasonable restraint is in its very nature a matter of debate and change. Those who do not understand this, and who do not want such rule of law anyway, argue that debates on the Court and changes in basic opinions indicate a lack of authority in our basic law. But in fact what such arguments and changes indicate is rather that such authority is reasonable and not totally blind. The very fact that the justices disagree on what is reasonable proves the rule of reason in the law.

Nor does the fact of the Court's activism detract from its position as guardian of the rule of law. Judgment can be self-directive, as much as legislation can, and although justices accuse other justices of legislating and not adjudicating, the realm of adjudication is seen by each justice as the proper realm of the activities of the Court. The extreme pragmatist, Justice Holmes, was willing to recognize an enormously wide realm for legislation and the interplay of interests, but he always insisted that the Supreme Court itself be above such movements of opinion and power and continue to embody the rule of reason rather than biased evaluation. The Court was not to make blind responses to past traditions or present notions of expediency, but to guard the rational limits of such responses. Holmes' insistence that such legislation and economic wrangling be allowed came from his views that the Court could only preserve its independence and objectivity by refraining from involvement in such matters. Whatever Holmes thought of the final rationality of the universe and man's life, the role of the Court, in his view, was to preserve a realm of objectivity and rational judgment above the flux of powers and passions.

The ability of men of opposite views to argue peacefully, and with great resulting changes, can be seen in the arguments between Holmes and Brandeis and the results of their combined arguments on constitutional law. Furthermore, before the pragmatist Brandeis came to the Supreme Court, Holmes' best friend on the Court was the ultra-legalist Fuller, a man whose position in law was exactly the opposite of Holmes' views. Similarly, in terms of formal jurisprudence, Justice Black brought about great changes in the law by insisting on formal arguments from the propositions in the Constitution itself, irrespective of precedents and the pragmatic considerations of current and established interest groups. In Black's theory, the Court can stand above political passions by doing its proper job, but if this doing of the job has vast emotional consequences for some people, that is their problem, for involvement in such considerations would lead to the rule of passion and interest rather than reasoned adjudication. Thus no matter what the juridical position, changes are to be expected—changes deriving from the deeply felt duty of the justices to declare the law and maintain the law free from passion and bias. The dynamics of the battle of reasonings is argument itself, and freedom and practical reason, and all these together comprise the rule of law. If the reasons and the changes stopped, the rule of law would be over.

This chapter will present two recent and controversial changes in the law, the *Mapp* case and *in re Gault*. In both cases, there is argument between justices who hold to pragmatic determinations and those who maintain determinations through formal process and rights. The *Mapp* case majority opinion was written by the politically conservative Justice Tom Clark, while the *Gault* decision was written by the politically liberal Justice Abraham Fortas. But that some kind of legal reason, rather than political bias, controls the determination of the cases should be proved by the fact that these cases both tend in the same direction: a narrow pragmatism is rejected for some larger combination of pragmatism with independent considerations of form and due process of law. The cases also illustrate the continued ability of the law to remain aware of opposite arguments in relation to practical cases, to move in practical ways, and to determine affairs by adjudication. Past changes are reviewed and new changes contemplated in these adjudications, as part of the functioning process of the law in action. After an exposition of these cases and their significance in showing the confrontation of pragmatism and formal rights at the present day within the confines of the law, the final section of the chapter will be devoted to a return to the main argument about the foundations of practical action, the great issues between law and reason on one hand and authority and power on the other, as alternative modes of achieving survival in the continual changing circumstances of practical life.

Clark: Mapp v. Ohio

A "common sense" approach to jurisprudence, not entirely formal, but derived from practical applications of formal demands, is explicitly the basis for Justice Tom Clark's majority opinion in the recent crucial case of *Mapp* v. *Ohio*.[1] In Justice Clark's view, the pragmatic emphasis on constitutional jurisprudence as a recognition of facts and interests has gone too far. Following the lead of Holmes, Justice Frankfurter had held, in the earlier ruling case *Wolf* v. *Colorado*,[2] that state court decisions were primary normative facts for the Supreme Court, and that the Court could do no more than recognize these decisions. In the *Wolf* case, this meant that evidence which had been illegally obtained could be used in state courts in criminal trials. Clark argues both pragmatically and formally. He indicates that the course of decisions in the state courts is in the same direction as the course he is taking, but then he also states that, strictly speaking, pragmatic recognition of such facts should not determine the course of constitutional law. The formal considerations of logic are more important: if the Fourth Amendment guarantees a right against illegal searches and seizures, then it should have effect in both the federal and the state courts. It is illogical that the right should mean one thing in the federal courts (where evidence obtained in such ways was inadmissible) and another thing in some state courts. The right should lead to the same consequences in any court.

Finally, Justice Clark turns to what he appropriately terms "common sense": there is no good sense in allowing a state prosecuting attorney to use illegal evidence, while across the street the federal attorney cannot use such evidence. Thus the "activist" conclusion was reached that all state courts would have to follow the federal law and exclude evidence illegally obtained. The dichotomies maintained in the earlier Supreme Court opinion in the *Wolf* case were destroyed and the case bluntly overruled.

The basic pragmatic axiom in the *Wolf* case was that the law should be based on the actual going norms of the community. If the community wanted to make illegal searches and use evidence so obtained in its criminal trials, the Supreme Court should not dictate to it other standards. The due process of the law is the recognition of the standards which in fact obtain in a society. As Frankfurter stated the issue:

> Due process of law conveys neither formal nor fixed nor narrow requirements. It is the compendious expression for all those rights which the court must enforce because they are basic to

1. *Mapp* v. *Ohio*, 367 U.S. 643 (1961).
2. *Wolf* v. *Colorado*, 338 U.S. 25 (1948).

a free society. But basic rights do not become petrified at any one time, even though as a matter of human experience, some may not too rhetorically be called eternal verities. It is of the very nature of a free society to advance in its standards of what is deemed reasonable and right. Representing as it does a living principle, due process is not confined within a permanent catalogue of what may at a given time be deemed the limits or the essentials of fundamental rights. To rely on a tidy formula for the easy determination of what is a fundamental right for purposes of legal enforcement may satisfy a longing for certainty, but ignores the movements of a free society.[3]

Therefore due process has a substantive meaning, but that substantive meaning changes with time. For Frankfurter it was a matter of sensitivities to the public's feelings about injustices. He has carefully explained the problems of discovering or stating these feelings in other cases.[4] But with regard to the right to privacy of one's belongings in one's own home, free from arbitrary police searches, Frankfurter stated that the matter was clear, and there was such a right: "The security of one's person against arbitrary intrusion by the police is basic in a free society." He went on to say that such illegal searches by the police are "condemned as inconsistent with the conception of human rights enshrined in the history and the basic constitutional documents of English-speaking peoples."

However, Justice Frankfurter, and the majority of the Court with him, then went on to apply "self-restraint" to the Court's action in enforcing rights. This basic constitutional right should be enforced by the people in the states or by the police departments, not by the Supreme Court. The Court would not apply the remedy of denying admission of illegally obtained evidence in the state courts. The remedy should be in some form of local democratic action: "We cannot, therefore, regard it as a departure from basic standards, to remand such persons to the remedies of private action and such protection as the internal discipline of the police, under the eyes of an alert public opinion, may afford."[5]

Justice Frankfurter supplemented his opinion in the *Wolf* case with statistical tables indicating the course of judicial and legislative opinion on the use of illegally obtained evidence since the *Weeks* case (which had ruled such evidence inadmissible in federal courts).

3. *Ibid.*
4. "Other cases"—see *Rochin* v. *California,* 342 U.S. 165, 169 (1952) and *Haley* v. *Ohio,* 332 U.S. 596 (1948).   5. *Wolf* v. *Colorado,* supra.

The tables revealed that state supreme courts and legislatures had taken various actions with no clear direction, but that most of them had *not* switched to the federal court ruling of excluding illegally obtained evidence. This was meant to supplement the majority finding, indicating an absence of any public mandate to exclude illegal evidence, but it was not the key proof of the majority opinion, which was rather that there were other remedies for victims of illegal searches and seizures, involving local rather than federal controls, and that in the interest of judicial self-restraint and the encouragement of local effective democracy, the other remedies were declared adequate. This view of local prerogative was applied in unusual instances[6] by Justice Frankfurter but is part of a philosophy of the recognition of local autonomy that carries back to Holmes' dissent in the *Lochner* case,[7] and to a crucial dissent in the *Black and White Taxicab* case.[8] The general pragmatist view is that the interpretation of constitutional terms, such as due process of law, can only be given with candid recognition that the going values of society are inevitably involved in such a process; there are not, and cannot be, any fixed formal meanings. The pragmatist view also holds that federal jurisdiction is a matter to be determined by the Court on policy grounds. The Court can extend its power or not, depending on its own interpretation of that power.[9] Thus in the *Wolf* case, the Court decided not to extend its power.

In the *Mapp* case, the Court reversed *Wolf* in a five-to-four decision. To dispose of the Frankfurter arguments, Clark noted, as stated, that times have changed: "While they [factual considerations] are not basically relevant to a decision . . . we will consider the current validity of the factual grounds on which Wolf was based. While in 1949 almost two-thirds of the States opposed the exclusionary rule, now more than half of those since passing on it have wholly or partly adopted it. Significantly, among those now following the rule is California, which, according to its highest court, was 'compelled to reach

6. "Unusual instances"—see *Minersville* v. *Gobitis*, 310 U.S. 586, discussed *supra*.
7. *Lochner* v. *New York*, 198 U.S. 45, 74.
8. *Black and White Taxicab and Transfer Company* v. *Brown and Yellow Taxicab and Transfer Company*, 276 U.S. 518, 532 (1928).
9. See discussion in W. W. Crosskey, *Politics and the Constitution*, chapter 25, pp. 818-937. H. L. A. Hart's notion that jurisdiction of courts is given by rules about what the judges do is not always applicable in the federal system of U.S. constitutional law (consider *Marbury* v. *Madison*), and probably not applicable to historical extensions of common law, such as under Mansfield in the eighteenth century or Coke in the seventeenth century.

that conclusion because other remedies have completely failed.' "[10]

Clark went on to explain that Cardozo's "weighty testimony" against the exclusionary rule was now no longer applicable, that "Time has set its face against *People* v. *Defore*," and concluded: "It therefore plainly appears that the factual considerations supporting the failure of the *Wolf* Court to apply the exclusionary rule when it recognized the enforceability of the right to privacy in 1949, while not basically relevant to the constitutional consideration, could not, in any analysis, now be deemed controlling."

Clark turned from pragmatism to logic. If the Fourth Amendment and the Fourteenth Amendment prevented the federal courts from using illegal evidence, then, since the Amendments were now understood to hold against the states, state courts should be prevented from using illegal evidence: "Since the right of privacy has been declared enforceable against the States through the Due Process Clause of the Fourteenth Amendment, it is enforceable against them by the same sanction as is used against the Federal Government." Logic and consistency demand the move from the statement of the right to the full exercise of the right: "In short, the admission of the new constitutional right by the *Wolf* opinion could not consistently tolerate denial of its most important privilege, the exclusion of the evidence forced by an illegal search. To hold otherwise is to grant the right but in reality to withhold its privilege and enjoyment. . . . The philosophy is . . . that no man is to be convicted on unconstitutional evidence."

Justice Clark does not want to be fully identified with the rationalists, however, since he has in other places claimed, with Holmes, that the life of the law has not been logic.[11] For Clark it is common sense: "Our holding is not only the logical dictate of prior cases, but it also makes very good sense. There is no war between this Court and common sense. Presently, a federal prosecutor may make no use of illegal evidence, but a State's attorney across the street may." In common sense terms, there was a "double standard recognized until today." With *Mapp*, the double standard disappears.

Justice Clark's insistence that the thinking and the decisions of the Supreme Court are an independent variable with respect to the powers of states and the rights of citizens, and are not merely dependent on the recognition of state interests, also means that Clark

10. *Mapp* v. *Ohio, op. cit.*, p. 651.
11. "Other places"—*Linkletter* v. *Walker,* 381 U.S. 618, 629 (1966).

and the court recognize the fundamental role of formal law in guaranteeing rights. The law may determine the norms in a community; it does not merely have to mirror these norms. Objective thinking, applied to practical situations with the use of good sense, may be taken as higher than mere sensitive recognition of the popular will or the popular lack of will.

Frankfurter's thought, to repeat, was that the power of the federal courts should be limited by recognition of the priority of genuine state and local community processes. The philosophic backing for Frankfurter's insistence that constitutional jurisprudence should be seen as recognition of going norms can be found in Kant's *Metaphysics of Morals,* where it is said that the law, as an external imposition of norms, does not and should not operate where there is no subjective and internal motive in the life of the man or community under consideration. Although the objective commands of the law and the subjective norms of ethical life are two sides of the same coin, in both Kant and Frankfurter the subjective grounding is more basic. The relative failure of the Prohibition Amendment in the United States is an example which illustrates the problem from Frankfurter's view. The alternative view rests on logical analysis of the statement that the Constitution is the supreme law of the land.

The *Mapp* case, like the *Wolf* case, had its strong dissents; the Court remains a citadel of discussion and argument, affirmation and reply. Justice Harlan stated that the Court had abandoned all its written and traditional limits and now expressed only its own will to power. The *Mapp* case had gone against the classic principle of *stare decisis* and also had ignored the sound reasons in the *Wolf* case for the independence of state criminal processes. The Court, said Harlan, was losing all outside respect in so doing. Justice Frankfurter, needless to say, concurred with Harlan. But the general outcome of the *Mapp* case was a new confrontation with the principles of pragmatic jurisprudence and an attempt to include the arguments of pragmatism in a larger synthesis which also included logic and a common sense role of the dominance of federal law in the nation's legal practices.

Fortas: in re Gault

A second crucial case is the Supreme Court's review of the rights of juvenile delinquents under state laws, which had established a paternalistic authority outside of normal criminal procedures for dealing with such immature law violators, in *in re Gault*.[12] In that case Justice Fortas presents a full review of the pragmatic reasons given for excluding juveniles from the normal processes of the law and then criticizes the results, both in pragmatic terms and in terms of a full formal jurisprudence of rights.

In the *Gault* case, a 15-year-old boy, living in a trailer camp with both his parents, who, it happened, both worked, was accused of making obscene phone calls to a neighborhood woman. On the strength of the woman's complaint and the testimony of a comrade, Gerald Gault was declared "delinquent" by the juvenile court judge and ordered to be placed in a state industrial school for the rest of his minority, six years. The opinion of Justice Fortas and the Court was that this decision deprived Gault of basic rights.

Under the juvenile law, Gault was not charged with any crime; the fact that he and a friend were making lewd phone calls was evidence that he needed the protection of the state and the Juvenile Court. The theory of such action was explained at some length in the Supreme Court opinion on the case: "The early reformers were appalled by adult procedures and penalties, and by the fact that children could be given long term prison sentences and mixed in jails with hardened criminals. They were profoundly convinced that society's duty to the child could not be confined by the concept of justice alone." The state's mercy was to replace the law's justice: "They believed that society's role was not to ascertain whether the child was 'guilty' or 'innocent' but 'What is he, how has he become what he is, and what had best be done in his interest and in the interest of the state to save him from a downward career.'" The problem was seen as outside the criminal legal system: "The child— essentially good, as they saw it—was to be made 'to feel that he is the object of the State's solicitude and care,' not that he was under arrest or on trial. The rules of criminal procedure were therefore altogether inapplicable." The methods and the concepts of law were both rejected: "The apparent rigidities, technicalities, and harshness which they observed in both substantial and procedural criminal law were therefore to be discarded. The idea of crime and punishment was to be abandoned."

Therefore, in the original juvenile "hearing" in Arizona, Gerald Gault was not charged with a crime, and his placement in the industrial school was not punishment. The Arizona Supreme Court

12. *In re Gault,* 387 U.S. 1 (1967).

had refused to change the original judgment, on the grounds that the juvenile system had special needs and problems.

The Supreme Court not only reversed the Arizona high court, it also subordinated the pragmatic conception of law as recognition of social needs and interests to the alternative conception of the law as formal processes guaranteeing rights and even facts.

Justice Fortas reasoned primarily from the principles of a formal, rule-oriented jurisprudence, but secondarily, he also used pragmatic principles to show they developed unpragmatic results when institutionalized. Fortas assumed it is the crime, and not the boy's character, that is the proper and only subject for adjudication. (This was not the assumption of the juvenile judge, who said that Gerald was "habitually immoral.") The crime was trivial—"of the irritatingly offensive, adolescent, sex variety." The juvenile "hearing" lacked basic elements of due procedure: the lady who made the charge never appeared, and the boy who gave evidence as a witness, stating that he and Gerald made the calls, was never cross-examined. The fact that Gerald had refused to admit stealing a baseball glove two years earlier was taken as weighing against him in this case, and he was asked to testify against himself in this case again. Finally, Justice Fortas declared that the "protection" of the Juvenile Court was in fact "punishment": placement in the Receiving Home or the State Industrial School was forced incarceration, and the term "delinquent" had criminal, not merely civil, connotations and consequences. The position of the juvenile authorities, that there was no crime and no punishment, was declared to be without basis in fact.

Within the opinion, the pragmatic principles of non-legal treatment of juveniles are explored by Justice Fortas, and he finds the principles questionable but the practices in contradiction to the principles themselves. There is no careful and benevolent search into the entire situation with regard to individual offenders. Rehabilitation does not occur in the "homes" and "schools," and in fact most juvenile offenders are repeaters, i.e., they have already spent some time earlier in a State Home. The general problem of juvenile delinquency has not lessened. What was to be parental guidance has become arbitrary determination and extended punishment. Gault was to be "protected" for six years, as the result of an action for which the maximum adult criminal sentence was two months.

Justice Fortas went on to state the rules of ordinary criminal justice that would now be applicable to the juvenile courts. There should be formal notice of charges, the right to counsel, the right to confront the accuser and to cross-examine witnesses, and the right against self-incrimination. But since children were different from adults, other criminal court rights did not apply, such as the right to bail, the right to grand jury indictment, the right to a public trial, the right to trial by jury, or the right to appeal the court's determination.

Now what the Court did in Gault's case can be described either pragmatically or in terms of a jurisprudence of rights. (a) Pragmatically, the judges extended their jurisdiction, changed the meanings of words to suit themselves, and changed therapy procedures for confused children. The juvenile courts had previously been considered a matter for state legislative prerogative in the civil jurisdiction; now these courts were within the purview of the Federal Courts and in the criminal jurisdiction. In that new jurisdiction the judges created entirely new rules of procedure for courts that were not entirely the same as the previous criminal courts. The judges had changed analogies; before, the juvenile courts had been "like" civil courts, while now they were "like" criminal courts. The new analogies led to revised language-procedures in talking about juveniles. The word "delinquent" is now like "offender" and not like "upset but basically good child." "Industrial School" is now like "forced incarceration" and not like "ordinary home" or "ordinary school." The open paternalism of the older system was wrong, for the juveniles actually felt better when their cases were conducted with the appearance and the reality of "fairness, impartiality, and orderliness." A trial according to "certain essentials of due process" could be "more impressive and more therapeutic as far as the juvenile is concerned."

To emphasize this pragmatic interpretation of the results, it should be noticed that the jurisdiction of the problem had formerly rested in the states, but was assumed by the Supreme Court on its own fiat. The new rules were developed simply by stating them; they are a new interpretation of the Due Process Clause of the Fourteenth Amendment to the American Constitution, and these rules are only similar to rules for adult criminal jurisprudence. Two justices of the nine thought there should be a right to appellate review, for instance, but the majority did not so opine.

(b) On the other hand, formal jurisprudence of rights can better describe the decision of the Court: a court of defined powers and jurisprudence, the United States Supreme Court, considered an issue confronting it for the first time—the rights of juveniles with regard to the power of juvenile authorities. This is the dominant mode of argument used by Justice Fortas (although, to strengthen his position, as lawyers do, he argued both ways). Formal, independent law is basic for any personal rights and is necessary with regard to processes of evidence to discover the relevant or significant facts. Formal law means basic regard for the intrinsic due processes of the law. The rules involved in the process of the law establish rights and freedoms within the legal system. Fortas is quite explicit on this: "Due process of law is the primary and indispensable foundation of individual freedom. It is the basic and essential term in the social compact which defines the rights of the individual and delimits the powers which the State may exercise."

The rules of evidence and procedure allow an escape from the confusion and relativism of the world of evaluated data and clarify practical facts the way scientific method clarifies scientific facts. Facts are not prior to the law; they are the results of the due processes of judicial consideration. The due process of the law is the formal practical equivalent of scientific method in modern theoretical research: "Procedural rules which have been fashioned from the generality of due process are our best instruments for the distillation and evaluation of essential facts from the conflicting welter of data that life and our adversary methods present. It is these instruments of due process which enhance the possibility that truth will emerge from the confrontation of opposing versions and conflicting data. Procedure is to the law what scientific method is to science." For Justice Fortas, the due processes of the law began when the case was finally and appropriately heard before the Supreme Court. That Court then properly recognized that the rights of juveniles could only be guaranteed by the establishment of rules of procedure in the juvenile courts. The Court did not "make" rights for the juveniles, since that was done by the Constitution; it ensured that the processes of adjudication would recognize those rights, and this could only be done by rules.

In Fortas' brief historical exposition of the problem of the treatment of juvenile offenders, he states that the pragmatic juvenile system can be traced back to chancery practice. Legal pragmatism is not new and not American, but can be seen as simply another version of the English equity jurisprudence. Thus we have Justice Fortas himself summarizing the theses of this book: the struggle be-

tween the formal rules of the Supreme Court and the authoritarianism, supposedly benevolent, of the juvenile court system is simply
another round in the match carried on at the beginning of the seventeenth century between Edward Coke, for the law and rights, and
Francis Bacon, for authority, paternalism, and Chancery. In Peacham's Case, Bacon thought it was a waste of time to run Peacham
through the processes of a criminal trial, since the King had already
decided he was a traitor, and even though he had been obstinate
enough to refuse to admit this fact (as Gault also refused to admit
his guilt, which the juvenile judge took as a count against him). Coke
had insisted that Peacham had a right to a trial in which the decision
was not known beforehand. Coke insisted that the formalities of trial
gave rights to the accused; they did not simply provide a method for
the power of the state to act. In the same fashion, Fortas insisted that
the juvenile system could not argue its professional benevolence, and
that it could best provide effective treatment for maladjusted persons
in the face of Gault's rights under the law. Justice Fortas is quite
explicit on the difference of manner of formulation of the problem,
in pragmatism and in formal law: "The child was to be 'treated'
and 'rehabilitated' and the procedures were to be 'clinical' rather
than punitive. The proceedings were not held to be adversary, but
rather that the State was proceeding as *parens patriae.* The Latin
phrase proved to be a great help to those who sought to rationalize
the exclusion of juveniles from the constitutional scheme. The
phrase was taken from chancery practice, where it was used to
describe the power of the State to act *in loco parentis,* for the purpose of protecting the interests and person of the child."

In the Bacon-Chancery-Holmes legal realist view, state inter-
vention "does not deprive the child of any rights, because he has
none. It merely provides the 'custody' to which the child is entitled."
The arguments for chancery, including Holmes' arguments for politics tempered with judicial aloofness, are met by Fortas with arguments that the law is better than benevolence: "The highest motives
and the most enlightened impulses led to a peculiar system for juveniles, unbeknown to our law. The constitutional and theoretical
basis for the peculiar system is—to say the least—debatable. Un-
bridled discretion, however benevolently motivated, is frequently a
poor substitute for principle and procedure. The absence of substantive standards has not necessarily meant that children receive
careful, compassionate, individualized treatment."

The linguistic changes demanded by the Gault decision can be seen not merely as matters of changing analogies, but as a matter of placing terms in a proper framework. In the paternalistic system previously used in juvenile cases, an attempt had been made to take away criminal connotations simply by changing names. But the new names soon acquired derogatory connotations in the context. Thus "delinquent" had been a neutral term, but after being used in the juvenile system, had come to mean criminal offender. It was replaced by "person in need of supervision," but even that, shortened to "pins," had come to have the same derogatory meaning in actual practice. The law-as-rules jurisprudence, according to Fortas, should not try to hide "realities" under "sentiment," but simply recognize that the defendant was a "juvenile offender." Where the pragmatic system had euphemized incarceration through such terms as "home" and "school," the law would state the facts, that these were actually "places of forced confinement." Only with a proper and realistic linguistic usage could rights be determined, for punishment is punishment, even if called rehabilitation or vocational training.

The conclusion reached as the result of the linguistic definitions found was that the juvenile court's power, exercised on behalf of the state, could no longer be unlimited, but must proceed according to legal processes, and these processes must be considered adversary proceedings in law, and not "findings" in civil law or chancery.

In the Gault case, the pragmatic jurisprudence of Holmes (and Bacon) is defended in dissent. Justice Stewart objected to the majority holding, and in his dissent, the opinion was "unwise" because professional social workers, who had "dedicated their lives to the young," would be unrealistically constrained in their work.

Thus in the current confrontations of pragmatic jurisprudence with a jurisprudence of rights there have been continued controversies and dissents, but there has also been a tendency for the formerly dominant pragmatism to be overruled in terms of a new notion of independent formal law and independent rights. The best opinions, such as those above, do not ignore pragmatic considerations, but attempt to show that genuine pragmatic considerations can be harmonized with, albeit subordinated to, the establishment of legal rights. This is not to say that these decisions are the end of the process of argument and discussion that makes our constitutional law both free and reasonable—we would then be stultified in a mechanical jurisprudence—but rather it is to indicate that the principles of law can proceed in terms of opposite notions of jurisprudence, and that these oppositions are resolved peacefully and reasonably in the debates and discussions found in the majority opinions and the dissents.

There has been a discussion of differences in conception of the notion of due process in the law: some have held that the term incorporates substantive rights, while others have held that the term meant procedural processes only. I hope it can be seen, from the *Gault* case and earlier discussions, that the distinction is meaningless. The procedural rights, of hearing all relevant arguments and regarding all relevant evidence, guarantee substantive rights: the two are one and the same. Coke was talking about rights of independence and security which were both substantive and procedural, and the same is true of the rights discussed by Justice Fortas. The basic substantive right is to be treated as a free citizen, with such treatment primarily implying the protections of the due processes of the Constitution, in elections, and in court trials.

Conclusion

The preceding section was concerned with how reason can function to bring about changes and determinations of issues in the law, which indeed has been the topic of the book. But major issues of politics and change are not confined to the various oppositions and rationales within the legal process, but rather include solutions which depend upon force rather than thought. The reasonable solution to man's political conflicts assumes that we have the ability to criticize ourselves and to tolerate others, that we have the Lockean awareness that not all the good reasons are on one side, that we fulfill the Jeffersonian expectations that public government can proceed on the largely self-governing talents we have in our own affairs. But in the oppositions that changes bring, another position arises: when men are opposed to each other tooth and nail, and feel that their ideals and their wives and children are threatened by another group of men who feel the same way about the first group, then the only earthly blessing is the domination of some arbitrary power. War can only be stopped by force, and internal as well as external peace demands the efficient and forceful authority of a strong administration, acting in the crises, saving the country by breaking through the checks and balances which lay our freedoms bare to the fangs of the enemy.

There is an element which has not been discussed earlier in relation to changes in man's affairs, but which enters into all such changes: this is the *negativity* of man's reactions, his resentment of his situation, the frustrations of "a world he never made," the emptiness of ordinary life, and the resultant hatred of law and reason and freedom. This factor can be seen in the symbolist literature of France at the turn of the century; it can be seen in the Dada movement in Germany in the 1920's; it is most explicitly stated in the philosophy of Nietzsche; and it exists in American life and popular literature.

In Nietzsche's philosophy, the basic realities of life are subhuman irrational vitalistic drives, wild Dionysian energies that create and destroy. Reason exists as a sublimation of these energies, but in itself has no independent substance; in fact, reason and intellect taken too far kill the spirit. Logic and thought are myths by which we make the terrible energies of nature civilized and conformist; but these myths mask the truth which is the reality of force and the unreality of reason. The philosophy has its classic variations in Marx, who held that the human reality is economic war, with the law and rights mere fetishes of the myths of peace which hide the basic conflict, and in Freud, who asserted the reality of the Id, the energy of desire, and the derivative and parasitic dependence of conscience and reason. In human conflicts, decent manners require that we negotiate in the first instance on the level of diplomacy and reason, but when the conflicts are real, then they move to the fundamental area of force and violence. Obedience to law is "conformism" and is both untruthful and unmanly. Activism of any sort is preferable to reflection, for in thought all we find is the utter meaninglessness and emptiness of life.

This sort of thinking, which in European academic circles is still fashionably shocking, is taken in America as either comic or simply prosaically true. A recent American commentator on Nietzsche noted that he wrote an excellent style and openly wondered why Nietzsche won no writing prizes in Germany in the 1880's. The Nietzschean philosophy was adapted by Shaw to British conditions, and Shaw wrote a play in which he indicated that all British civilization was based on the surface sham of accent and diction, and that the difference between the outcasts and the law was a matter of speech therapy. This play became the American "Cinderella story" hit *My Fair Lady*. Earlier the Hollywood writer Ben Hecht read Nietzsche and realized the philosophy could be adapted directly to the American scene. He invented the James Cagney gangster movie, in which Cagney played the gangster villain-hero, treating women with the roughness they deserve and adore, committing great crimes, and ultimately being killed by the conformist police, who represent mass-man stifling genius. The recent success of *Bonnie and Clyde* is a return to the same theme. The literary success of Capote's *In Cold Blood* is based on the same negativisms, with the added horror of its literal truth: an unseen underworld of the crippled and perverse killers without motive, in an idyllic Eden of innocent and prosperous wheat farmers. The killers are presented with sympathy; their letters are printed, showing both great writing skill and remarkable psychological insight and sensitivity, while the killed remain two-dimensional. Capote's book became an international success.

The standard drama of television westerns is the same. The good man wins, but because he can shoot faster. The peaceful man, who has sworn never to use a gun again, is finally driven to the truth that only violence solves problems. He takes his gun belt and his shooting irons off the nail, with his son looking on with new admiration, and "wipes out" the gruesome bad guys. In every detective story, the "real man" who solves the crime goes outside of the law and defies the police in order to get the elusive criminal; this is as true of the gentle Perry Mason as it is of the oversexed sadist Mike Hammer.

The purpose of these illustrations is not to deplore them, as in standard editorials and sermons, but rather to face the reality of such motives in human nature. There is an ontology of resentment, fear, emptiness, and violence, with an effect on the political order the opposite of man's urges toward reason, freedom, and law. Such negative themes may come out more in poetry than in life, and we may use the violence of television to escape from the humdrum of the peaceful living room, but the factors of raw negation and hatred of reason and law are there no matter what. The violence of the artists is not entirely an escape from the routines of ordinary middle-class existence, for the greatest literary figures of the twentieth century have insisted on such negativities and anti-heroisms in their writings. If Hemingway had written some of his later novels in German he would have been condemned as a Nazi writer; men without conversation overcome *nada* by shooting animals or making love, and they fight without any conception of rational themes or motives in the political order.

But such anti-rational themes are not simply part of the poetic imagination. Periods of change bring such empty unrest and real violence to the fore. The attempt to change the country to a temperate nation, with the Prohibition Amendment, brought about organized crime and the acceptance of a recognized "underworld" in reaction, factors which did not disappear with the repeal of the amendment. The changes in the world scene have brought reactions from both the fanatical rightists and the fanatical leftists. The changes in race relations have brought hatreds and violence and riots. Even the new affluence has brought a sense of alienation to the American scene.

Since the realm of the practical is the realm of change, no one is going to stop completely such reactions of negation, frustration, apathy, and violence. It is better to recognize them as permanent factors than to attempt to exhort them out of existence. The question is which shall be king, negation and resentment and violence, or law and tolerance and reason? This reaches the heart of the Nietzschean problem: if Nietzsche is right, then the negations are more real than the rational formulations, and the very ontology of the practical world is violence and sub-rationality. But if reason is independent and self-determining in its awareness of practical realities, including its awareness of negation, resentment, frustration, violence, and meaningless reaction, then the rational processes of the law are paramount. When the purely positivistic and scientific social scientists have refused to recognize the intangible factors of resentment and anti-rationality, the artists have made them the overwhelming reality. It is up to the judges and the people to place them in proper perspective.

Thus the movement for greater functional status for Negroes in this country can be seen in two opposite ways: it is either a movement which started with "phony" appeals to Christianity and non-violence and is finally moving to the Nietzschean "realism" of mass organized violence and arson, or it is a movement which started changing with the Supreme Court decision in *Brown* v. *Topeka*, and has proceeded along lines of judicial and legislative change since that time, admittedly with vast but subordinate reactions in terms of hate, violence, and anti-law emotions and activities. The ramifications for the future of American politics depend a great deal on how the question is formulated in the minds of the public, for the negative and pessimistic formulation leads to demands for charismatic personal rule, a powerful administration which can put down violence, or, on the other side, a powerful revolutionary who can overthrow "the Establishment." The positive way leads to renewed emphasis on adjudication and legislation for open discussion and debate of the problems and issues, and determinations of these issues in terms of the rights and interests of the citizens and the public as a whole. The latter way maintains the freedom of the country; the former way, in the name of saving the country from oppression, leads to arbitrary and irrational power, and to "final solutions."

It is no weakness in the rule of law that the Supreme Court should be a storm center of controversy; indeed, just the opposite. It is a sign of the basic rationality of the country, when the Court is a topic for debate and discussion. In the recent history of the Supreme Court, it never had such prestige as when it was attacked by Franklin Roosevelt and the more fanatic New Dealers, in connection with the administration's Court-packing plan of 1937. Granted that the Court "reversed itself" on some of the New Deal legislation reviewed, most notably the Agricultural Adjustment Acts, still Chief Justice Hughes lost some battles and won the war, and the executive and legislative plan to humble the Supreme Court not only collapsed, the entire New Deal program of domestic reform largely lost fire. It was obvious that the citizenry as a whole regarded the maintenance of the rule of law as more vital to the country than the reforms of the current administration, the problems of the then current depression, or the existence of possible bias due to age and independence of the justices of the Court. The Warren Court, in again becoming a storm center, again fulfilled the function of maintaining discussion about the rule of law in the nation. The great problem of maintenance of the rule of law is not the possibility of lack of respect for particular views expressed by particular justices, for that is really healthy and sound; the great problem is that the public and the government become so concerned with other issues, such as the atomic bomb or foreign policies, that the entire domain of problems connected with the rule of law is forgotten. Thus when the "liberal scientists" who were concerned about "proper and peaceful" uses of atomic energy began political activities and launched the supposedly uplifting "Bulletin of Atomic Scientists," they were truly denigrating the rule of law in the country more than the Birchers who place "Impeach Earl Warren" signs along the highways. What the scientists want is for the public to forget the importance of everything else and concentrate on the horrors of atomic attack and its sinister implications for all of humanity. If we all did this, with supposed enlightenment and benevolence we would find ourselves totally dominated by pseudo-scientists and their political allies, who would be constantly "saving" the country from greater dangers by continued concentration on atomic attack and defense. The National Security Council would dominate not only part of our national policy, it would dominate all of it. The Supreme Court and the rule of law would disappear in the lack of attention to such old-fashioned matters. The same threat is posed by foreign policy. Those who want us to think entirely about "proper" and "liberal" and "saving" solutions to our foreign policy want the endless concerns of Viet Nam, France, Nigeria, the Near East, India, Argentina, Cuba, and so on to be our dominating and ruling interests. Concentration on important issues in Washington would not be between law and administration, but between various parts of the administration, between the Defense Department and the State Department, or between the State Department and the CIA, or between the administration and its popular critics of our foreign affairs, such as Lippman and Conor Cruse O'Brien and William Buckley and Ronald Reagan and all the student riot protesters of the war. In such total fights over particular issues, the rule of law and all larger concerns disappear in the noise. In such dangers the liberals who wanted to overwhelm Chief Justice Charles Evans Hughes and the conservatives who wanted to rid the high court of Chief Justice Earl Warren have done the nation the profound service of reminding the public of the larger concerns and the basic issues. If the Supreme Court were above public criticism and controversy, it would be dead as an institution, and the rule of law would no longer exist.

The rule of law does not destroy other modes of political action. They all continue, for the good or evil of the nation and individuals in it. Everything that is most deplorable in American culture and politics is not stopped by the debates in the Supreme Court. Thus moralists have lamented that presidential candidates now adjust their principles to a current "popular image" created for them by public relations advisers. Others have lamented the biases and stupidities of the mass media, and their acceptance of such opportunistic propaganda in supposedly responsible communications to the public —none of this can be stopped. All that can happen with the rule of law is that such practices do not ultimately dominate all government in the country. Propaganda and persuasion will exist, whether for health or for confusion, no matter what. The rule of law at least places such political rhetoric in a subordinate position. The same is true of raw force. The rule of law does not mean that governments no longer need the use of force to preserve the peace. The policeman is a necessary and effective part of American city government, and the National Guard and the Army are necessary on the larger scene, but only in their place. The horror would be if the police, the guard, and the Army totally dominated the country. People can deplore police brutality and Army stupidity all they want; the rule of law will never end such things, and it is difficult to see how ultimate disorders could be stopped without having some such force behind the referees and umpires of our life. The rule of law guarantees that we do not end up as many South American nations have, entirely subordinated to their armies, who rule in some cases in conservative fashion, in other cases supposedly for the people and the workers, but whose arbitrary whims cannot be discussed or debated in determinations of long-range national policies.

The rule of law, then, does not end crooked politics, brutal force, crime, or immorality. It does not stop rape and thefts, and even guarantees that the rapist and the thief will get a fair trial. It does not stop laziness or homosexuality or dirty political deals. It is the wisdom of the rule of law to distinguish itself from immediate political or moral reform. This has ramifications with respect to the usual analysis of the problem of the Prohibition Amendment. The usual description of the failure of prohibition is wrong in stating that this law, however "noble" in its conception, ignored the resistance of cultural mores and the weakness of men. But a proper attack on the Prohibition Amendment is rather that it was not law at all. It was an attempt to force permanently on the public one set of moral values, ending all discussion of the rationally opposite moral opinions. The Prohibition Amendment was brutal force and thus could only be resisted by brutal force. Law operates in terms of rational tolerance of opposition views. What was wrong in the situation was not the mores of the public, but the abuse of the rule of law to disguise propaganda and force.

The alternative modes of politics are three. Problems can be solved by full debate and determination after such debate, with the freedom to continue discussion maintained at all times, and this is termed the rule of law. Problems can be solved through one side actively persuading the other sides that its view is the best, through a campaign of biased propaganda and image-building in which alternatives are dismissed without much fair consideration. This is the usual mode of personal and administrative politics and of party politics in general. Or problems can be solved by force, with the literal destruction of the opposition and opposing views; this is called "war" on the international scene and various other things domestically. Now the uniqueness of the rule of law is that it allows the other two modes of solution of problems to continue within its confines. The rule of law does not stop the dominance in the nation of one political party or another at any one given time: the politics of rhetoric and persuasion continue. And the rule of law does not stop the forceful quelling of civic disturbances, the forced imprisonment or execution of criminals, nor international wars. In its openness, the rule of law even allows discussion and debate on the best operational method for solving any particular dispute: should persuasion and negotiation be used in some international dispute or should force? Should a new poverty program be installed in an urban area or should the police buy armored cars? These alternatives are kept in open and realistic perspective. The characteristic of the so-called tough-minded political analyst, who believes that all politics is "power politics," and force the only real answer to social problems, is that they can never allow the alternative modes of political analysis to function. The politics of force and the politics of rhetoric and persuasion are confining and restrictive, while the rule of law is the opposite and, in fact, admits the necessity of persuasion and of force when subordinated to debate and law. In a country where respect for law exists, partisan politics is not only healthy but it is basic in preserving the rule of law, since law is only realized in the transition from opposition to power and back again by the major party organization. But if one party achieved permanent domination, then dissent would gradually be swamped with government propaganda, and law would cease. The politics of persuasion would end the politics of freedom and reason, if it became totally dominant, but in a country where several alternative parties follow the politics of persuasion, then flexibility and sensitive reaction to political problems are assured. In the politics of sheer power, even such flexibility and sensitivity disappear; the propaganda machine is given fixed goals and fixed lies to use to achieve victory in the struggle. Again it must be granted that there are crises in the affairs of the nation where such demands can be made, as during the depressing years of Axis victories in the first part of the Second World War. But if the rule of law basically obtains, then the society can "come out" of such periods and return to the recognition of rights and freedoms, while if not, then somehow the country involved is always in such a crisis that no return is admissable "at this time." Thus those Russians who felt that Stalin was not allowing adequate progress toward a workers' republic in the Soviet Union in 1936 were all executed. Somewhat more amusingly, the East German economic advisers to Castro's regime, who recommended a change in incentives policy for workers in Cuba, were put in prison as traitors and capitalist subversives.

The four mainstays of the rule of law in America have been delineated, but will be summarized here, as the necessary bases for the continuation of such law and reason in the politics of the nation. They are: (1) a tradition of private independence, maintaining the *mores,* the subconscious and traditional security for private persons in their economic existence and their private thought and opinions; (2) a basic philosophy of practical freedom and toleration of opposing views, grounding on a conscious and rational level the freedom to reason and dissent in law and politics; (3) an actual politics of party oppositions and changes in ideology and personnel at the levels of highest political power; and (4) a fundamental constitutional law which itself is a forum of opposing rationales and dissenting views which can and do become majority views over periods of time. The unknown institutional contribution to the rule of law in America was begun in the acts and books of the now forgotten Edward Coke. The philosophic bases of toleration and the rule of law in politics were developed by John Locke. The political bases of open dissent and party changes within the constitutional framework were accomplished by the Jeffersonians. Thomas Jefferson also had a great deal to do with the institutionalization of seriatim opinions and reasonable argument and dissent in constitutional law, but such dissent in its full nature can only be understood by comprehension of the consequences of the dissents of Justice Field and Justice Holmes. The rule of law continues in current controversies: the great argument for law is the arguing itself.

DATE DUE

DEMCO 38-297